The Last Destroyer:

The Story of the USS Callaghan

By
Barry J. Foster

Copyright © 2002 by Barry J. Foster

ISBN 978-0-7414-1275-1

Published by:

PUBLISHING.COM

Info@buybooksontheweb.com
www.buybooksontheweb.com
Toll-free (877) BUY BOOK
Local Phone (610) 520-2500
Fax (610) 519-0261

Printed in the United States of America

Published January 2013

Dedication Page

This book is dedicated to my father, Allen Foster, the crew of the Callaghan and the families who waited for them back home. Let us not forget that nearly 50 of them never returned.

I especially want to thank all the men who took time out of their lives to help me with their personal stories, stories of the ship and either gave me material or told me where to find it. I cannot thank them enough. Many of these fine men are no longer with us. I remember with pleasure talking to Captain Bertholf, Doc Parker, Francis Dunne, Admiral Wulzen, Mark Ahrano, Howard Gray, George Pitts, Vinnie Policano, my father's dear friend, Eddie Mello and all the others too numerous to mention here.

I would like to say a word of special thanks to the men of the Callaghan who will read this. You have all helped me more than you will ever know. I thank you for your patience all these years.

These men left their simple homes and went off to fight a terrible war. We are free and America is a great nation because of them. We must never, ever, forget.

Barry Foster

The Last Destroyer:
The Story of the USS Callaghan

After shooting down 12 Japanese planes, sinking one submarine and firing thousands of rounds at shore targets, the Callaghan met its fate at the hands of one of the last kamikaze attacks of World War II.

By Barry Foster

2002

Table of Contents

INTRODUCTION

Prior to World War II the US Navy began to emerge from the malaise forced on it by isolationism in the US and ridiculously tight budgets. One of the ship types ordered each year in increasing numbers was the destroyer.

Destroyers were the utilitarian warships of the fleet. They were originally meant to launch torpedo attacks on the enemy fleet. The two great fleets of destroyers built for World War I and World War II were designed with that in mind. All featured large numbers of torpedo tubes to launch the 3841 pound steel monsters at the enemy. But during World War I it was discovered that the destroyer was valuable for another extremely vital duty. That duty was to protect convoys of merchant ships and the fleet itself against the dreaded German submarines called U-Boats. In fact, US Navy destroyers never made a torpedo attack against any fleet of any kind in that war. Virtually the only combat duty of destroyers in WWI was to defend against submarines.

World War II was different. The US Navy knew this even before it got officially involved in the war. Based on British experience it was clear that destroyers would be called upon for all kinds of duty. These duties included defense against submarines, anti-aircraft defense, shore bombardment and even occasional minesweeping and troop transporting. The original purpose of the destroyer also began to stand forth as the British made several torpedo attacks against units of both the German and Italian fleets.

As in World War I, one design of destroyer was selected by the US Navy to be mass-produced in great numbers. The World War I design, the "flush-deck" or "four-piper" was distinguished from other designs by having an unbroken deck line from fore-to-aft. Hence the name "flush-deck." The World War II mass-produced design called the Fletcher class also

1

sported a flush deck. This was done largely to cut the time required for production. A flush deck was easier to produce than a broken-deck design and, therefore, could be manufactured in less time. This was all-important in wartime when Admirals were virtually screaming for more destroyers, the workhorse of the fleet.

Our story is about one of the flush-deck Fletchers. In all, 175 Fletcher class destroyers were built. It is virtually certain that no Navy in the world will ever again produce so many destroyers of one design. Of course, the Fletchers were part of the largest ocean-going fleet the world has ever seen: the US Navy.

The Fletcher class was designed and ordered in the first part of 1940. Since war was still almost 2 years away for the US fleet, this could be called a pre-war design. But it was the first design unhindered by treaty. The Washington and London naval armament treaties had limited the size of destroyers. By the time the Fletcher class was ordered, these treaties were no longer in effect. So the Fletchers were to be big, robust and bristling with weaponry.

The first three destroyers of this type were commissioned in the summer of 1942. For various reasons it took some time to get them to where they were badly needed, the South Pacific. It was there that the ship this class was named for, the USS Fletcher, met up with a man whose name is central to our story.

Rear Admiral Daniel Judson Callaghan

Rear Admiral Callaghan was born in San Francisco, California, July 26, 1890. He graduated from the United States Naval Academy in 1911. He went on to a distinguished career with the US Navy serving in the first Nicaraguan campaign, the Mexican Campaign, World War I, various destroyers, battleships and cruisers. On July 14, 1938 he was appointed Naval Aide to President Franklin Roosevelt. He served in that capacity until May 1941 when he assumed command of the

Heavy Cruiser USS San Francisco. On May 2, 1942 he was transferred to Headquarters, South Pacific Area and South Pacific Fleet. He was promoted to Rear Admiral on June 22, 1942.

While serving as chief of staff of the South Pacific Fleet, Dan Callaghan had to standby while the terrible battles around Guadalcanal erupted. The Marines held Guadalcanal while the Navy fought the Japanese Fleet in the surrounding waters. Battle after battle was fought between American and Japanese task forces resulting in great loss of ships and lives on both sides. "Iron Bottom Sound" got its name from the sunken ships lost during those battles. At that point, Dan Callaghan asked for and finally got the chance to try his hand as Task Force Commander.

He could not have joined the battle at a more critical time. The Japanese had decided to make their last great effort to force the Americans out of Guadalcanal. They were determined to use their superior strength in surface ships to force aside the American Navy and bombard the Marines. They had done this successfully on several occasions. Dan Callaghan would lead the fight during the first night of a two-night battle that would defeat the Japanese surface forces decisively. From this defeat the Japanese would be forced to evacuate Guadalcanal and never return. But the victory would be won at a terrible cost.

On the night on November 13th, Dan Callaghan led Task Force 67.4 up the slot. His force consisted of 13 ships, an auspicious number. Task Force 67.4 included two heavy cruisers, three light cruisers and eight destroyers. He was delighted to have his old command, the San Francisco, as his flag ship. His mission was to stop the Japanese bombardment of Guadalcanal.

Admiral Callaghan disposed his task force in a single column with four destroyers ahead followed by the cruisers Atlanta, San Francisco, Portland, Helena and Juneau with four destroyers trailing. One of the trailing destroyers was the USS Fletcher. Many historians have criticized this disposition as it prevented the destroyers from playing the role they were meant for: torpedo attack. In addition, he was criticized for not using the best radar-equipped ship, the Helena, as his flagship. That meant that he had to depend on radio-relayed reports from his best "eyes" (the radar) aboard the Helena.

The Gods of War were happy that night, for the Americans ran smack-dab right into the Japanese. In fact, that battle was unusual because the two forces were unwittingly steaming straight at each other. The situation developed so quickly that the American column of ships ended up splitting the Japanese formation by colliding with it.

The US force got three breaks that night. Otherwise they would have surely been annihilated. First, the Japanese did not spot the Americans until it was too late. Second, the Japanese ships had bombardment ammunition in their ready ammunition spaces around the guns. This meant that they could not quickly switch back to the armor-piercing ammunition used to fight other warships. Lastly, the Japanese Admiral was not expecting to be intercepted before the planned bombardment. He was quite surprised at the fierce battle which erupted so quickly. As a result he gave no really useful orders during the entire battle.

The Japanese had 14 ships including two battleships, one light cruiser, and 11 destroyers. This would be the first time that American surface forces would challenge Japanese battleships. The Japanese were very confident. They knew the Americans were desperately short of battleships since the attack at Pearl Harbor. The Japanese had always felt that their battleship fleet was the finest naval fighting force in the world. This battle would be at night and the Japanese were the acknowledged masters of night- fighting. They trained endlessly for night battle. They searched the entire fleet for sailors with superior night vision to serve as lookouts. The Japanese optics, telescopes and binoculars, were the finest in the world.

So it began on Friday the 13th, November 1942. There was no light at all from the moon or the stars as a completely overcast

4

sky kept everything in blackness. Five of the American ships were equipped with radar but not the flagship.

The Helena's clocks said 1:24 a.m. when blots appeared on her radar scopes. The report was flashed to Admiral Callaghan on the flagship San Francisco: Three groups of ships off the port bow, at distances ranging from thirteen to fifteen miles!

Course was changed to head directly for the enemy. The two fleets closed rapidly and the radar aboard the Helena showed that the enemy was split into three distinct groups. To the right was a large group of Japanese destroyers. In the middle were a couple of destroyers who were out of formation. They were followed by the cruiser Nagara and the two battleships. On the left was another group of destroyers.

The lead American destroyer was the Cushing. Since the American formation was in a very long single column, the Cushing quickly found itself in danger of colliding with the leading Japanese destroyers. The skipper of the Cushing turned hard left and requested permission to open fire with torpedoes. Permission was granted but the Cushing's aim was thrown off by the sudden turn and the rapid closing speed of the enemy. The Laffey, just astern of the Cushing, also had to swing hard to port. These two destroyers would become separated from the rest of the American formation.

By now the Americans were sighted. The Japanese fleet commander, Admiral Abe, ordered his battleships to switch back to armor-piercing ammunition. This created confusion and delay aboard the battleships in the middle of combat. Admiral Abe did not know what kind of American ships he was facing or their disposition.

The lead Japanese ships opened fire. Admiral Callaghan countered with the order: "Odd ships fire to starboard, even to port!" Like the Japanese Admiral's order, this one was not designed to add clarity to a confusing situation. One can imagine the immediate questions in each American skipper's mind. "Am I odd or even? What about the Japanese ship on the

5

wrong side that is firing at me?" Very quickly this order was ignored as each ship fought for its life against superior Japanese forces.

One by one the American ships confronted the Japanese flagship, the battleship Hiei. Each recognized the foe for what it was and yet immediately decided to take it on. Small destroyers fired their 5" guns and machine guns at the monster. Some got in so close that the Japanese gunners on the towering battleship could not depress their guns to hit the little destroyers. More than one destroyer deliberately fired its machine guns at the bridge of the battleship trying to disrupt command of the monster. They succeeded. Admiral Abe's Chief of Staff was killed. Admiral Abe himself had to take cover and was badly shaken. Fire control of the battleship was poorly coordinated.

But the Japanese were hitting the American ships. Destroyers Cushing and Laffey were smashed. The cruiser Atlanta was devastated in a matter of minutes. Heavy cruiser Portland's steering was disabled but continued fighting. Heavy cruiser San Francisco and Admiral Callaghan went right into the middle of the fight.

San Francisco slugged it out directly with battleship Hiei. An 8" shell from San Francisco put Hiei's steering out of commission. But the cruiser paid dearly. It was hit by many of the huge shells thrown by the Japanese battleships. The smaller shell-hits were too numerous to count. At the end of the battle it was a floating junk pile. The Captain and most of the others on the bridge were killed. Admiral Callaghan died on his flag bridge.

This battle came to be known as the First Battle of Guadalcanal. It was followed the next night by the Second Battle of Guadalcanal which was fought by a different US task force. The first battle resulted in the sinking of the Japanese battleship Hiei. The second battle resulted in the sinking of her sister ship, the battleship Kirishima. The Japanese never again risked battleships or carriers in the waters near Guadalcanal. Within a month they began withdrawing their troops by night from Guadalcanal. That was the turning point of the warfare in the South Pacific. From that point on, the Japanese would always be on the defensive.

On December 9, 1942, President Roosevelt awarded the Medal of Honor posthumously to Rear Admiral Callaghan, and presented it to his son, Lieutenant (junior grade) Daniel J. Callaghan, Jr., USNR. Following is the citation for this award:

"For extraordinary heroism and conspicuous intrepidity above and beyond the call of duty during action against enemy Japanese forces during the Battle of Guadalcanal on the night of November 12-13, 1942. Although outbalanced in strength and numbers by a desperate and determined enemy, Rear Admiral Callaghan with ingenious tactical skill and superb coordination of the units under his command, led his forces into battle against tremendous odds, thereby contributing decisively to the rout of a powerful invasion fleet and to the consequent frustration of a formidable Japanese offensive. While faithfully directing close-range operations in the face of furious bombardment by superior enemy fire-power, he was killed on the bridge of his flagship. His courageous initiative, inspiring leadership and judicious foresight in a crisis of grave responsibility were in keeping with the finest traditions of the United States Naval Service. He gallantly gave up his life in the defense of his country."

CHAPTER ONE: A WAR-TIME WARSHIP

In the winter of '42/'43, several future destroyers, ordered but not yet built had their names changed. They were now named after destroyers that had been sunk in the South Pacific or naval officers killed in the war up to that point. One of these was the DD 792. It was renamed The Callaghan.

The Callaghan was the lead destroyer in the so-called "repeat Fletcher" group. There were originally 115 Fletchers ordered before the war began. After Pearl Harbor it was quickly decided to expand the class to 175, the largest single class of destroyers in the history of the world. The additional 60 Fletchers were ordered despite the fact that a new class of larger destroyers, the Allen Sumner class, had already been planned. Being wartime, speedy construction was considered to be most important. New Fletchers could be built faster than Allen Sumners because of the experience already gained in building the existing ones. The first of the Allen Sumner class would not be commissioned until mid-1943.

Several changes were ordered for the "repeat Fletchers". Some, like the new squared-off bridge, were designed to make construction easier and hence faster. Others, like the five twin-40mm guns were a result of war experience which called for all the anti-aircraft gunnery possible. In fact, due to the much larger numbers of 40mm gun mounts, the design was getting very top-heavy. Top-heavy in a ship means instability particularly in bad weather with big waves and high wind. To compensate somewhat, the main director for the 5" guns was lowered 6 feet. But that was not enough compensation and the Fletchers were known to be overloaded.

The Callaghan was assigned to be built by the Bethlehem Steel shipyard in San Pedro, California. Before the war that yard didn't build ships of any kind. It was a humble repair yard. Then it was converted into a yard to build merchant ships. Later it was decided that the yard would build warships. Many people and many places were called upon to do duty which was not dreamed of before the war clouds gathered.

The Bethlehem Steel corporation knew how to build ships well. It had built ships of several kinds in World War I. It had to cut back to producing just a few merchant ships between the wars. But when called upon to once again produce warships for its country in the naval build-up prior to World War II, it did so with great skill and industry.

On February 21st 1943, the keel was laid for the Callaghan. Over the next several months, a form took shape. The form was that of a simple hull because the Fletchers were flush decked. No superstructure took shape until after the hull was basically finished. Even then just the rudiment of a superstructure was in place prior to launching. Consequently, the Callaghan looked odd at that stage. It would have been difficult for the untrained eye to see a warship in that simple hull. But the trained eye would see power and speed that would provide the foundation for a greyhound of the sea, a destroyer.

A solemn ceremony was held for the launching of the Callaghan. The Navy asked Mrs. Daniel Callaghan to christen the ship. She did so with the dignity that would be expected of an Admiral's widow. The traditional champagne bottle was broken over the bow of the Callaghan and she slid down the ways into San Pedro bay. Surprisingly, almost every man who rode her down those ways was a civilian. The shipyard was still firmly in charge in nearly every respect. The officers and enlisted men of the crew had not yet arrived. That was about to change soon.

The Callaghan was moored (tied-up) to the pier for completion. Soon after that the Navy started sending men to her to serve on the commissioning crew. One of the first to arrive was the chief engineering officer, Floyd Hoskins. Engineering officers always arrived early because they had to oversee the powerplant installation, among other things. At this point, the construction became more of a joint effort between Navy and shipyard.

Lieutenant Hoskins was a mustang, an officer who had come up through the enlisted ranks and because of special talent and leadership, was selected for officers' school. Hoskins was serving on the aircraft carrier Saratoga at the start of the war. He twice experienced the "Sara" taking a torpedo from Japanese submarines. Both incidents were serious but the second time it threatened the very life of the Saratoga. Off San Cristobal, near Guadalcanal on Aug. 25th 1942, the Saratoga took a torpedo in a vital area. The Saratoga, the largest carrier in the US fleet, was crippled and came to a complete stop. The engineering department worked frantically to overcome the damage and supply power to the engines once again. A warrant officer named Hoskins came up with an idea for an electrical jury-rig to get the Saratoga going again. It worked and the Saratoga was saved. Hoskins received a Silver Star for his efforts.

Hoskins was rewarded with a couple of rapid promotions to Lieutenant. He was then assigned to new construction: the Callaghan. Lieutenant Hoskins was instrumental in making the Callaghan a smooth running ship. A ship is a steel hull with machinery in it. Most of that machinery was Lieutenant Hoskins responsibility.

One of the most important men to arrive early was Chief Petty Officer Maiwald. Gene Maiwald was to be the gunnery Chief. That meant that he would be responsible for the training of all the enlisted men aboard who would serve the guns. Although there would, of course, be gunnery officers, on a small warship such as a destroyer during this part of the war, the junior officers would not have a great deal of experience. Therefore a lot of reliance would be placed on the shoulders of the senior enlisted man with more years of experience with the type of guns the Callaghan would carry.

Maiwald was a Godsend to the Callaghan. He had joined the navy in 1935 and served on several different types of ships.

Then he was sent to the Naval gun factory to become an expert in medium caliber guns such as a destroyer carried. From there he became a gunnery instructor. Gunnery instructor was a post that Maiwald excelled at.

However, he quickly became dissatisfied with it. He had joined the Navy before most of the students he was teaching, yet he was not seeing any combat. He applied for sea duty but his commanding officer, recognizing his valuable contributions to the school, turned it down. Finally he saw his chance. A navy bulletin came out which stated that any enlisted with a certain number of years of service could apply for sea duty directly to the bureau of personnel. He did and a couple of anxious months later he got orders to report to the Callaghan in San Pedro.

When Gene reported to the Callaghan, Captain Johnson spoke to him privately. The skipper solemnly told Gene that he would be depending on the Chiefs a great deal because the Callaghan was receiving so many inexperienced officers and men. He said that the Chiefs would be central to the success of the ship particularly in light of the inexperienced officers. He told Maiwald that if Gene had an problems with any of the officers that would interfere with the function of the gunnery department, then he should bring those problems to the skipper.

Shortly thereafter, the gunnery officer reported for duty. Luckily for Gene Maiwald the new gunnery officer was experienced, educated and knew his guns. Lieutenant Jake Heimark was a Minnesotan who had graduated from Annapolis in '40. He had served in the battleship Washington and the destroyer Earle before reporting to the Callaghan. On both of those ships he became very familiar with 5" 38 caliber guns and with gun directors. Those skills along with Gene Maiwald's would be put to the test very soon.

But of course, the most important person to report to the San Pedro shipyard during construction of the Callaghan was Commander Francis Johnson, the Captain. Whenever any

Captain takes over a ship he puts his indelible imprint on that ship. Whether strict or loose in discipline, aggressive or calm in temperament, skilled or unskilled in seamanship, the Captain sets the tone for the ship. Because a ship is a single machine, no matter how complex, a single authority must hold sway. Any ship with two authorities aboard will have a very palpable tension that cannot help the crew in their daily lives. That is why even when there is a higher authority aboard such as a Commodore or Admiral, they must defer to the Captain of the ship in the running of the ship. Otherwise the all important authority of the Captain might be compromised at the wrong time leading to dire consequences. Since the sea is not forgiving, the Captain must rule. The same principle applies to aircraft and that is why the chief pilot of an aircraft is called the Captain.

Francis Johnson was an Annapolis graduate of the class of '29. He had a reputation at Annapolis of being extremely competitive and temperamental. He was involved in water sports and was known to dunk opponents if necessary to win a match.

Johnson married into a military family; his father-in-law was an army General. This may have been hard on Johnson during the latter part of his career which did not go as high as his father-in-law's did. In any case, Francis Johnson did not feel like his career was going the way it should. During the early part of World War II, Johnson served on the staff of the Southern Pacific command. He specialized in ordnance which was undoubtedly an important function during those desperate early campaigns.

But it was not what he wanted and not what he felt he deserved. He watched as others of his class at Annapolis received their own commands. Some of them even went on to higher positions and ranks after their first command. Francis Johnson was a very frustrated naval officer.

Finally the word came that he had been waiting for. He would detach from his current duties and report for command school.

He was going to get command of a destroyer. He felt like this was his final chance to prove himself to his family and to those in the Navy who had passed him over. He was not going to drop the ball. He was determined to have the best destroyer in the US Navy. That was a very tall order to fill during the biggest war the world had ever seen.

When Francis Johnson reported to San Pedro to assume command of the Callaghan, he could not believe what he found. First, the Callaghan was a mess. Ships under construction are always a mess but they were even worse during the breakneck construction days of World War II. Lines, hoses and various types of equipment were everywhere. Because of the non-stop work and cramped working areas, the Callaghan was dirty. Francis Johnson did not like dirt.

However, it was not the condition of the Callaghan that bothered him the most. It was the experience of the crew, or rather the lack of it. He was familiar with the cracker-jack, combat experienced crews of the South Pacific warships. Now he was getting a bunch of kids straight out of boot camp. Most of the crew had never been to sea at all. Many of them, far too many for Johnson, were draftees. He hated the idea of civilians drafted for the duration of the war. He wanted a salty crew but most of these kids were completely green. Incredibly, most of the officers had never had sea duty. Commander Johnson had his work cut out for him and he knew it.

A warship in the United States Navy is organized into departments. There are some differences in organizations between warship types but every destroyer had the same departments. These included gunnery, engineering, navigation, deck force, and medical. The Navy tried to staff the department heads with experienced naval officers. However, in the case of the Callaghan, they were barely able to do so. Hoskins was a mustang, Heimark was young and didn't have many years in the navy, and the first Lieutenant was a young reservist!

The first Lieutenant was responsible for keeping the ship in clean, workable condition. He was in charge of the deck force and damage control. In the case of the Callaghan, the first Lieutenant was Buzzetti who had previous experience on the China station on an old destroyer named Edwards. The Edwards was one of two destroyers from the Asiatic fleet which made it down to Australia without being sunk or captured during the first year of the war. He came to the Callaghan and was a strong right arm in every direction and was a solid officer for the Navy. Competent, able, dependable, fun to be with, all of those things. One couldn't ask for a finer shipmate than "Buzz" Buzzetti. His contribution to the ship was very substantial in terms of morale and in terms of being a very solid citizen in every situation.

The officer who was second in command was the executive officer. The executive officer was essentially in charge of administration, discipline and the day-to-day details of running the ship. Depending on the Captain, the executive officer might have a great deal of room to shape the way the ship operated. In the Callaghan's case, the executive officer was a Lieutenant Commander who was already designated for future command of a ship. But as was standard procedure with the US Navy, a prospective commanding officer often served first as an executive officer on the same type of vessel as would be his future command. For the Callaghan, the executive officer may well have been selected to balance the personality and heavy-handed manner of the Captain.

Don Wulzen was a very intelligent, civilized, patrician officer who exemplified the finest traditions of the Navy. Unfortunately, he was to remain with the Callaghan for only about six months. While the Callaghan was in the middle of the Pacific ocean, Lieutenant Commander Wulzen left to take command of the USS Pritchett, another Fletcher class destroyer in the same squadron.

When Don Wulzen left, Jake Heimark, the third senior officer on board, fleeted up to become the new executive officer. That left the gunnery department without an experienced officer to take over. Ed Calvert, the junior gunnery officer, was a former

Chief Yeoman who had been commissioned about a year earlier. Captain Johnson had no choice but to put Calvert in charge of the gunnery department. But he did so with the proviso that Heimark would remain an overseer of the gunnery department.

Of course, no ship could operate without the enlisted men, the sailors who worked at the direction of the officers and chief petty officers. The enlisted men began arriving for duty with the Callaghan immediately after the first group of officers and petty officers. They arrived in very small numbers at first but prior to the commissioning of the ship the numbers grew larger and larger. Many of them were attending various Navy technical schools around the country before their journey to the Callaghan. Many of the deck force came straight from boot camp on hugh troop trains bringing thousands of sailors and marines to the West coast every week. The largest contingent of sailors destined for the Callaghan were sent to Treasure Island Naval Station in San Francisco. While there, they received training specific to duty aboard ship. They were sent by train to join the Callaghan just before it was commissioned.

Glen Schroder experienced a crowded troop train which traveled the northern route to California. There was a navy administrative type who was in charge of buying the food for the hundreds of sailors. Unfortunately he was not doing a very good job. Schroder suspected he was keeping some of the funds and buying the cheapest breakfasts and sandwiches he could find. It backfired. At one stop late in the trip the sailors spied a vendor at the railroad station who was supplied with delicious looking fruit, decent sandwiches and candy. Dozens of sailors tore into the food despite the vendor's protests. In just a few minutes he was cleaned out and the sailors cleared out as fast as they had appeared. The irate vendor went to the authorities and the purchasing agent had a lot of explaining to do. It is assumed he also paid for the pilfered food.

Upon arriving at Treasure Island, San Francisco, the sailors in Schroder's contingent were divided up between two destroyers:

the USS Longshaw and the USS Callaghan. As each sailor stepped up, they called out Longshaw, Callaghan, Longshaw, Callaghan; and so evenly divided the sailors. As it turned out, neither ship would survive the Pacific war. Schroder was grateful much later that he got the Callaghan. Both ships were sunk off Okinawa but the Longshaw's destiny came first and she suffered nearly a hundred casualties. The Callaghan would have only half that loss.

A couple of brand new torpedoman's mates arrived at the Callaghan fresh from Torpedo school. They quickly discovered that there wasn't much to do. Since the ship was still being outfitted, the torpedos weren't on board yet. They worked the normal details but got frequent liberty. San Pedro was next door to Los Angeles and that meant heaven to these sailors! Compared to San Diego, there weren't many sailors here. But there were plenty of girls!

One of these torpedoman was a smooth talking Italian-American named Eddie Mello. He still remembers how they were rudely taken out of paradise. One day the junior officer in charge of the torpedo gang decided that the new torpedomen should go back to torpedo school for advanced training. Torpedo school, like most of the Navy's technical schools on the West coast, was in San Diego. A shore-based sailors nightmare was tens of thousands of sailors and a city with girls that were bored with sailors. That was San Diego.

Slowly, the Navy's personnel bureaucracy assigned sailors to the Callaghan. Actually the Navy was assigning thousands of sailors to ships all over the United States. But this was the peak production time for Naval ships in World War II and there were so many ships to send sailors to. Occasionally, a sailor didn't serve on the first ship he was assigned to. Allen Foster was designated to ship out with a destroyer and then came down with an illness that confined him to the base hospital. He doesn't know what the original destroyer was but he ended up being reassigned to the Callaghan.

Soon, it was time to get ready for the commissioning of the ship. The pace of work picked up. Captain Johnson became very demanding of his officers that they get their departments squared away. He became obsessed with obtaining all of the equipment that the Navy listed for a destroyer and then some. Unfortunately at this time of the war, ship production was outspeeding certain equipment production. Some things were just not available. Johnson unofficially authorized his men to requisition scare equipment items any way they could.

Thus was born the can-do spirit of the enlisted men of the Callaghan that would serve them so well throughout the life of the ship. Bosuns' mate Simonton became the head of requisitioning. Whenever Captain Johnson wanted something for the Callaghan that supply said it didn't have, he turned to Simonton. The orders were simple. Get what was wanted, no questions asked. On one occasion it was discovered that the Captain's gig was delivered without a rudder. Simonton found out about another destroyer's gig that was on shore being worked on. He got together some men and marched them over to the gig. He then loudly announced "Ok men, there's the rudder we gotta fix." His men detached the rudder and left without interference because Simonton knew how to make it look like it was suppose to happen.

Meanwhile, Chief Engineer Hoskins was having a hard time getting ready for the commissioning. The real meaning of commissioning for him was that the ship would be required to go through ship trials immediately following the commissioning. That meant he had to get the engines in working order and a engineering department capable of operating them.

The latter problem was the more serious. The shipyard was responsible for delivering a fully operating destroyer. But providing a trained crew was the Navy's problem. The Chief Engineer did not have enough trained engine and fireroom personnel. He would get by for awhile by overusing his Chiefs and working long hours but those tactics would not hold up steaming for weeks at a time at sea.

Finally the big day arrived. The San Pedro shipyard was ready to turn the Callaghan over to the Navy. The Callaghan even sported a new coat of paint, olive green! On November 27th, 1943 a special ceremony, steeped in the long tradition of the sea services, was held at San Pedro on the pierside next to the Callaghan. For the first time the officers and crew wore their dress whites. After appropriate speeches by the senior officer present and by a representative of the builder, Bethlehem steel, Captain Johnson read his orders from "Bureau of Naval Personnel." The colors were raised on the mast and the U.S.S. Callaghan was officially a warship of the United States Navy.

Unlike a peacetime commissioning, this one did not take all day. In fact after it was over, Captain Johnson issued orders for all available hands to make ready for a work-party to load ammunition. He wanted his warship to be a warship in every sense of the word. In fact, he intended to get underway within just a couple of days for the Callaghan's first shakedown run.

The next couple of days were a blur for most of the crew. They were under unrelenting pressure from Captain Johnson to get the ship fully ready for sea trials. Every warship goes to sea for trials to determine her capabilities and what needs to be fixed if anything. Captain Johnson made it be known that he wanted to test everything there was to test as soon as possible. Every day brought more news of the war in the Pacific and he was itching to be a part of it.

Then the morning came when everybody took their places for that special moment in a ship's life: the first time out under its own power. For a naval warship, it's a time of testing for the crew as much or more as it is a test of the new ship. In a peacetime merchant ship the crew is likely to be mostly experienced sailors so the maiden voyage focuses strictly on any problems the ship itself may have. But a new destroyer in the middle of a world war is certain to have a mostly green crew that has never been to sea. That makes the maiden voyage a far more tension laden experience than normal. To add to the tension, the Callaghan had the most demanding skipper imaginable.

The first time out was a real trial for the green crew. Coupled with the fact that few of the enlisted sailors had been to sea was the state of the sea itself. Although there was no storm, there were waves and a destroyer has a natural tendency to roll or pitch given the slightest excuse. Many of the new sailors found themselves at the rail divesting themselves of the entire contents of their stomachs. Worse was when a sailor didn't make it to the rail. When this happened, even the experienced sailors suddenly found themselves nauseated. One of the sailors on the bridge didn't quite make it to the rail and this caused a commotion.

On this first time out, the Callaghan got to fire its main battery of 5" guns. This was indicative of the rest of the life of the Callaghan. The skipper was determined to test the destroyer's weapons and would conduct endless drills, often involving live firings. Within just a few days of the commissioning, every weapon on the Callaghan had been test fired except the torpedoes. Torpedoes were very expensive and hard to replace. Therefore, test firings required support from auxiliary vessels to recover each torpedo.

In fact, the Callaghan would only fire torpedoes a couple of times and never in anger. But one would never know that by the way the torpedo gang was drilled. Every known torpedo procedure applicable to destroyers was practiced and practiced again. The torpedo gang would attain not only memorization of all of these procedures but would come to detest and deeply resent the endless drills forced on them. The truth was that most torpedo firing procedures were not overly complex. Without the ability to actually fire the torpedoes, the procedures became boring, almost silly drills. Sighting on neighboring ships, swinging out the torpedo tubes, spinning the dials on the torpedo directors all became meaningless drill.

Meanwhile the gunnery crews were being worked equally as hard but they had the satisfaction of firing their guns. Chief

Maiwald and Lt. Heimark held classes and drills for the gun crews every day and many evenings as well. Although their was some resentment from some of the gunners, Maiwald was able to keep them going with his easy going, down-home ways. He carefully explained to the boys why they needed to know their guns inside and out, by memory and without having to look it up in a book. He and Heimark had been at sea for months at a time with no support available except the expertise aboard your own ship. They knew very well why procedures had to be memorized. The trick was to convince these boys who had never been to sea the value of something that they could barely imagine.

Almost immediately a major problem arose for the gunnery department. For some unknown reason, the main battery could not maintain accuracy while under director control. As with all modern warships, there was a main director, mounted high above the bridge, that was used to sight on targets and control the fire of the main battery. This was extremely important because without it the main guns would not only be basically inaccurate but also uncoordinated. It was the main director coupled with a fire control system that allowed accurate firing at great distances. For U.S. navy destroyers, the 5" guns could be fired accurately at surface targets up to 9 miles away. In the previous world war, that kind of accuracy was only possible from battleships and battlecruisers.

At first, it appeared that the guns were not calibrated correctly. Heimark and Maiwald led the gunnery department through a tedious process of calibrating the guns and the director. The Callaghan went out to sea again and target practice was, as always, included. Once again the main guns would not stay on target especially when the Callaghan was maneuvering. Captain Johnson was not pleased at all. He suggested that maybe Heimark didn't know what he was doing. Since Johnson was an ordnance man, he thought he knew what the problem was and kept telling Heimark so.

The gunnery department next went through a calibration process at night while sighting on the star Polaris. This was the most exacting way any of them had heard of to align the main director. Disastrously, it didn't work. Captain Johnson was now thinking about replacing Heimark. But luckily, the fire control group came up with an idea.

The heart of the U.S. Navy's fire control system at that time was a modern marvel called a Mark I fire control computer. Electronic computers had not been invented yet so the computer referred to was a mechanical device. In this case, the Mark I fire control computer was a large refrigerator sized metal casing full of gears and cams that interacted to perform calculations that kept the guns on the target despite whatever wild maneuvering the Callaghan might be doing. When the director moved fast as when it was slewed onto a target, the cams inside spun at a very high rate of speed.

The important clue was that the guns seemed to operate with accuracy when a static target was fired at while the Callaghan maintained a steady course. The inaccuracy developed whenever either the target was moving fast (an aerial target) or the Callaghan was maneuvering or both. This suggested something wrong with the computer. The firecontrol men opened up the computer and carefully measured and observed. Eventually they discovered that the cams were slipping especially after they were spun at very high speeds. Lt. Heimark was greatly relieved and a report was immediately prepared for the Navy's ordnance department.

Weeks later a letter was received from the Bureau of Ordnance thanking the U.S.S. Callaghan for alerting them to a very serious problem. It turned out that the manufacturer of the fire control computer had traced the problem back to the installation of the cam shafts in the computer. The original computers all worked just fine. But in the middle of the war some women were put on the production line. They did a fine job of installation except for one thing. The cam shafts were manually installed. Power tools were not used. The women did

21

not have the same hand strength as the men who originally performed the installation. They could not snug the cam shafts down as tight. As a result, the cam shafts were prone to slippage when great forces were exerted in high speed operation.

One by one the problems of the Callaghan were resolved. Meanwhile the sailors and officers were getting used to life on a warship. It was one thing to live in a barracks on shore. It was quite another to live in very cramped quarters in a warship. The main living quarters for the sailors was in an area immediately below the main deck in the center/aft area of the ship. It had bunks three deep and six wide. That meant that most of the men were sleeping with two other men real close on either side of them. The only other time most of these men would sleep this close to another human being would be with their wives. But of course, there was only one wife to share the sleeping area with. Not fifty or sixty!

During this intense time around the commissioning an incident occurred that illustrates what life was like with Captain Johnson in charge. One day while the Callaghan was moored to the pier, the Chief Engineer decided to shut down the power plant for maintenance of some type. Usually the Captain was informed of such things but this time he did not get the word. Unfortunately he chose to take a shower soon after. When the Callaghan was alongside the pier, it was easy to get electrical power and cold water provided from the navy facility. However, they did not get hot water. On board ship, the steam power plant provided the hot water and, as a consequence, there now was none. A frantic call came down from the Captain's cabin: "Chief Engineer, Chief Engineer to the Captain's cabin!" Lt. Hoskins rushed in and to his astonishment found a disgruntled skipper with a towel around him demanding to know why there was no hot water.

Most of the officers who came to San Pedro to join the Callaghan were reservists. Before the war, they were civilians who happened to serve weekends and a couple of weeks in the summer in the U.S. Navy. Or in some cases, they did not serve at all before the war.

The new ship's doctor was a good case in point. Philip J. Parker was in medical school at Jefferson in Philadelphia when the war broke out. A few months later a Navy officer came by to make a pitch to the students about joining the Navy after graduation. To Parker, it sounded good. At least it sounded better than some army field hospital in God knows where. So he joined the navy in 1943.

The Navy put Parker and all the other new doctors through a specialized set of courses at the Navy Medical Center in Bethesda. Those courses were designed to prepare them for Navy life and military medical needs. The training lasted for three months and at the very end the new doctors received their assignments from the Navy. Lt. Parker found out that he was going to the West coast for assignment to a new ship.

After a couple of weeks off, Parker traveled west to San Pedro. On arrival, he didn't know what he was supposed to do for accommodations so he got a room at the YMCA. He was unaware that the junior officers were assigned to the Base Officers Quarters (BOQ). So he enjoyed more privacy and less military control than his contemporaries. This was indicative of how Doc Parker's military career was going to unfold. He was a Doctor with a sense of humor. A military officer he was not.

For the first few weeks, Doc Parker spent his working hours at a small infirmary and dispensary at the prison at San Pedro. The military had taken over the prison and was using it for housing, feeding and the medical needs of the enlisted men. There were about four destroyers building at San Pedro so each one had an assigned time for sick call at the dispensary. The Callaghan's men came over at a certain time of the morning and Parker would work sick call until all of the men were tended to. The rest of the day was spent in acquiring medical supplies in preparation for setting up a medical suite aboard the Callaghan.

23

But "painless" Parker, as he was affectionately known, had it pretty easy. He had a Chief Pharmacist Mate named Jones from the state of Iowa. Jones was regular navy and had been in the navy for a number of years. He was completely familiar with the Navy paperwork. So it took no time at all for Parker to relinquish all the daily mundane activities including all things administrative to Jones. Parker became one of those rare doctors who just practiced medicine and never had enough of that to do.

But Captain Johnson was soon to remedy that. After departing westward, he assigned Doctor Parker and Supply Officer Mark Ahrano to hours of work daily in the coding room, typing and decoding messages at sea. This normally would be an enlisted man's job but the two officers were literate and good typists. Johnson resisted all opposition to this unusual procedure and the two officers had to do it for months, quite unwillingly.

After a month or so, the San Pedro shipyard was finished installing equipment and fixing any malfunctions that the Callaghan's crew had identified. It was time to join the real Navy. There wasn't a fleet in the Los Angeles area and as a consequence, limited training facilities. The fleet was in San Diego and the Callaghan transferred there.

Captain Johnson was very relieved to be in San Diego. He wanted the Callaghan to be with the fleet and operate with the fleet. That meant that the crew would learn what it was like to operate the destroyer in company with other naval vessels. In addition, they would experience what it was like to be a part of a fleet; something they could not experience while they were living on shore in a small facility such as San Pedro.

San Diego was another world. It had arguably the largest naval base in the continental United States. There were sailors by the tens of thousands. There were dozens and dozens of ships of all kinds and sizes. The awesome sight of great battleships and aircraft carriers greeted the Callaghan's green crew when they arrived.

The shipyard civilians were gone from the Callaghan as well as the naval personnel from San Pedro. The Callaghan's officers and crew were on their own now. Captain Johnson would put them through their paces.

CHAPTER TWO: PREPARING FOR WAR

From just after Christmas until the first week of February 1944 the USS Callaghan conducted intensive training exercises in the waters of Southern California. In peacetime the chance to cruise off the Southern Californian coast in wintertime would be considered a wonderful vacation. The officers and men of the Callaghan had no such thoughts as they worked through the endless drills and maneuvers that the Navy and Captain Johnson thought up for them.

The Navy, of course, had publications for the many procedures that a naval warship was required to be familiar with. Captain Johnson was grimly determined that the Callaghan would be more than familiar with each and every one of those procedures if it was at all possible. He had the executive officer prepare a rigorous daily schedule of exercises that the Callaghan would carry out.

It is difficult for most civilians to appreciate the extensive number of procedures and drills that the Navy published. Anti-aircraft drills, anti-submarine drills, surface action drills, torpedo firing drills, smoke generation, collision, man overboard, and more. These are but a small sample of the procedures that were expected to be carried out without mishap. Some of the drills could only be practiced rarely because of the effect they had beyond just the ship that was conducting it. Smoke generation, for instance, had the nasty side effect of causing a potential hazard to navigation.

The Callaghan resided at one of the many berths in the San Diego Naval station. The days in San Diego were a blur for the Callaghan's crew. The Callaghan might get underway at any time of the day to go out for some test of the equipment or exercise.

The most common exercise was for anti-aircraft gunnery. The navy had planes out towing sleeves for target practice nearly every day. A sleeve was a long cone shaped cloth held open at the forward end by a wire hoop. It was attached to the tow plane by a cable that, for obvious reasons, was pretty lengthy. In a typical exercise the 5" guns would fire first. When the 5" guns were finished, they would be followed by one or more of the 40mm guns. Then if time and targets allowed, the 20mm guns would get a chance at an aerial target.

Meanwhile, the Engineering department had a junior officer named Low Stern who was another mustang like Lieutenant Hoskins. Unlike Hoskins, this mustang felt closer to the enlisted men then he did to the officers. Unfortunately for him, this camaraderie came to the attention of Captain Johnson. Captain Johnson talked to Hoskins about Ensign Stern. Even though Hoskins verified the Ensign's engineering capability, Captain Johnson insisted that they get rid of him. By the time the Callaghan left the West coast for the Pacific war, Stern had been transferred.

The confusing unscheduled activities continued with overnight cruises out to sea or up the coast, late night or early morning departures and no certainty of what would be asked of the crew next. Most of the crew tried to settle into some type of routine but found it difficult to do. Captain Johnson had his own agenda in mind and a comfortable routine for the crew was not on it.

One of the things Captain Johnson was obsessed with was to have, as much as possible, a self-reliant ship. This meant trying to obtain certain equipment which was not issued to destroyers. In particular, he wanted to be able to effect repairs or modifications with his own resources. This led to a couple of interesting situations as Captain Johnson, although a strict disciplinarian, did not mind having the rules broken in his own favor.

Just before the Callaghan left San Pedro, a welding torch that belonged to the shipyard disappeared. It was last used aboard the Callaghan so the shipyard accused the Callaghan's crew of stealing it. When no-one came forward to confess as to its whereabouts, the shipyard brought aboard a couple of federal agents as part of a search party to find the missing property. This was not a unique situation, other crews had been known to appropriate useful shipyard items in the past and hence the aggressive stance by the shipyard personnel. An exhausting search did not produce the missing torch so the Callaghan was allowed to leave. A few days later the torch was brought up out of one of the ships oil tanks and thoroughly cleaned for future employment as part of the ship's metal working facilities.

Several of the officers had wives staying in the San Diego area while the Callaghan was stationed there. Captain Johnson's father-in-law, the retired Army General, was a resident of San Diego. Just after the New Year, Captain Johnson held a party for the officers of the Callaghan at his home. Many of the officers were apprehensive about the party since Captain Johnson was not known for being amiable or forgiving about any perceived slip in social behavior. Yet surprisingly, most of them found the party to be a pleasant affair. This was the one time Captain Johnson seemed to display genuine regard for his officers. Both Captain Johnson and his father-in-law were gracious hosts for the young men. Perhaps it was the moderating effect of the women present, perhaps it was the holidays, perhaps it was the realization that their time at home was drawing to a close. In any case, the young officers had this one fascinating opportunity to see the human side of their commander before they would leave with him to join the greatest naval conflict the world has ever known.

However, Ensign Dunne was still the butt of jokes at the party. As a former merchant mariner and junior Ensign, Dunne was always singled out for special treatment by the Captain. Ensign Dunne was glad to have the party over. He simply wanted to get to sea and do his job.

Back aboard the ship, the routine, if it could yet be called that, returned to the tension and stress they had come to expect. During one of their first night time deployments from San Diego, a submarine alert was declared. The crew never found out what evidence of a real submarine there was but they found out how their skipper treated such alerts. He immediately brought the Callaghan's crew to General Quarters. He shouted out orders for a search pattern including active sonar pinging. He shouted out more orders for the depth charges to be armed and set at a depth he thought appropriate.

Most of the green sailors were scared to death. By the Captain's behavior, they assumed that a submarine attack was immanent. After all, an alert was declared, they rushed to GQ (General Quarters), the ship suddenly leapt ahead in a burst of speed and the Captain was rapidly shouting out orders. Sonar even reported elusive contacts. Instead of going to war, the war had come to them. Or so they thought.

Nothing came of the submarine alert and eventually the Callaghan proceeded on her mission for the night. For the crew this was but the one of many panicky alerts that would send them scrambling to their GQ stations and send the Callaghan dashing about looking for an enemy that never could be found. Although it was unpleasant and stressful, the crew was being prepared for the real thing. Months later when the real shooting would begin, the crew would react like a well oiled machine. A combat team was in the making.

Many of the crew joined the Callaghan in San Diego. Until she left the States, new crew members would show up every week to join the roster. Of course, this aggravated the training problem as the training and experience was never at the same level for the whole crew or for even one department. Many functions were handled by teams such as a gunnery crew. The crew for a five inch gun might have nine or ten men in it. Just as the men were all getting familiar with their individual functions within that team, along comes a new guy with no experience who must be integrated into the team without disrupting the efficiency of that team. This was difficult and could only be handled by a great deal of training and drill.

A couple of men aggravated the manning problem by leaving the Callaghan. Seaman Schroder, whom we have met before, found a young lady that took far too much of his time and interest. Enough so that he failed to make it back to the ship after one leave. Many sailors were punished for getting back to the ship an hour or two late. It usually meant extra duty, loss of liberty or a fine. But Schroder was a couple of days late. That meant a court martial and jail time. He would be in the brig, a Navy term for jail, when the Callaghan left the West coast. But he would not be completely gone from the story of the Callaghan as we shall see later.

While the Callaghan was in San Diego, Captain Johnson met a Reserve officer whom he took a liking to. The officer's name was Hugh Owens and he had been a lawyer in his civilian life before the war. Hugh wanted to go to sea so he asked Captain Johnson if there was any chance of getting an officers position on the Callaghan. Johnson promised to ask for Owen's transfer to the Callaghan.

Captain Johnson did ask for Owen's transfer but there was one little catch. Owens had never been to sea and had no training for any type of ship duty. As a result, the Navy personnel bureau changed his file so that he was given a future assignment to the Callaghan. But first he had to go to officers school to make him acceptable for command at sea. Unfortunately, the time it would take to get Hugh Owens to school, complete his training and then make his way across the Pacific to the Callaghan would be longer than the time it would take for the Callaghan to complete its training and first three missions in the combat zone. The Callaghan would be ready for the big time when novice Owens would report aboard.

The Callaghan returned to the San Pedro naval station at Los Angeles on Jan. 15, 1944. The shakedown testing and training was over and the ship went into post-shakedown availability at the U.S. Naval Dry Docks at Terminal Island. The ship would spend 15 days being worked over by technicians and laborers to fix bugs that had been discovered and to get the ship ready for combat duty in the Pacific. One important change that occurred here was that the green camouflage paint that earned the nickname "Green Hornet" would be replaced with a conventional scheme of blues and greys.

Soon the time came to prepare for leaving the West coast to join the war. Captain Johnson reported to the Navy authorities that the Callaghan was ready for action. A set of orders came back with directions for the Callaghan to depart for Pearl Harbor, Hawaii on Feb. 5th, 1944. The Captain wasted no time in informing his officers who, in turn, informed the crew.

This set off a round of frantic activities as officers and men alike made final preparations to say goodbye to their loved ones, whether in person or by some means of long distance communication. A lucky few had a wife or girlfriend in the area. The vast majority either wrote a quick round of letters, or scrapped together the money for a phone call or telegram. A phone call was best because they could then tell their loved ones the whole story, at least as far as they knew. An officer would censor a letter so the men could not disclose where they were going. It could only say something vague like "We're leaving soon and won't be back for a long time."

Captain Johnson was still not satisfied with the readiness of the ship or men. He was particularly annoyed that the Navy had not yet given him a full crew. But Navy personnel assured him that he would get the rest of his enlisted men in Hawaii. There was nothing else he could do about it as he had his orders to get the Callaghan to Hawaii to join the Pacific command.

A day before the Callaghan was to leave for Hawaii, the squadron commander and his staff moved aboard, thus making the Callaghan the flag ship of the squadron. Squadron 55 was a brand new unit of the United States Navy and its purpose was to assimilate eight new Fletcher class destroyers into a cohesive fighting unit. The practice in World War I and between the wars was to train squadrons of destroyers to operate together in anticipation of fleet sized battles. The squadron would protect a battle line unit from attacks by enemy destroyers, submarines or aircraft. Equally as important, when the squadron's fleet went into battle with the enemy's capital ships (battleships and/or battlecruisers), the squadron might be ordered to make a torpedo attack against those giant ships. Such an attack by German destroyer squadrons against the British battle line at the Battle of Jutland in 1916 was credited by many with saving the German fleet from destruction.

But, as has been pointed out earlier, the reality of World War II naval conflict seldom allowed squadrons to operate intact much less execute a spectacular torpedo attack against enemy battleships. Even when such attacks did occur, they were almost always failures. A British squadron made such an attack against the German Battleship Bismark in 1941 with no apparent success. In the bloody Solomon Islands campaign, many torpedoes were fired from US destroyers against larger Japanese warships, again with no credited success. True, US torpedoes were found to be defective and destroyer squadrons were usually unable to make the kind of optimum, coordinated torpedo attack that tactical doctrine called for. The fact was that naval conflict was changing. The conditions that allowed a full squadron of destroyers to make an attack as a unit, separate from the larger ships it was assigned to protect, were disappearing.

Naval warfare in the Pacific was so brutal and desperate that warships were often sent to the conflict individually as soon as they were available. Loss of ships in conflict and maintenance problems in forward areas with limited support meant that squadrons often existed only on paper. Too often, whatever ships were available were put together in a task force and sent out on short notice against the enemy. Not until mid-1944, the third year of the war, were destroyer squadrons able to operate intact for any length of time.

So it was that Captain C.R. Todd came aboard the Callaghan as commander of destroyer squadron 55 which consisted of exactly two ships. The other destroyer was already at Pearl Harbor. The six ships that should have filled out the squadron were still building or being equipped. In peacetime, the

Callaghan would have remained in San Diego waiting for the other ships to join it. Instead, the Callaghan was ordered to proceed independently to Pearl Harbor.

Captain Johnson was not thrilled to have the squadron flag aboard his new ship. He was having problems enough readying his ship for combat operations without the additional pressure of having a higher authority aboard. Although Captain Todd was fully aware of the inadequate supply situation at the time, there was nothing he could do about it except note it in his reports. He was just as powerless in this respect as Captain Johnson.

Even with the Commodore aboard, the responsibility for the Callaghan lay completely with Captain Johnson. The squadron commander's responsibility regarding the Callaghan was administrative only. The majority of his decisions affecting the Callaghan were put in reports copied to Captain Johnson. The Commodore was never in command of the Callaghan even when he was on the bridge. Operationally, as far as the Callaghan was concerned, the Commodore was just a passenger.

There was a side effect of not having a full crew. That meant that there was room for passengers. In due course, Captain Johnson was informed that fifty-one Marines would be boarding the Callaghan for the trip to Hawaii. In addition, twenty-three Navy enlisted men and three officers would be catching a ride to Hawaii via the Callaghan.

The big day arrived for the U.S.S. Callaghan and crew. At dawn, the special sea detail was set and all was in readiness. At Captain Johnson's command, the lines tying the Callaghan to the pier were singled up. After giving the appropriate commands, the last line was let go. With a now smooth and precise skill, the Callaghan departed San Pedro harbor. As soon as the Callaghan cleared the harbor, Captain Johnson ordered speed increased. All those topside who were not

33

absorbed in their duties watched in silence as the shore and harbor buoys quickly disappeared.

Captain Johnson made one of the most dramatic announcements these men would ever hear. He said "We are heading into the war zone and some of you men will not be coming back. However, those who are fortunate to survive will return as heroes." Most of the men wondered who would see that shore again and who would not. The U.S.S. Callaghan and almost fifty men would not.

Most of the sailors had by now adapted to the motion of the ship at sea so that they no longer suffered from seasickness. Some of the experienced sailors had made known their disdain of the weakness of the "green" crewmembers. Now it was the turn of the new sailors to make fun of someone else's seasickness.

The marines had come aboard with the rough-tough swagger of new marines eager to show the world that they were the best fighting troops in the world. After all, they had been through the famous marine boot camp, hadn't they? They looked over the Callaghan's new sailors with an air of superiority.

Unfortunately, they did not fully comprehend the warnings they had received about seasickness. As soon as the Callaghan got out to open sea, they suddenly found that this substantial warship that they thought was solid and powerful would not stay still. It rolled and pitched and swayed, endlessly. Soon their stomachs were in revolt. Marines were soon either on their knees in the head or lined up at the rail offering up the contents of their stomachs to the sea Gods. The Callaghan crew found themselves feeling superior to fellow fighting men for the first time.

After the first day or so of the transit to Hawaii, things settled down to a semblance of a routine. By now the crewmembers knew basically what was expected of them at sea and they performed their regular duties with ease. Each man stood watches on a regular basis. A watch lasted eight hours, three watches to each day. The schedule was midnight to eight, eight to four and four to midnight.

Life became a blur of watches stood, meals and drills, seemingly endless drills. Although drills were usually planned in advance by the Captain and the Executive officer, they were never announced. Sailors who had just come off the midnight to eight watch might just be settling in for some sack time when General Quarters would come blaring over the Public Address system. After all stations reported in as manned and ready, a drill would be announced. "Now hear this, now hear this, anti-aircraft drill will now commence". Or, "Anti-submarine drill" or "Man overboard drill" or "Torpedo firing drill". Soon the men were sick of drills.

Little noticed by the men, but noticed by some of the officers, the drills, training and instruction were having a remarkable effect. Teams had been formed and were now becoming remarkably efficient. General Quarters was held in a very respectable time. The gunners were batting out shells like a well oiled machine. Shells were closing in on targets, sometimes hitting. The Callaghan could execute maneuvers with speed and precision. The torpedo gang was positively bored. The Callaghan was no longer green, either in appearance or in the experience of the crew.

After the crew had rushed through the first day or so at sea and things settled down somewhat, they began to make friends with their passengers. Almost immediately a time-honored tradition in the armed services came alive. The sailors began trading with the marines. The hottest item was the one item the marines had which no other service seemed to carry: the jungle knife. At first the marines were reluctant to part with the knives. After all, it was the only unique weapon they had and it might not be replaceable. But the sailors offered increasing amounts of cash or items in trade. Before the Callaghan docked at Pearl Harbor, almost every knife had been traded away.

Each knife was a treasure but none of them remained intact as government issue jungle knives. When the first sailor showed off shiny custom-made Plexiglas handles, all the other knife owners wanted a part of the action. Soon the repair shop was doing a small but brisk business in plastics. The knives were all converted to Plexiglas.

When radar first reported land *early* on Feb. 10th, word spread quickly. The new sailors and passengers were eager to catch their first sight of Pacific islands. As travel was far more expensive in that era then it is now, none of them had ever been to Hawaii before. Hawaii was still a territory of the United States and was not developed at all compared to today. As a result it still retained the mystique of an exotic tropical paradise. Sailors that were free from duty for the moment gathered to catch the first glimpse of the high island-mountains of Hawaii.

After the first island came into view the sailors quickly disappeared below. Some of them had duties to perform but most of them wanted to check on their dress whites. They were coming in to the Gibraltar of the Pacific, Pearl Harbor and nearly everyone from the Captain on down wanted to look good. Of course, there were a couple of old salts who downplayed the excitement of the newer sailors. They had seen Pearl Harbor and Honolulu before and, more important, they knew that the both were flooded with sailors.

There was one last chore to fulfill before the Callaghan's sailors would see Honolulu this time. Much to the chagrin of the eager sailors, an announcement was made to prepare for Anti-aircraft gunnery practice. There was undoubtedly a general groaning and muttering under the breath against the endless drills and authority in general.

The navy provided a plane towing target sleeves. The Callaghan made four firing passes. The crew knew that only one thing would shorten the firing practice. That would be to shoot down the target sleeves. In four passes firing just thirty-one 5" shells, Jake Heimark's gunners shot down three target sleeves. Since the supply of target sleeves in the sky at that moment was limited, the Callaghan was finished with anti-aircraft practice and returned to Pearl Harbor. Although the Captain did not express it to anyone, he was secretly pleased. He made sure that the shooting down of three sleeves with only thirty-one shells was recorded in the log book. He would later incorporate that fact into the war diary of the Callaghan.

Soon the first islands disappeared and then the island of Oahu was visible. The distinctive Diamond Head volcano told them the trip was nearly over. After entering through the channel into Pearl Harbor, the Callaghan headed for pier K-1. Mooring was completed at 11:20 on a bright Hawaiian morning. But the Callaghan sailors were not to get liberty on this first day.

After the marines and navy passengers departed, the crew got the word that the Callaghan was receiving torpedo warheads and detonators from the navy yard. Following that, the ship would be refueled. Liberty would not be granted until tomorrow.

After the Callaghan moored to pier K-1 again, the crew began to anticipate liberty in Honolulu. Work details prevented liberty for most of them on that first day. The next day, however, a large group of sailors were granted their first experience of a tropical port of call. Like most sailors, they set off with a great deal of enthusiasm.

Meanwhile, the Captain and senior officers were making plans to get the Callaghan ready for war. Captain Johnson and the Commodore had already reported to the office of the Pacific Destroyer command at Pearl. There they received general instructions on what was expected of the Callaghan while it was in Hawaii. More specific instructions on training procedures and schedules, local policy and area charts were also obtained.

After the mundane requirements were met, Captain Johnson began to seriously consider how to obtain a piece of equipment that he badly wanted for the Callaghan but had failed to requisition so far. Based on his experience and what had happened to ships in the South Pacific, he had decided that the Callaghan would benefit from a metal bending machine. The problem was that such a machine was usually found on repair ships or large aircraft carriers. Probably no other destroyer in the entire fleet had a metal bending machine. None-the-less, Captain Johnson was determined to get one.

He began to make inquiries to every naval officer he could find that might be involved with work that would require such machines. He soon determined that there were some at Pearl but that most of them were being used or were being jealously guarded by their owners. Obtaining one was not going to be easy at all.

Over in Honolulu, the enlisted men who were lucky enough to have leave were fanning out around the city. Little groups of sailors were engrossed in the pursuit of various forms of entertainment and enlightenment, some their families would approve of and some they would not. Some of the men were simply being tourists in a tropical port of call they had never been too.

On the morning of Feb. 12, 1944, the world for the Callaghan men suddenly changed. Orders arrived directing the Callaghan to prepare to leave within a couple of hours for their first war mission. The play acting was over and the war had arrived. The Callaghan was ordered to proceed in company with the destroyer Tingey to join Task Unit 50.14.1 consisting of Washington, Manlove, and Franks to supplement the escort to Pearl.

Behind this cryptic order was the fact that the battleship Washington was limping back to Pearl Harbor after a collision with the battleship Indiana. The Washington was having a very difficult time because its bow had been sheered off by the collision. A temporary repair job had been accomplished at the new fleet anchorage at Majuro but it was not satisfactory at all. The Washington was experiencing vibration and could not steam more than 14 knots. To accentuate its vulnerability, it maneuvered poorly due to its now flat nose and the fear of putting too much stress on the temporary repair. The Washington was in great danger from any Japanese submarine that might get within firing range. It was slow and vulnerable and only had two destroyers escorting it. The authorities at Pearl wisely decided to send out reinforcements to help get the Washington back safely.

At 12:11pm, the Callaghan got underway with a new purpose. No longer was it heading for yet another destination for equipping or training. Without the additional training they had expected to get in Hawaii, the crew of the Callaghan found themselves checking their equipment and ammunition with a new found enthusiasm. This was not for another bothersome inspection. This time it might save their lives.

The Callaghan, in formation with the destroyer Tingey, set a course to the southwest and set a brisk pace of 20 knots. Normal cruising was 15 knots, a speed designed to be economical with the fuel. This time it was decided that speed was more important than fuel mileage. The Washington needed help as soon as possible.

The tension aboard the ship affected everyone from Captain Johnson down. Just after sunset, surface radar picked up a vessel ahead. The crew was still at sunset GQ so the only disturbance was to the nerves of the crew. Luckily it soon turned out to be a friendly patrol craft on the fringes of the Hawaiian defense zone. Still many sailors had trouble sleeping that night.

The next morning just after breakfast, surprise target practice was called. The Tingey fired a 5 inch anti-aircraft round which burst well away from both ships and the Callaghan gunners were ordered to fire on it. Seventeen rounds of 5 inch were expended in this drill that occurred as the two ships continued their run toward a mid-ocean rendezvous. The Tingey also exercised its gunners skills with a few 5" rounds after the Callaghan was through.

The drills and inspections continued during daylight hours on this little voyage to no-where. Relentlessly, the two groups of ships drew closer together until they found each other.

A little after 1:30 pm on the afternoon of St. Valentine 's Day, radar contact was made with friendly ships. Soon the men topside could make out the heavy masts of the Washington. Shortly thereafter, the two destroyers joined the battleship's little task force. A decent escort was now formed around the damaged ship with four destroyers instead of only two. The Callaghan began performing the duty it had been built for. It proudly took the lead position in the front of the task group.

Since the Callaghan was busy guarding the Washington and looking out for Japanese submarines, the incessant drills that had characterized its time at sea so far suddenly stopped. This meant that much of the crew had little to do. Routine maintenance and chow time became the focus of the crew not standing watch.

Yet one little group remained overworked and under pressure. That group was the quartermasters. A select group of enlisted men aboard every naval warship was trained to carry out navigation related duties. These men had been sent to school to learn the theories and procedures used for navigation in the US navy. Such skills as using a sextant to record the angle of the sun or a star above the horizon were practiced. The duties these men would perform were extremely important to the safety and proper function of any naval ship.

Like many men in wartime, the quartermasters aboard the Callaghan were cross-trained to perform other important duties. Since the Callaghan had never received the trained radar operators it was suppose to have, Captain Johnson decreed that the quartermasters would perform this vital duty. So it was that in addition to taking turns at the wheel of the Callaghan, exercising the navigation equipment, logging the navigation data hourly, these men spent endless hours in CIC staring at the radar scopes that would indicate a possible air or surface contact. They were also cross-trained as sonar operators.

At 2:00am, the sonar shack reported a sonar contact, 1400 yards distant and just off to the left. The Callaghan immediately went to General Quarters and altered course directly toward the contact. A message was broadcast to the task group which caused the Washington to plow into an emergency turn away from the location of the contact. Using standard procedure, the Callaghan prosecuted the contact while the rest of the task group steamed away.

Captain Johnson was using the small sea cabin adjacent to the bridge as his quarters so he was on the bridge within moments of the GQ alarm. As expected the contact disappeared when the Callaghan was almost on top of it. This happened because the noise of the destroyers own engines and turbulence from the hull and propellers blotted out sonar returns from directly beneath or behind the ship. Destroyers had to wait until opening up some distance from a submarine to reestablish contact.

Unfortunately, the contact was not heard from again after the original pass. Captain Johnson aggressively quartered the area for about a half an hour with no luck. At that point the Commodore ordered the Callaghan to rejoin the task group. In other circumstances the search might have been made for much longer. But the whole purpose of the mission was to protect the Washington and it was now out of range of any submarine that might have been at the original location. To protect the Washington, the Callaghan had to get back into position in the escort screen of destroyers.

The Callaghan went to full speed to rejoin the escort screen. Meanwhile, Captain Johnson decided that the original contact was a false one and had it recorded that way in the log book. Sonar was a new technology in those days and the equipment was very crude, especially by todays standards. False contacts were caused by many things: whales, a school of fish, sometimes even a thermal layer a couple of hundred feet down could cause a return. The Callaghan was particularly handicapped because it had no experienced sonar operators. It took serious experience to determine a false echo from a the real thing.

The Callaghan took its place at the head of the little task force again. The sailors not on watch went back to their bunks knowing that all too soon morning reveille would get them up again for morning duties and breakfast. This was a pattern that would repeat itself again and again throughout the time the Callaghan would spend at sea in the Pacific. The threat of submarines or unidentified aircraft would result in General Quarters being sounded and force all the men to their battle stations in the middle of the night. Sleep became a very precious commodity.

The next morning, not long after breakfast, the Callaghan experienced another submarine scare. This contact was more serious in one regard. The range was reported as 400 yards. At 400 yards, the Callaghan could only hope to circle back to make an attack. Again, contact was quickly lost. It was also evaluated as a false contact and logged as such. The quality of Callaghan's contacts might have been called into question at this point except for the fact that the Tingey now reported a contact. The task force commander called for a change of course to clear the area. He was not going to take a chance on the assumption that these contacts were false.

There would be one more "submarine" contact before the task force would reach Hawaii. This time most of the crew reacted much differently than during the first two contacts. The heart-racing anxiety was replaced with a more professional interest. Finally on Feb. 18th, the task force was within radar range of Hawaii. Strangely, they took time out for the Washington to get in some AA practice. A plane was sent out from Hawaii and at 9:00am the Washington commenced a two hour gunnery practice session. This from a ship that was considered both extremely valuable and, at this time, extremely vulnerable. The authorities had to know that the Washington

42

would soon be laid up in a dry dock unavailable for any combat of any kind. Yet here they were, banging away at target sleeves while essentially crippled!

The task force began steaming through the Pearl Harbor defensive nets a little after 2:30 in the afternoon. The Callaghan took time for boat practice before mooring. The deck force lowered both of the Callaghan's boats into the water and then retrieved them again. The destroyer then went to the same anchorage berth as before and tied up alongside the destroyer Halsey Powell. The Callaghan's first mission had been exciting but not, apparently, dangerous.

At 5:00 that day, Captain Johnson served sentences to the latest offenders of Navy justice in the Callaghan crew. As usual the sentences were very harsh. Following that event the ship was refueled. Some of the crew was beginning to think that this was not paradise after all.

The next day was a Saturday and a relatively quiet day in port for the Callaghan. The one significant event was that a hundred rounds of red dye projectiles for the 5" guns were received aboard. The next few days were going to be gunnery days for a squadron sized formation of destroyers and would include several new experiences for the Callaghan.

On Sunday, official passengers from a different armed service boarded the Callaghan. It was a U.S. Army shore bombardment spotting team. In preparation for the great island invasions that everyone knew the destroyers would be involved with, they were going out to a small island in the Hawaiian chain that was used for gunnery and bombing practice. For the first time the Callaghan would have someone ashore in radio communication with it to give the ship targets and correct the fall of its gun fire.

Four destroyers left that Sunday morning and made their first stop at an approved naval gunnery practice area where they were met by some support vessels. The Callaghan fired radar calibration practice in order to insure the accuracy of its 5" guns while under radar control. Later it fired the 5" guns under local control. This meant that each gun turret's crew relied on its own periscope sighting system rather than the much more accurate main director mounted high above the bridge of the ship. Such practice was necessary in case the main director was knocked out by enemy action or by mechanical failure. The other destroyers in the formation carried out the same practice while the Callaghan waited.

That night just before 10:00pm, the formation met with a vessel towing a target sled. The destroyers were about to perform the type of practice that had become so important in this war: night surface gunnery practice. This was seldom practiced before the war and the consequences were dire. All of the surface battles fought in the South Pacific were slugged out at night. After the battles of Coral Sea and Midway, it was obvious that surface forces stood no chance of surviving against determined opposition from the air. Therefore, surface vessels of both sides stayed safely under their own air forces protection during the day. It was at night that they headed out at top speed to find the enemy and use all those many gun barrels and torpedo tubes that were developed for great fleet actions.

After the U.S. navy suffered such heavy losses in the night fighting around Guadalcanal in 1942 and 1943, a new emphasis was put on night practice. The Japanese navy had been training at night for decades. It took blood and lost ships to get our Navy to break its peacetime habit of practicing only during daylight and good weather.

The Callaghan fired star shells for illumination and standard ammunition at the target sled. Crewmembers topside enjoyed the fireworks like show provided by the star shells. After the practice was complete, most of the crew was dismissed for much needed sleep. The Callaghan steamed off to a safe, distant position to wait while the other destroyers completed their practice. The Callaghan usually got to practice first simply because the Squadron Commodore was aboard her. Rank hath it's privileges.

Just about dawn the next morning the group of destroyers headed for the small island of Kahoolawe Island. At 7:12am, off Smuggler's Cove the Callaghan stopped engines while landing craft came alongside to receive the shore spotting personnel. The Callaghan rejoined the other three destroyers. Shortly thereafter, maneuvers were conducted with the four destroyers in a dry run preparatory to conducting the shore bombardment. At 8:37am, the crew was sent to their G.Q. stations.

It took some time for the shore party to get ashore and get their communications established. During this time the Callaghan conducted fighter director exercises. This was a new role for destroyers that was a direct outgrowth of experience in combat. In the beginning of the war, the necessity of maintaining control over the protective fighter cover that would guard against enemy air attack was only appreciated by aircraft carrier commanders. After a couple of years of war in which devastating air attacks occurred in all kinds of situations, it became apparent that smaller vessels would often have to take over this task. Because destroyers always were among the forward forces and were being used increasingly for picket duty in advance of major combatants, it became obvious that they were the logical candidates for the fighter direction function. In fact the Callaghan would seldom be called upon to perform this function until late in its wartime career. But when this task was performed, it became a life and death matter.

While exercising with the local fighter forces, a surprise anti-aircraft drill was sprung. A tow plane came by with a target sleeve behind and a few rounds were quickly thrown at the sleeve. The rest of the morning was spent simulating all the various kinds of air attack that a naval vessel could expect. Torpedo planes, dive bombers and fighters all made "attacks" on the Callaghan. The communications personnel talking with the fighter cover were kept very busy trying to get the fighters in position to ward off each of these attacks.

Finally after lunch the shore bombardment problem was begun. For about an hour and a half, the Callaghan received targets from the shore party and blazed away with its 5" guns. When a target was judged to be destroyed a cease fire was ordered. Within just a few minutes, a new target was assigned and the drill was repeated. Again, this practice was for a skill that would not be called upon for months. But during the last phase of the Callaghan's career, this skill would be called upon frequently and would gain the Callaghan a reputation for excellence.

The shore bombardment exercise was divided into three phases. The exercise began at 1:25pm and because of the three phases and the waiting intervals in between phases, it took up most of the afternoon. It was nearly 5:30pm before the last destroyer was finished with the firing exercise. Luckily this was just in time for dinner so the crew got a good hot meal.

After dinner the crew was called to General Quarters again. This time it was in preparation for night anti-aircraft practice. Once again this was a rare opportunity as anti-aircraft practice was always held during daylight. Careful coordination was required to conduct such firing at night in order to prevent shooting down a stray patrol plane or the target tow plane. As was the case for the previous exercises, the Callaghan got to practice first. When this exercise was complete the Callaghan secured from general quarters but set condition two which was the next highest level of readiness.

A final exercise involving starshell illumination was held before the ships knocked off for the night. Another cruising disposition was assumed and the little task force steamed back and forth for the rest of the night while their tired crews not on watch enjoyed the night's sleep knowing that more was going to be demanded of them the next day.

As usual the crew was awakened before dawn. This time, along with their usual morning routines of shaves and showers, they were treated to a friendly bombing attack. The topside crew got to see how difficult it was to pick out and identify aircraft in the pre-dawn half-light. After breakfast it was back to general quarters and more exercises. The entire morning was occupied by the difficult task of trying to shoot down target drones. The first target drone made the exercise particularly difficult by going out of control and crashing in the water. Luckily the rest of the drones were more cooperative. 56 rounds of 5" anti-aircraft ammunition was fired at these drones.

The drone exercise was finished at 11:37am so the crew was sent to lunch while the Callaghan was sent at high speed back to the little island of Kahoolawe. At 1:00pm the crew was back at General Quarters and preparing to open fire. The next three hours were spent at various shore bombardment and anti-aircraft exercises. Then at 4:00pm the gun crews got a real workout. A "Call Fire" exercise was conducted with the shore party controlling the gunfire. In just a half hour, 128 5" rounds were fired. After this unusual fast paced exercise the Callaghan pulled off to wait while other destroyers conducted the same type of practice.

Just before 6:00pm the Callaghan steamed in close to the island for a little 40mm gunnery practice. The crew then secured from General Quarters and the Callaghan stopped to pick up the shore party. A short time later the shore party was transferred to other destroyers. At 10:00pm, it was night battle practice against a target sled. Like they had two nights ago, the Callaghan fired starshells to illuminate the target and then high explosive shells to try to hit the target.

The Callaghan did not fire any more after it was finished with the target sled. But various formations and maneuvers were conducted with the other destroyers to simulate night combat conditions. As a result the crew got a very short night's sleep. This time at sea with the endless exercises, the frequent firing and the lack of sleep would prepare the Callaghan crew as nothing else could for the actual battles that were to come.

Reveille came as an unwelcome intrusion early next morning. After breakfast it was back to General Quarters again and more battle practice. This morning it was to include firing against a surface target and radar torpedo practice against one of the sister destroyers.

After lunch the Task Group dissolved with the various destroyers free to conduct exercises on their own or with other willing destroyers. The Callaghan spent the first part of the afternoon making or receiving dry run torpedo attacks with the destroyers Tingey and Edwards. In mid-afternoon the Task Group formed up again in a long column headed for Pearl Harbor. General Quarters was sounded again in preparation for anti-aircraft practice.

Tow planes pulling target sleeves were soon flying over the column of destroyers. In contrast to the Callaghan's previous experience with target practice, all of the destroyers were given permission to fire at will at any of the targets that were within range. Consequently the Callaghan got in a more than the usual amount of target practice in a very short period of time. This target practice looked and sounded like a real battle as 5" guns, 40 mm and 20 mm automatic guns were all firing more or less simultaneously from the various destroyers.

In this practice session the Callaghan fired off 82 rounds of 5", 549 rounds of 40 mm and 296 rounds of 20 mm ammunition. When the session was over the decks were littered with shell casings. The crew secured from General Quarters and were ordered to clean up and stow away the shell casings.

At 5:00pm the Callaghan was working its way up the Pearl Harbor channel. After stopping to lower its boats to send some personnel ashore, the Callaghan proceeded to its assigned anchorage and moored to a couple of buoys. A very tired crew was happy to be back in port. There were, however, still duties to be performed which including refueling the ship after dark.

The following day, Thursday February 24th, was a welcome quiet day in port. The Callaghan took on provisions and the crew performed the usual routine maintenance tasks.

The quiet was not to last. Early the next morning, the Callaghan prepared to get underway once more. The destroyer steamed out of Pearl Harbor and set a course to an assigned practice area. There it joined another Fletcher class destroyer, the Franks. The morning was spent in torpedo practice drills which this time included live firings.

The Callaghan carefully fired a single torpedo at 10:36 and then another one at just before noon. The second torpedo was seen to rise to the surface at about 1000 yards out in its run. It was definitely not supposed to do that and no trace was found of the torpedo after that. Torpedoes used in practice were set to rise to the surface only at the end of their runs after the engines had run out of fuel. They were then designed to float in order to facilitate their recovery for reuse. This torpedo was clearly defective.

After lunch the torpedo exercises were continued. Another practice torpedo was fired at 1:00pm with the auxiliary vessel Swan standing by to recover the torpedo. This time the practice torpedo was speedily recovered. Most of the rest of the afternoon was spent conducting torpedo practice including one more live firing.

Just before dinnertime, the Callaghan was back in Pearl Harbor moored next to the USS Edwards at a pier. After dinner, four replacement torpedoes were delivered to the Callaghan to replace the four fired in practice that day. Later a fuel oil barge came alongside to top off the Callaghan's fuel bunkers. As if to demonstrate that the Callaghan really was in a war zone after all, an ammunition truck arrived to transfer ammunition to the

Callaghan at 11:30 at night! The sailors rousted out of their bunks to load ammunition could not have been happy.

Luckily the next day, a Saturday was another quiet day in port. Some of the luckier sailors received liberty. At noon four torpedoes were exchanged for routine maintenance reasons. In mid-afternoon the Callaghan got underway to go back to its previous berth at buoys in the anchorage. Very late that night sailors Brunton and Chedester reported aboard five hours after their leave was supposed to end. They were not so lucky after all.

Sunday was an even quieter day than Saturday while the crew not on liberty prepared the ship for its next sortie. Right after breakfast another fuel barge pulled alongside to top off the Callaghan again. This was a good clue that the Callaghan would not be idle long. Soon the scuttlebutt (rumor mill) was stirring things up with the story that the Callaghan was going to leave Pearl Harbor bound for the real war zone in the Central Pacific. Most of the officers were informed of the Callaghan's next destination but were sworn to strict secrecy.

The next morning Chief Henderson was transferred to the Naval hospital for a broken rib. This did not sit well with the Captain as he jealously strove to hold on to his experienced men. At 10:00am the Callaghan cast off and proceeded to leave Pearl Harbor.

CHAPTER THREE: MUCH ADO ABOUT NOTHING

Shortly after clearing the entrance to Pearl Harbor, the Callaghan joined formation with six other destroyers and increased speed to 19 knots. The destroyer group settled down on a course of 256 degrees in a cruising disposition. The Captain announced to the crew that their little task group of destroyers was on its way to the fleet anchorage at Kawajalein. Immediately crew members were asking each other, where in the heck is Kawajalein? Crew members in the know smugly answered that it was in the Marshall Islands. That was followed by the question, where is the Marshall Islands? Usually the answer to that question did not really illuminate the minds of these young civilians turned sailors.

As usual the crew of the Callaghan was run through some exercises on this first day out. Knowing that they were on their way to the war zone helped them take the exercises seriously.

Late that night the destroyers met an inbound Naval task group and exchanged greetings by radio. Although the Callaghan's crew could not then realize it, this was now to be their world. The Callaghan would spend its career at sea in contact with other Navy ships and planes but with only tenuous and infrequent contact with the world and the lives they had grown up with.

Soon after passing the other Navy task group, the USS McDermutt left the formation and went ahead at full speed. The McDermutt was going to provide a target for exercises to be held early the next morning. The McDermutt disappeared in the darkness and was only tracked by its solitary echo on the surface radar screens in each destroyer.

At 3:30am a heavy rain storm was encountered. Although it was relatively brief, its violence helped remind the crew on watch that the ship was now crossing the great open space of the central Pacific ocean. The distance from Pearl Harbor to Kawajalein was over 2000 miles of absolute emptiness.

At 8:00am, the six destroyers left in the formation divided into two divisions of three destroyers each. About a hour later, day division battle practice was started using the McDermutt as a target. No live ammunition was used in these exercises. The whole morning was spent in first one exercise and then another with the divisions alternating the practice. The exercises were called off just before lunch time and the seven destroyers reformed one task group in an anti-submarine disposition.

Later that afternoon, Captain Johnson held the time-honored Navy tradition of the Captain's Mast. The Captain's mast was the most common way of carrying out justice aboard a US Navy vessel. The Captain was responsible for administering justice for all but the most minor offenses. During the days of sail the court was held by the Captain near a mast of the ship, hence the name Captain's mast. Since the days of steam, it had nothing to do with an actual mast of the ship but the name remained.

Five sailors were up for Captain's mast. For once, Captain Johnson showed some leniency. Possibly it was because the ship was finally headed for the war zone. Whatever the reason, four of the sailors received extra mid-watches to stand in addition to their normal duties. This included our two friends, Brunton and Chedester, who were five hours late returning to the ship on its last Saturday in Pearl. The fifth sailor received a Summary Court Martial which meant that his offense would wait for a formal court including other officers of the ship.

Another sailor had previously been tried by Summary Court Martial for Absence over Leave. This afternoon the result of his court martial was published, official jargon for announced. This case showed no leniency at all. The sailor was sentenced to confinement for 20 days and a loss of pay of $80. Since this was approved by Captain Johnson's superior officer, the sentence would be carried out immediately. This meant that the sailor would be spending at least the next few days in the ship's brig (jail) until arrival at Kawajalein.

Late that night, the USS Newcomb steamed ahead of the formation just as the McDermutt had the night before. The opportunity to be the target for the next day's exercises was being rotated among the destroyers. On this voyage as usual, the Navy was showing its preference for a pattern, a routine.

Just like the previous day, the morning was spent in drills beginning with fake torpedo attacks against the Newcomb. After the various "attacks" against the Newcomb were finished, Captain Johnson put his crew through a couple of rescue drills. The rest of the day was uneventful.

After nightfall, the Halsey Powell left the formation to get into position to serve as the morning's target. The only difference this time was that it left earlier so that it could use a slower and more economical speed to get ahead. This voyage had to be made with the existing fuel on board since there were no plans for refueling at sea.

The morning dawned party cloudy and temperate on Thursday, March 2nd. Soon after breakfast the squadron of destroyers focused on the target up ahead for more exercises. It was largely a repeat of the previous two days with two divisions formed of three destroyers each. Each division was varied to rotate each destroyer to different positions within each division during the exercises. Positions in battle changed rapidly due to maneuvering so it was important to reflect that in training.

After dinner that evening the crew was put through the abandon ship drill. This was a drill that obviously no crew member ever wanted to carry out in reality. There was a lot of wise cracking among the inexperienced sailors. Officers and men who had seen combat before didn't joke about this drill.

The formation remained together that night with the Callaghan proudly in the middle. No destroyer was sent out ahead as before. The squadron was drawing closer to the war zone and there were enemy islands that had been by-passed by the Allies that within aircraft range now. This increased the risk of attack so the protective formation was kept intact for the remainder of the voyage.

On Friday morning, more exercises and drills were carried out. Just after lunch, a radar contact was made at about 7000 yards. Other destroyers confirmed the contact so the McDermut dashed off to check it out. Nothing was found and after a very short search the Callaghan resumed its position within the task group. The contact was evaluated as false. It was an anomaly of radar that couldn't be explained.

At 1:30 in the afternoon, the Newcomb and the Halsey Powell left the task group on assignment to another destination. The task group was no longer intact. This was a sign that they were getting close to their destination. They were almost past the great empty expanse of the central Pacific ocean. Up ahead lay the Gilbert and Marshall island groups.

A hundred or so coral atolls formed each of the island groups. United States forces under Admiral Nimitz's command had invaded the Gilberts starting in November of previous year. In January, U.S. forces invaded the Marshall islands. The Callaghan and its task group were headed to Kawajalein which was an important fleet anchorage in the Marshall islands.

Actually the U.S. forces only held a few islands in each major island group in the central Pacific. If each and every island had to be invaded where Japanese forces held or occupied in the case of unoccupied islands, the U.S. forces would still be working there way through the Gilberts. Fortunately, the Pacific command figured out early on that most unoccupied islands were of little value and could remain unoccupied. More importantly, they also figured out that not every Japanese island needed to be taken for a successful campaign.

Several Japanese held islands had already been bypassed. The great Japanese base of Rabaul on New Britain island in the Solomons had been bypassed and isolated by taking strategic islands in a giant ring all around it. In the Marshall islands,

Wotje, Maloelap and Mili were bypassed. The pre-war Japanese bastion on Truk island had been pulverised by a devastating carrier plane strike in February. Truk would also be bypassed. Some of these bypassed islands were going to have an immediate effect on the life of the Callaghan.

Task Group 12.6 had altered course during the morning to 242 degrees. This was a direct result of a couple of those bypassed islands which just happened to be on the direct route from Pearl to Kawajalein. The Japanese were known to have batteries of coastal guns on these islands so any Allied shipping had to be diverted around them. So the Callaghan and company were going further south than normal to get to their destination.

Not long after the Newcomb and Halsey Powell left the Task Group, the remaining destroyers changed formation to one they seldom used. They were now cruising side by side with 3000 yards between each destroyer which caused the Task Group to stretch about 6 miles across the ocean. This was the formation that filmmakers preferred especially before the war. It made the destroyers look like a group of graceful greyhounds racing each other across the sea.

All afternoon and all night the greyhounds raced, curving around unseen enemy islands. General quarters the next morning held new meaning. Anxious eyes roamed the sea and sky looking for the enemy which, for once, was known to be present in some form not too far away.

Just before 8:00am, the surface radar picked up land. The ships reformed into a column formation. Within short minutes the land was sighted by lookouts. Here was another new experience for the fresh sailors. Unlike the towering volcanic Hawaiian islands, these islands were low to the sea. Coral had built itself up over centuries to form these islands and as a result they squatted over the sea with only the trees and man-made structures to stand upright.

The formation was changed yet again to a double column in preparation for entering Kawajalein lagoon. Perhaps the Commodore wanted a purposeful looking display of naval ships as they joined the fighting fleet. Whatever the reason the destroyers steamed up the lagoon with the Callaghan and the Laws in the lead.

At 10:21 the Callaghan anchored in 23 fathoms of water which was about as deep as she had ever laid her anchor. Kawajalein lagoon was huge and deep. It would be the best fleet anchorage the U.S. Navy would ever find. It was good that it was so large and deep since the largest fleet the world had ever seen would soon gather here.

But for now there was not much here. The fleet that was in was only three heavy cruisers, the destroyers that had arrived with the Callaghan and assorted other auxiliary vessels.

Just after lunch the Callaghan got under way to cross the anchorage to visit the tanker Gazelle. After filling its nearly empty fuel bunkers, the Callaghan returned to its assigned berth which was really just a spot next to a buoy. It spent the rest of the day quietly anchored while the crew went about normal in-port watch and maintenance duties.

The next day was Sunday, March 5th 1944. In contrast to past normal in-port routine of one boiler being lit, two boilers were kept in readiness all day. The idea was to be ready to get under way in no more than 30 minutes at any time. This was a war zone and air raid alerts had been experienced at Kawajalein since it was taken over by the U.S. Navy.

Someone in the local Navy bureaucracy decided that the Callaghan needed to be in a different berth. Accordingly, at 1:12 in the afternoon the Callaghan pulled up its anchorage and got under way for berth KD16.

The trip took a lot longer than anticipated though because within minutes an air raid alert was flashed to all ships at Kawajalein. General quarters was immediately sounded and the crew dashed to their stations. Captain Johnson naturally kept the Callaghan out in the navigation areas of the lagoon during the alert. After 25 minutes the alert was canceled and the Callaghan's crew was returned to "Readiness II." This meant that most of the crew could return to normal routine while half of the gun crews remained with their guns.

The excitement was over and the Callaghan anchored at KD16. Just before dark a sub chaser tied up alongside the stern of the destroyer. This was the first time such a small patrol vessel had been immobilized next to the Callaghan so it gave the new sailors a chance look one over. No doubt most of them were glad to be assigned to a large fleet destroyer rather than a small, slow, poorly armed craft made of wood.

Late that night the engineering department was put on 15 minutes notice for steaming. That meant that they had to be ready to get underway in just 15 minutes. This put a strain on the black gang that was on watch. They had two hot boilers going with lots of steam ready to be put through the engines. The watch standers had to check and re-check the boilers and the dozens of gages they had attached to the boilers and engines. All this in a warm tropical anchorage!

At eight o'clock the next morning the Callaghan sailors had to say goodbye to their new friends from the subchaser. In minutes it cast off all lines and pulled away from the side of the Callaghan.

That morning Captain Johnson held mast again for an unfortunate sailor who had transgressed against Navy regulations by falling asleep while on watch. He was ordered to stand trial by Summary Court Martial.

As soon as the Captain was done with Captain's mast, the main battery, the director and plot were called to General Quarters for an anti-aircraft exercise. The Salt Lake City was kind enough to supply a couple of planes to make simulated attacks against the Callaghan. These were float planes that all U.S. heavy cruisers carried to provide aerial reconnaissance and spotting for gunfire. They were not very fast but they could still give the gunners a workout. It was vital to keep the gunnery skills honed to a fine edge.

In mid-afternoon a Summary Court Martial was held with Lt. Heimark serving as the senior officer. Four cases were tried and found guilty. The cases were then filed awaiting sentencing by the convening authority, in this case, Captain Johnson.

The following morning, just after breakfast, the Callaghan got underway. Much of the morning was spent in crossing Kawajalein lagoon and then finding an anchorage off Roi island. The whale boat was then lowered with the Captain and Executive officer aboard. The whale boat headed out the North Pass. The little group was serving as a sounding party to check the depth of the North Pass. Kawajalein had been captured so recently it was not known if the North Pass was deep enough for destroyers to safely steam through. It took fully four hours to sound the channel to the Captain's satisfaction.

Luckily for the assigned mission of the Callaghan, the Captain determined that he could take the Callaghan through the North Pass safely. The deck force hoisted the whale boat back aboard and the anchor was weighed. In a few minutes the Callaghan was, in a small way, breaking new ground for the U.S. Navy.

At 6:00pm the Callaghan was on anti-submarine patrol on the other side of North Pass. An hour later sunset GQ stations were manned. Around 9:00 that night the Callaghan met up with two LCIs (Landing Craft Infantry), an LST (Landing Ship Tank) and a Mine Sweeper to form a convoy. The Callaghan took station out front and led the small convoy away from Kawajalein bound for Wotho Island.

The Callaghan's crew now experienced the reality of escorting landing craft: deadly, agonizing slow speed. The convoys speed was all of nine knots! The Callaghan maintained 12 knots by zigzagging in front of the convoy. Even at twelve knots, the watch spent a long, slow, tense night of watching and listening for the dreaded signs of a Japanese submarine. At this slow speed, how could any submarine armed with 40 knot torpedoes possibly miss?

Luckily the Japanese missed their opportunity and morning found the little convoy within sight of Wotho Island. Just when the Callaghan's officers were sure they were through with this dangerous duty, an unexpected problem reared its ugly head. The Landing craft could not find the entrance to the lagoon!

So while the LST wasted over two hours searching for the hidden entrance to the lagoon, the Callaghan patrolled endlessly back and forth at the irritatingly slow twelve knots. Finally, at 11:30am the LST entered the lagoon and the Callaghan was free to leave.

And leave they did! Within minutes the Callaghan had reversed course and increased speed to a comfortable 19.5 knots. A little after 3:00pm the Captain decided to up the speed to 23 knots. He wanted to get back to Kawajalein before dinner. At 5:37pm they entered the atoll through the West pass named Gea. One hour later they moored alongside tanker YO 160. The Callaghan's first mission in an area of known enemy activity was over.

After taking 711 barrels of fuel from the tanker the Callaghan got underway to move over to it's assigned anchorage, RD16. The destroyer anchorage in 26 fathoms of water with 90 fathoms of chain out. That length of chain was over 160 feet longer than the entire length of the Callaghan itself!

After a quiet night, the next morning the crew went about cleaning up the ship for an important inspection. Since Captain Johnson had arranged for the Commodore to inspect the ship, he was even more fanatical than usual about the preparation beforehand. The officers and Chiefs were harried. The enlisted men felt like they were under siege.

Captain Johnson's inspections became legendary among the crew. He used white gloves to check for dirt or dust and he checked everywhere. He was particularly careful to check under things. This not only included the obvious places such as under desks, but also included looking under refrigerators, sinks and storage lockers in the galley.

The one positive result of this fanaticism was that the inspection by the Commodore went quite well. There wasn't much for him to find wrong after Captain Johnson got through. The officers and men were quite relieved when the inspection was over and ship life was mostly back to normal routine. There were, of course, things to be taken care of that the Captain had noticed before and during the inspection.

Late that night there was an air alert. These were quite common at Kawajalein as the Japanese sent over "snoopers" on a regular basis to check on the whereabouts of units of the U.S. fleet. On at least one occasion, a night-time visitor dropped a couple of bombs in the hope that some damage might be done. The only real damage was that everyone's sleep was disturbed. As many sailors and soldiers had before them, the crew of the Callaghan came to hate these nightly interruptions with a passion. Although night fighters were now available in the Pacific, the radar was too crude to be very effective. Most "snoopers" escaped untouched.

On this occasion the alert was a false one. The aircraft was determined to be a friendly one. The crew secured from general quarters and most went back to their bunks. With a pre-dawn reveille, this was going to be another night with not enough sleep.

In mid-morning the Callaghan got underway to leave it's solitary anchorage to go alongside the U.S.S. Cascade and tie up to it. This was a welcome event for most of the Callaghan's crew. Since the Cascade was a larger auxiliary ship, certain items could be obtained from it that the Callaghan would not have it stock. These not only included repair or maintenance items but also luxury items such as ice cream or movies.

Within a couple of hours, another ship came along to tie up alongside enjoy the hospitality of the Cascade. A destroyer escort, the Greiner, tied up alongside the port (left) side of the

Callaghan. This meant that there were now two ships companies for the sailors of the Callaghan to socialize with. This would be increasing important to the men as their time away from civilization stretched out. There was a lot to be learned from other sailors that could not be learned from official channels or ones own shipmates.

In this case a lot of questions were asked. What was going on in the Central Pacific area? What was available at Kawajalein? What could the Callaghan crew expect of duty in this area? Unfortunately the answer to all of these questions was "not much."

Thus was spent a Friday and Saturday in March of 1944. When most civilians back home were enjoying a relaxed weekend, the Callaghan crew got maintenance and routine work livened up through comradeship with fellow sailors from other ships. It was, of course, short lived.

On Sunday morning the Callaghan pulled out. The destroyers at Kawajalein shared the duty of guarding the entrances to this most important fleet base in the middle of the war. It was the Callaghan's turn to patrol outside South Pass. Just before noon it relieved the Longshaw which promptly steamed back inside the lagoon for it's period of maintenance and rest.

The next couple of days were spent in endless boring, patrol outside of the South Pass. The patrol tied the Callaghan to an arc 7000 yards from the entrance to the Lagoon. At twelve knots speed, the Callaghan plodded out to one end of the arc, turned around and plodded back. The lookouts had to be hard pressed to stay alert after hours of looking back and forth over the same little stretch of sea and sky!

This boredom was punctured by a middle of the night scramble to general quarters the first night. Radar had a surface contact at only 1200 yards. Luckily no shooting resulted as the contact turned out to be a Navy patrol craft exiting the lagoon. As too often happened, somebody didn't get the word.

Just before lunch a plane was sent out to tow a sleeve over the Callaghan for more gunnery practice. This time it was the turn of the 20's and 40's. 128 rounds of 40mm and 334 rounds of 20mm were fired at the sleeve. This was the kind of practice that made the US Navy warships the best in the world at anti-aircraft fire.

The following day the gunnery practice for the machine guns was repeated. This time the expenditure of rounds was significant with the 40's firing 356 rounds, only 5 fewer than the 361 of the 20's. Right after this practice round, the patrol duty was over.

The USS McDermut came through the South Pass to relieve the Callaghan. The Callaghan immediately steamed off to the Gea Pass. There she entered the lagoon to head for the berth containing the USS Sepulga. The Callaghan moored alongside and took on 675 barrels of oil from the tanker. This time she also took on 36 barrels of diesel oil.

The diesel oil was used for the auxiliary generators. This was an often overlooked need of modern warships. In order to take the strain off the engineering plant and to provide an emergency backup power system, auxiliary generators were installed aboard all US navy warships. These allowed production of electricity even when the ships engines were shut down. Since all of the weapons systems relied on electric power this was a very vital function. This had proven especially critical in battle when ships received serious battle damage that temporarily shut down one or all of the engines. The auxiliary generator ensured that the weapons could continue to fight while the engineers repaired the ship's engines. In this manner, many ships were saved that otherwise might have been lost.

After fueling, the Callaghan cast off and returned to berth KD-16 where she had anchored before her patrol duties. 26 fathoms of anchor chain were let out again. This was becoming the Callaghan's home away from home.

A quiet night was spent in the anchorage. At dawn, preparations were made to get underway. The Callaghan didn't go very far though as it merely shifted berths from KD-16 to KD-12. This, however, was in preparation for the next mission.

The ship was alive with rumors again. The word was that the Callaghan was going out with another destroyer to Majuro to join the fleet. The big question: "What would transpire after that?"
Were they going to be involved in some big fleet action? Was an invasion forthcoming?

Once again vigorous and exacting cleaning and maintenance was carried out all morning and part of the afternoon. This was followed by one of the Captain's famous and feared inspections. Then just before 6:00pm, the Callaghan got underway.

About a half hour later, the Callaghan went through Gea Pass with the USS Longshaw following. A two ship task force was formed with the express purpose of seeing what they could find in enemy territory. At dusk, general quarters was sounded as usual. There was a definite sense of purpose this time. If they were going to join the fleet, it was time to get it right!

Four minutes after exiting through the pass a surface radar contact was picked up nearly dead ahead at 22 miles range. Speed was stepped up to 18.5 knots and a watch was placed on the bearing of the contact. As so often happened with contacts like this, it disappeared when the destroyers drew close. A short search was made in the vicinity with no results. Course was then changed to 110 degrees and general quarters was canceled. Most of the sailors then went off to their bunks although many might find it hard to drop off to sleep.

Just after 7:00am, the Callaghan entered Calalin channel to pass into Majuro atoll. Once inside the topside sailors were greeted by a stirring sight. The fast battleships were here. These were the modern battleships all built since the pre-war naval treaties had expired. This allowed them to be built unrestricted in size and weight. They were all armed with main batteries of nine 16" guns firing shells that weighted well over a ton each. This was the most powerful battle fleet in the world.

The first order of business was to go alongside the USS Platte to top off the oil bunkers. Only 351 barrels were required but this allowed the destroyers to stay fully ready for whatever mission would occur in the future. Then it was off to an assigned berth.

The only further thing of consequence that occurred that day was a court martial convened to try two cases. It was adjourned after an hour and forty-five minutes with it's conclusions prepared for the Captain's review.

The next day the Captain held mast for minor offenses by four sailors. All received varying amounts of extra duty as punishment.

Finally on Saturday, the 18th, the Callaghan got underway again in company with the Longshaw. The two destroyers had a mission after all although not at all what the rumors had envisioned. Instead of going out on some grand fleet action, the two destroyers were on their own for a sweep by the nearest enemy held islands. Since these islands had been by-passed but were still quite close to Majuro, they had to be kept under a close watch.

Around mid-afternoon the destroyers slowed to 12 knots. About 30 minutes later, the first island that was not occupied by friendly forces came in sight off the starboard bow. It was not believed that Loj island had Japanese troops on it but it was treated as if it did. Many curious eyes on the two destroyers looked it over carefully as they steamed by at a respectful distance.

The rest of the afternoon and early evening was spent steaming to Wotje atoll, a known enemy base. The two ships changed course several times to get around reefs and small islands. At dusk, general quarters was set and the ships were darkened. No lights and no cigarettes were allowed. Then minutes later, with the Callaghan in the lead, Wotje came in sight.

All optics that could be brought to bear scrutinized the southern part of the island and its entrance channel. The tension and excitement could be felt by everyone. Finally, after all those months, each crewman knew they were in the presence of the enemy.

However, there was no visible sign of any enemy activity. The Callaghan and Longshaw marched and counter matched within sight of Wotje for several hours. With a mixture of frustration and relief, the two crews began to realize that the enemy was not going to challenge them this night. After moving away from the island to the West, general quarters was canceled at 10:21pm.

Five minutes later a plane was sighted but it was quickly determined to be friendly. With that short burst of excitement, the night became quiet again and the crew not standing watch went to their bunks to sleep. This sleep would be precious as an early general quarters was planned.

After steaming back and forth all night, course was changed to due north at 5:30am. General quarters was sounded at 5:40am. This was fully 45 minutes before dawn but the Commodore and Captains were taking no chances. Part of the purpose behind patrols such as this one was to intercept any vessels whether surface or submarine that might be coming to Wotje to resupply or reinforce the Japanese garrison. A submarine might sight the destroyers in the pre-dawn period when the sun's effect on the upper atmosphere begins to lighten up the sky. With this danger in mind, the destroyers were made ready.

At 6:00am speed was increased to 19 knots. 25 minutes later, with dawn blooming around them, the ships were lightened. This meant that the internal lights could be turned on without risk that a light leak would reveal their presence to the enemy. Destination was Erikub atoll.

About a half hour after lighting the ship, the Callaghan began to enter Loj pass into Erikub atoll. Not long after, the anchor was let go and the Callaghan was anchored in the middle of an unoccupied atoll. What a strange feeling for experienced officers as well as the new sailors. In all their previous experience, a US warship anchored or tied up in a location that had the presence of at least other allied ships. Here there was nothing but sand and coconut trees.

Captain Johnson put extra crewmen on watch both as lookouts and on the anti-aircraft guns. It would be very awkward to be anchored in a deserted lagoon if a Japanese plane or submarine suddenly decided to pay a visit. Normal work routines were executed as the Callaghan spent almost the whole day anchored in the middle of Erikub atoll. The Longshaw left in mid-afternoon.

Finally at 5 minutes before 5:00pm, the Callaghan got underway. In minutes she was exiting Loj pass and turning toward Wotje. This time she would skulk around enemy waters all by herself.

At sundown general quarters was sounded as usual. It was called off an hour or so later. At 11:00pm, as the Callaghan was moving near Wotje, the Callaghan abruptly reversed course to close on the channel entrance to the enemy island. Captain Johnson decided to sound general quarters again as insurance since they were moving into shore battery range of the island. The Callaghan was alone this time and he wanted to be as prepared as possible. By this time with the on, off and back on again general quarters anybody would have been edgy.

The Callaghan cruised back and forth a couple of times before it was decided to cancel the general quarters status and let part of the crew get some sleep. The destroyer continued its watchman like march back and forth around Wotje island until dawn. No sign of enemy activity was ever seen. It is not known to this day if the Japanese on the island were aware of their visitor that night.

66

Dawn general quarters came and went while the Callaghan was on a western leg of one of its marches. This time the destroyer did not turn back again but altered course to the northwest and kept on going. Soon they were back again to Erikub Atoll where they went inside and anchored again.

20 minutes after they anchored their sister ship, the Longshaw, reappeared and did likewise. Erikub Atoll had been appropriated as the staging area for a two ship task force of U.S. destroyers. As during the previous day, routine was maintained but at a lower level so that some of the men could catch up on their rest during the day. This was primarily a night mission designed to prevent any traffic to the by-passed Japanese occupied islands.

A little earlier than on the previous day, the two destroyers pulled out of Erikub and headed southwest again. The two destroyers stayed together this time and formed up abreast with the Longshaw maintaining station 2000 yards to the port of the Callaghan. All night long they marched back and forth in the vicinity of Wotje but again nothing was seen of the enemy at all.

In the dark of the early morning well before dawn, the two ships left enemy waters behind. Pre-dawn general quarters was sounded again but with much less urgency since the word was out that they were on their way back to port. While still at their G.Q. stations, the two destroyers passed through the entrance to Majuro Atoll.

What they saw woke them up.

Since the Callaghan left the West coast of the US they had looked forward to seeing the "real" fleet. They had seen the old battleships, the survivors of the attack at Pearl Harbor and their sisters at San Pedro. They had seen some Aircraft Carriers at San Diego. But they had never seen the great new combat fleet that was making a name for itself out here in the Central Pacific. Suddenly, while they were gone patrolling, the Fifth Fleet had arrived at Majuro.

Here it was, the might of the United States Navy. Large Essex class Aircraft Carriers were interspersed with the light Carriers built on cruiser hulls. The big new Battleships were here. Not one or two as they had seen before. Seven of them were anchored here in all their steel grey splendor. Plus more cruisers in one spot than any of the sailors on the Callaghan had ever seen. It was a thrill and it started the rumor mill into overdrive.

G.Q. was canceled and the Callaghan went alongside the U.S.S. Gargoyle. They stayed moored to the Gargoyle just long enough for the deck force to fill up the bunkers with black fuel oil from the tanker. That finished, they cast off and steamed over to berth #21 where they dropped anchor.

A tired crew went through the usual cleaning, resupply and maintenance routine that accompanied arrival back in port. Since they had been out on a three day night patrol mission, many of the crewmen simply wanted to finish up so they could get more sack time. The night patrols had really interfered with the normal sleep cycle so getting adequate sleep became a priority. Luckily this was a relatively quiet day in port, despite the presence of the fleet, so many of the crew got to indulge.

There was a reason that most of the men were allowed to take it easy. The officers were busy with other matters. Orders had arrived and it had the Commodore's staff busy. Captain Johnson conferred with his executive officer, Commander Wolzen. Something was up and the rumor mill caught wind of it.

The next morning, bright and early, the crew was hustled to breakfast and then to work. Preparations were being made for a voyage but the men still didn't know where to. The officers and Chiefs had been given their orders and they had the men jumping to it. At the same time, some of the men topside noticed that activity had increased greatly on and around all of the ships in the anchorage.

At 11:30am the Callaghan weighed anchor. All across the huge Majuro lagoon, ships were pulling their anchors up. The Callaghan steamed out into the channel to join up behind the Heavy Cruiser Chester. The men found out that the Chester was in charge of the particular task group with which the Callaghan was going off to war. That was the point of all of this. The Callaghan was finally getting to do what the officers and crew had thought about and dreamed about. The name of the fleet's operation was Desecrate One.

Soon after the Callaghan had left Majuro, Captain Johnson made an announcement to the crew. The Callaghan would serve with the Oiler (tanker) task group in support of the fleet. Although not as glamorous as accompanying the big carriers and battleships of the main task force, this was a vital function which allowed the big ships to do their job. No carrier task force on either side operated in the Pacific ocean without tankers along to provide refueling. The distances were too great and the maneuvering too hectic to operate without it.

The support function was considered so vital that heavy and light cruisers were attached to the task group. This was a sign of the abrupt change in the fortunes of the US Pacific fleet. So many warships were now available that such protection was now provided to even the tankers. Only a year and a half earlier, the cruisers often were the main punch and the tankers only had destroyers to keep them safe.

Captain Johnson went on to explain that the Fifth Fleet was out to strike the Palau Islands. Later on, crew members had to ask the quartermasters to explain where these islands were. They were not well known.

For some reason that this author does not know, the task group headed northeast first before changing course twice to end up on a roughly western course. It finished by departing from northwest of the atoll on a bearing a little south of due West. Possibly this was because Kawajalein was to the northwest of Majuro. This maneuvering would facilitate a rendezvous with units coming down from Kawajalein. In any case, around 3:30pm they were finally on their way.

Sunset G.Q. came and went. The task group cruised on at a steady 17 knots, zigzagging until 10:00pm. Then they settled down to a easy straight course of 255 degrees. At 2:00 in the morning the task group screen reoriented itself and the group changed course to 205 degrees. They were now heading almost due southwest.

The following day was a cruising day at sea. Nothing of any consequence occurred. The latitude was decreasing and Longitude was increasing with every hour of steaming. Soon they would cross the International Date Line. That would mean that all the ships would change their clocks and records to skip ahead a full day. Therefore their records would appear to be minus a day. In other words they were steaming from Thursday into Saturday.

More importantly for the crew, the task group was also going to cross the Equator on that same day. That meant that a very time honored Navy tradition called "Crossing the Line" would have to be conducted. All sailors who had never been to the Southern hemisphere were considered pollywogs. All the sailors who had been across the equator at any time in the past were called shellbacks. The shellbacks would initiate the lowly pollywogs into the fraternal order of shellbacks through a ceremony which today would be called hazing. This ceremony would be conducted aboard every other ship of the task group which had not crossed the equator recently.

So on Saturday the 25th of March, 1944 at about 10:00am, the Captain was informed that King Neptune was coming aboard because he had heard there were polliwogs aboard. The Captain, the senior officers and a skeleton crew of experienced sailors ran the ship while the rest of the shellbacks proceeded with "Crossing the Line." They immediately gathered the lowly pollywogs on the forecastle (the front part of the ship in front of the bridge).

The pollywogs were not dressed in uniform for the initiation. In fact, they were mostly dressed in their underwear. They were also astonished to find certain shellbacks dressed in a very un-Navy like manner. Chief Bosunsmate Simonton played the part of Davy Jones. He was dressed in something resembling a summer version of a Roman Toga which allowed his very ample belly to see the light of day. Petty Officer Campbell played the role of the Royal Queen and he was dressed like one! Lt. Hoskins (Chief Engineer) was King Neptune and wore the crown to prove it. Most of the rest of the royal court wore non-standard items to indicate their status.

The ceremony began with a bogus prayer for mercy by the lowly pollywogs after which they began their march back to the stern of the ship. It was a long, slow, arduous journey. It included running and ducking through a line of royal floggers. A stop was made at the royal barbers for a complete head shave. This was followed by crawling through a tunnel like contraption during which various disgusting substances were poured on each pollywog. At the end of the tunnel crawl, they were ordered to open their mouth and a pill was shoved in. The effect of the pill was not noticed until the next time the pollywog would relieve himself.

Luckily, no one was hurt and the shellbacks had the time of their lives at the expense of the pollywogs. Clean up took quite a while especially as the hot water soon ran out. Strangely although the shellbacks thoroughly enjoyed lunch, many of the pollywogs showed little interest.

The actual equator was crossed at about 3:00 in the afternoon. At 6:00 that evening course was adjusted to 245 degrees. The fleet was following a course that would curve them to the south of the enemy islands that included the famous Japanese fortress island of Truk. Before the war, Truk was heavily fortified by the Japanese and carefully guarded. It was even rumored that Amilia Eearhart crashed on Truk and the Japanese kept the crash a secret. In recent months Truk had been virtually neutralized by a severe pounding at the hands of the American Fleet Carriers. Now they were moving on to targets further to the West. Truk was added to the list of Japanese islands that would be by-passed.

On Sunday morning, March 26th the support Task Group began earning their pay. The tankers and escorts rearranged themselves into refueling disposition. Each tanker could refuel two ships at a time, one from each side. The ships ready for fueling formed up behind the tankers in lines. Each warship approached from behind the tanker at a slightly higher speed to slowly overtake the tanker. As the ship drew alongside the tanker it would slow to match the speed of the tanker. The skipper would then work carefully with the helmsman to bring the ship to a position very close to the tanker but not too close. The helmsman would then steady the ship so that lines and fuel hoses could be passed between the warship and the tanker. They would then cruise in tandem at a steady 8 knots on a straight course for up to 45 minutes while the fuel bunkers on the warship were filled.

Since the refueling process involved cruising at a very slow speed and on a unbroken straight line, this was a very dangerous time. Submarines would have found this a perfect time for an attack. The escorts not involved in refueling maintained an extra measure of vigilance. In addition, the nearby carriers provided aerial anti-submarine patrols in the form of torpedo bombers outfitted with special streamlined depth charges that could be dropped from aircraft.

As soon as the tankers were in position, a group of escort carriers and their destroyer screen joined up. Escort carriers, also known as baby flattops or jeep carriers, were built from merchant ship or tanker hulls. They were originally built as an emergency measure to combat the hordes of U-boats in the Atlantic ocean. They proved very effective in this role but even before the first half dozen had been completed they were diverted for other wartime purposes. Such was the great need for carrier decks to support invasions and raids against enemy installations that even these slow "baby" carriers were used.

For this operation, a group of escort carriers accompanied the support group to provide extra protection. This strike against the Palau Islands was much further West and deeper into enemy territory than any previous carrier strike since Dolittle's mission to Tokyo in 1942. There were just too many enemy airfields within range to risk important elements of the fleet without air cover. The escort carriers provided that cover for the tankers. In addition, if a major fleet action developed against the Japanese fleet, the escort carrier group would be one more weapon to use.

After the carrier group was fueled it was time for the tankers' escorts themselves. The Callaghan's turn came at 12:40pm and she lined up behind the U.S.S. Kashashia. Twenty minutes later a tow line was secured between the two ships. The actual fueling began about eight minutes later. Captain Johnson did his usual excellent job of ship handling and the fueling was completed with no hitches. Thirty-five minutes after starting the Callaghan had taken on a thousand barrels of fuel or well over fifty thousand gallons of the black stuff. Shortly all lines were cast off and the Callaghan smoothly picked up speed to take station four thousand yards ahead of the tankers.

All ships were fueled at 3:00pm and an hour and a half later the support group resumed a cruising disposition. Speed was increased to 12 knots and then later to 15 knots. The fleet course however, did not resume the southwesterly heading of the previous two days. They first headed due West but late that night changed course to west/northwest. The fleet had moved around Truk atoll and was now headed toward the target, the Palaus.

Zigzagging resumed in the morning at the same time that dawn general quarters was sounded. At 9:30 that morning they woke up to the fact that the enemy was near when an unidentified plane was spotted on radar at a distance of eighty miles. General quarters was again sounded and the plane was tracked very carefully. The plane did not close and was lost on radar

73

fifteen minutes later. G.Q. was canceled and a few minutes later the course was changed again to a Westerly heading.

More excitement came the Callaghan's way when one of the other destroyers changed position in the task group. The USS Cowell was crossing from the Callaghan's port (left) side when it suddenly became apparent that they were on a collision course. The officer of the deck on the bridge ordered left full rudder and a rarely heard "all back emergency." The engine room responded with the complex procedure to get the engines stopped and then reversed. In moments the 60,000 horsepower engines were straining to throw the big brass propellers in the opposite direction. Quickly the big destroyer slowed to ten knots at which point the collision had been avoided and the order to reverse the engines was canceled. While every man topside got his breath back, the Captain ordered speed increased to nineteen knots to allow the Callaghan to regain its position in the screen.

The day proceeded normally until 2:30 in the afternoon when a sound contact was suddenly made about 40 degrees to the left of the groups' course. The Callaghan immediately altered course toward the contact while the rest of the task group was ordered to increase speed. The Callaghan lost contact eight minutes later and the Commodore ordered her to resume position within the destroyer screen. That was the end of the excitement for the day. Word went around that tomorrow the task group would refuel the fleet carriers' escorts.

The following morning dawned warm and humid as it always seemed to be around the equator in the South Pacific. The task group was split up into three units to facilitate fueling the destroyers from the three fleet carrier task groups. The topside guys were looking forward to this in hopes of catching a glimpse of the big carriers nearby.

The tankers set a course northwest and again steadied up on a straight line and a slow speed. The Callaghan, her sister destroyers, and the support group Cruisers were as vigilant as ever while the Fleet's destroyers lined up behind each tanker for their turn at the pumps. Fortunately, no sound contacts or air alerts were made to cause the panic button to be pressed.

Refueling the destroyers proceeded at a rapid pace so that before lunch they returned to their task groups while the support group reorganized and changed course to the West. The guys topside had been disappointed that they could not see the big carriers. However, surface radar had picked them up so everyone knew the big decks were out there.

After lunch the support group changed course once again only this time they were backtracking to the east. Apparently they had gone far enough into enemy waters and were going to stay here while the big guys went on ahead to strike the Palaus. That suited the slow tankers and their nervous escorts just fine!

A couple minutes after 9:00 o'clock that night two radar contacts suddenly appeared only 26 miles away. Oddly they were separated by 75 degrees on the compass which was really alarming. Were these sneaky Japs planning to make a coordinated but divergent attack on the group? General quarters was quickly sounded and the air alert flashed to all ships. Just as mysteriously, the blips on the radar scopes faded away about 27 minutes later.

At 10:15pm, a sound contact was called out bearing 65 degrees and 1500 yards distance. So far this was not a good night for sleep! While the men ran to their battle stations again an attack course was set. Luckily in less than 5 minutes, the contact was judged to be false and the alert was called off. The crewmen not on watch stumbled off to their sacks once again hoping that this time they could stay there at least until their next watch.

At 4:00am the task group changed course to due south. They were steaming back and forth within a designated area now. Although they were within aircraft range of Truk, they were also within long range of the nearest Allied base. This meant that they were within the umbrella protection of air patrols that were always on the lookout for units of the Japanese fleet. These long range patrols would, in effect, replace the extra search capability and protection they lost when the Fleet carriers steamed away to strike the Palaus.

At about breakfast time, the task group changed course to the north. A half hour later they changed course again to the east. In mid-morning they suddenly got a aircraft radar contact only 22 miles out. The crew scrambled to general quarters as usual in such a case. 20 minutes later it was determined to be one of those friendly long range patrol planes that they were now depending on. General quarters was canceled and life returned to normal, if it could be called that.

The rest of the day and night were uneventful. The supply task group changed course back and forth from northeast to southeast. In an apparent attempt to throw off any enemy submarines that might be following them, the task group zigzagged for a couple hours at a time alternating with a straight course.

In the pitch darkness around 3:00 in the morning, an unwelcome sound contact was made. Luckily within 6 minutes the guys in the sonar shack decided that it was a false contact. The watch standers breathed a big sigh of relief and went back to anticipation of getting off watch.

It was now the 30th of March. At 7:00am the task group changed course and assumed disposition for refueling. The escort ships once again went in one or two at a time to top off their tanks.

While this was going on the Callaghan was being its usual very vigilant self. At 10:35am there was another sound contact. This time it seemed quite definite and the crew raced to general quarters again. The Callaghan was on course 040 degrees while the contact was 20 degrees to the left and about 2800 yards away. When the range dropped under a thousand yards the contact began drifting away to the left. At 700 yards the contact disappeared.

No matter, with four tankers behind him refueling other ships, Captain Johnson was taking this contact very seriously. The helm was adjusted to bring the Callaghan over the last known position of the contact. Captain Johnson gave orders for a full pattern of depth charges to be readied at medium depth settings.

As the Callaghan's propellers churned over the spot where sonar said the "sub" should be, the skipper gave the order to fire the charges. The six K-guns boomed throwing the smaller 300 pound charges high into the air either side of the Callaghan. Seconds later the big 500 pound barrel sized charges rolled off the racks at the stern of the ship. Nine charges in all were sent on their way. All hands waited for many long seconds while the charges sank to the designated depths. Then a series of deep rumbling explosions marked the pre-appointed self destruction of the depth charges. The surface of the sea boiled and lifted up over each of the charges and then sank back.

The Callaghan was brought around in the tightest turn she could make and the sonar operator kept the sonar beam pointed in the direction of the last contact. Tentative contact was made as the Callaghan finished its turn but the echo quickly faded.

The sonar operator turned the beam back and forth but no sign of any sub was found. While the task group steamed away the Callaghan made pass after pass in the area of the depth charge attack. Finally, after a half hour, the skipper decided that the contact was probably false and the Callaghan headed back to rejoin the task group screen.

After lunch, it was the Callaghan's turn to refuel. Captain Johnson ordered speed increased to 23 knots to overtake the USS Sabine. As before the refueling procedure was carried out. When the hoses and line had been cleared away, the Callaghan had taken on another 985 barrels of oil. Speed was increased again and the Callaghan sped away to find her position in the destroyer screen.

At 3:45 in the afternoon, cruising disposition was resumed.

Later on, before sunset general quarters, two course changes were made which reversed the course of the supply task group. They were now headed south.

The boredom of steaming in convoy was interrupted again with the excitement of a sound contact. But this time it was truly fleeting and little time was wasted on pursuing it. The crew was sent to general quarters anyway as it was nearing sunset. They were kept at general quarters a little longer than usual.

Just before 10:00pm, another sound contact was reported from the sonar shack. Again the Callaghan turned out of its station to investigate. Again this contact was determined to be a false one. One has to wonder what the bridge watch was thinking of the sonar operators abilities at this point. The Navy had made a serious error in failing to provide trained sonar operators to the Callaghan.

The task group changed course to the northwest. The rest of the night was spent steaming uneventfully to the northwest. This course was meant to put them closer to the carrier fleet that was attacking the Palaus.

At dawn, two of the escort carriers, the Chenango and Samgamon, left the formation to conduct flight operations. Aircraft carriers must face into the wind to provide the maximum possible lift for their aircraft to have successful takeoffs from their short decks. They could not do this while confined to the course that the supply task group was holding to.

At 10:02 in the morning, the Callaghan's sonar shack reported another possible submarine contact to the right (starboard). The Callaghan immediately turned towards the "contact" to investigate. The rest of the supply task group turned away in the other direction. By this time, no one was surprised to hear, a few minutes later, that the contact was considered false. The Callaghan turned back to rejoin the formation. After the

Callaghan was back in position, the task group resumed its original course.

That morning the latest punishments resulting from the previous Captain's mast were posted. Captain Johnson was back to his old self. Most of the offenses were for sleeping on watch. The men received solitary confinement ranging from 10 to 25 days and heavy fines. Two of the men were additionally sentenced to bread and water while in their solitary confinement. The men were a half a world away from home in more ways than one.

The rest of the day was quiet. Late that night the supply task group changed course to the east (101 degrees). The month of March, the Callaghan's first month in the combat arena of the Pacific, was over. April would open with a bang.

The first day of April opened quietly enough. At 1:30am the task group stopped zigzagging but continued its course of 101 degrees. At 2:25am the Callaghan got a sound contact 46 degrees to the right at a distance of 2000 yards. The depth charge battery was manned and the Callaghan swung right to check it out. A minute later a wake was sighted dead ahead and course was altered again to attempt to ram whatever it was.

Captain Johnson had been called to the bridge when the contact was first received. Now that a target had been apparently sighted, he became very agitated. There was danger and opportunity here. Danger because if there was a sub out there, they could be torpedoed. Opportunity because a successful depth charge attack could give Captain Johnson what he craved the most, credit for a combat kill.

At 800 yards distance, CIC (Combat Information Center) reported they had a pip on the radar scope dead ahead. Suddenly the elusive sound contact had become something much more sinister. There was something out there and Captain Johnson was convinced it was a Japanese sub. He began shouting orders. The entire crew was brought to general quarters.

The loud bonging of the general quarters bell lasted for approximately 30 seconds. That meant that it was still sounding while the Captain was barking out orders to prepare the depth charge attack. As the Callaghan reached the spot where lookouts and radar both had reported something should be, a swirl was noticed in the water. Captain Johnson ordered the depth charge battery fired. The torpedo officer repeated the order.

It wasn't fired. Allen Foster, lowly Torpedoman's Mate 3rd class, was manning the depth charge battery firing panel on the back of the bridge. He was in contact with the sailors manning each of the K-guns on each side of the destroyer. Procedure called for the men on the K-guns to report in when each gun was ready for firing.

Unfortunately this attack had developed very quickly in the middle of the night when the crew was tired, groggy and now frightened. Torpedoman Vanderwall on the number 2 K-gun projector was having trouble getting the 300 pound depth charge set for the ordered depth of 50 feet and squared away on top of the tube-like K-gun. He had not checked in. Foster reported that fact to the torpedo officer.

Captain Johnson began yelling at the torpedo officer to fire the K-guns. Foster had already reported the fact that there was no answer from the #2 K-gun. Unfortunately, the K-gun firing panel was not set up to fire individual projectors. You could fire all 3 K-guns on either side of the ship or all 6 at once. You could not leave one gun out of the firing action.

Captain Johnson now ignored the torpedo officer and screamed directly at Foster to "fire the Goddamn depth charges." Foster felt like he now had no choice and fired the entire battery. The guns fired, the 300 pound depth charges arched high in the air and, due to the shallow setting, soon exploded under the surface of the sea.

Within a few moments, would was relayed to the bridge of a casualty among the depth charge crew. Torpedoman

Vanderwall had been standing over his K-gun when it was fired. The flash of the mortar-like explosive charge used as a propellant caught him full in the face. He was down screaming in pain. Fellow crewmen rushed him to sick bay.

The crew was stressed to the maximum. Ten minutes after the initial sound contact, a possible torpedo wake was sighted off to the starboard side. Captain Johnson ordered the rudder over to right full. The ship was turned towards the possible torpedo sighting as it was safer to present the narrow, on-rushing bow to a torpedo than it was to show the broader retreating stern. It also put the destroyer in the best position for a counterattack.

But nothing more was seen or heard from the elusive "submarine." The Callaghan made several passes through the area but could not find anything. No more depth charges were fired. Finally at 3:10am the Commodore ordered the Callaghan to return to the screen of the task group. General quarters was canceled and the Callaghan returned at 24 knots.

A tired crew stumbled back to their bunks or their watch stations. Word had quickly spread about the casualty in the torpedo gang. Several members of the torpedo gang were not happy with Foster for firing the K-guns when Vanderwall failed to report in. It was not easy to explain what it was like to have the feared skipper of the ship screaming at you to carry out an order, procedure be damned!

Vanderwall was blinded. He would spend the next few days in sick bay under the care of Doctor Parker who did the best job he could. Vanderwall had cuts in the cornea of both eyes so he was in a lot of pain. When the Callaghan returned to Majuro, he would be transferred to a hospital ship.

At 6:00 in the morning, dawn general quarters was sounded. A lot of groggy sailors were looking forward to their morning coffee! Five minutes later word came in that one of the escort carriers, the Sauwanee had reported a man overboard. Since the Callaghan was not the nearest destroyer, it did not leave its station in the destroyer screen.

All was quiet until the afternoon. About 20 minutes after 2:00, a sound contact was reported from the sonar operator. It was 40 degrees to the left and about 3000 yards away. The Callaghan was turned to that heading and proceeded once again to run the contact down. This time sonar quickly determined that the contact was only a school of fish. The Callaghan wasted no time in turning back to resume its position in the screen. No one from the Commodore on down wanted to hear later about chasing schools of fish.

The supply task group was steaming in roughly a giant square now. It was marking time. It was maintaining a position that would allow Task Force 58, the fast carriers, to find them in a safe area where refueling could easily be accomplished.

The night was quiet as well as the morning. They continued to steam within the giant square until almost mid-morning. At 10:00am the lookouts were rewarded with the sight of the masts of the big ships coming up over the horizon to join them. At that point a curious ballet was performed.

First, the supply task group changed course to 105 degrees, a southeasterly heading. Second, the fast carrier task groups formed up on the left (port) quarter to be in position to join for refueling. Third, the supply task group reoriented itself in refueling disposition. This put the tankers in line with most of the cruisers behind them, zigzagging, and the destroyers in a big ring around all of them.

Next the ships with Task Force 58 peeled off in ones or twos to cruise up from behind a tanker to get into position to refuel. This was becoming old hat to the Callaghan crew by now. Captain Johnson saw an opportunity.

Since the refueling was going to take hours with the number and size of ships involved, the skipper decided to call a series of drills. The Callaghan crew must have groaned when the drills were announced. They had been free of drills since they had left Majuro.

Here we go again! Fire and rescue drill, rescue survivors drill, visit and search drill.

Finally at 2:30 in the afternoon, the drills were over. Shortly thereafter refueling of the Task Force 58 ships was finished. They departed from the supply group immediately.

Then at 4:48pm the unexpected and very unwelcome happened: a boiler casualty! A boiler casualty meant that a boiler breakdown had occurred. The four boilers of the Callaghan provided the power which gave the destroyer its great speed. With a boiler down for maintenance they were suddenly deprived of their top speed.

Luckily, Ensign Dunne's black gang quickly made good the necessary fix to the boiler. Less than 30 minutes after the breakdown, a sound contact was announced from the sonar shack. The Callaghan left its position in the screen to investigate. As it did so the contact disappeared and was not picked up again. The Callaghan quickly resumed its place in the destroyer screen.

Nothing further occurred of any consequence that day or on the following day. For two days the supply task group steamed steadily on an easterly course of 100 degrees. They were heading back to friendly territory. But first they had to make the long march back around the Japanese islands including Truk.

On Tuesday the 4th of April the supply task group changed course to the northeast. This meant that they were now well east of Truk and could start climbing the latitudes to return to their base well north of the Equator.

All day and night of the 4th through the 6th the task group steamed to the northeast. The only excitement of any kind came on the last morning of the journey when the Callaghan test fired its 40mm and 20mm machine guns. That afternoon at 3:25pm on the 6th, land was sighted.

As usual, the destroyers waited for their charges, in this case the tankers, to proceed into the anchorage. After all the big ships had entered, the destroyers were finally free of their escort duty. The Callaghan threaded its way through the channel to the area of its berth. Before anchoring, it stopped to lower the whaleboat and gig into the water. They had errands to run and the Captain preferred to lower them before anchoring to get them on their way. At twelve minutes after 7:00 o'clock, the anchor was dropped ending this first and lengthy fleet mission for the Callaghan.

An hour later the USS Porterfield came alongside. The inexperience of these new destroyers was demonstrated when the Porterfield crunched into the Callaghan causing damage to the #2 life raft and to the stanchions of the rail. The greatest damage was to the egos of the Captains and the Commodore. The Porterfield was a sister ship of Destroyer Squadron 55!

The next morning was Friday, April 7th. The Callaghan cast off all lines first thing and left the Porterfield behind. The Callaghan crossed the anchorage to moor alongside tanker X335. The Callaghan was nearly empty of fuel so the enormous load of 2650 barrels of fuel oil was pumped over from the tanker. The Callaghan then returned to the previous berth to moor alongside the Porterfield again. Captain Johnson was made sure that there was no repeat of the previous night's incidence.

The other significant thing that happened that day was that Norman Skylar reported aboard for duty. Seaman Skylar was a welcome addition to the crew. He was a fully trained sonar operator fresh out of the West Coast Sound School! The quartermasters who had been tapped to do double duty on the sonar were happy to have him take some of the burden off their shoulders.

The next day (the 8th) another court martial sentence of an errant crewmember was published. The sentence decided upon by Captain Johnson was severe as usual, confinement for 20 days and a $25 fine for 5 months. However, for the first time, higher authorities disagreed with the severity of this sentence. They decreed that it be reduced to time served and a $15 fine for 5 months. Higher authorities were not going to blindly rubber stamp Captain Johnson's draconian punishments.

Late that afternoon, an officer reported aboard for duty. Lieutenant Hugh Owens, United States Naval Reserve had caught up with the Callaghan. His fellow officers would quickly discover that this 90 day wonder was out of his element. Although sincere in his desire to do a good job as an officer, he was a landlubber through and through.

On Sunday April 9th the Callaghan lost its status as flag of the squadron. The commodore, Captain C.R. Todd and his staff transferred over to the USS Porterfield. This was easily accomplished since the two destroyers were moored side by side. The officers of the Callaghan were pleased as this meant the close up scrutiny from higher authority was over. It also meant there was a little bit more room aboard for the time being.

This Sunday also saw the transfer of two sailors to the USS Prairie for confinement in accordance with their court martial sentences. The Prairie was a destroyer tender, a large ship equipped to service a whole squadron or more of destroyers. It had a real brig (jail) and the means to properly take care of the prisoners. The point that was driven home to the crew was that these sentences were real and that confinement was not something to be taken lightly.

Over the next two days, three sailors were transferred to the USS Relief, a hospital ship, for medical treatment. One of them was Vanderwall, the sailor who had been blinded from the K-gun accident. Another was a Chief named Keilbart. These were men that Captain Johnson hated to see go. He was losing more men than he was gaining. That was a bitter pill to take especially when the Callaghan left the West Coast undermanned to begin with!

On Tuesday night the Callaghan received 14 depth charges to replace some of the charges expended on the Supply Task Group mission. There were 3 of the big 500 pounders and 11 of the 300 pounders for the K-guns. Although not at full capacity, the destroyer was now ready enough for whatever might come up.

What came up the next day was another cruise with Task Force 50.17, the tanker group. This had all the makings of a repeat of the last mission. The same ships were involved and the same initial course was set. There was, however, one big difference this time. This time they would be indirectly supporting an invasion force under General McArthur's command. This extremely important operation would include the invasion of Hollandia and Aitape on the northwest coast of New Guinea. It bypassed a major Japanese base at Wewak by several hundred miles and put the invasion force out of range of US land-based fighter support. It was a risky and daring move. It would result in the first verifiable meeting between the Callaghan and the enemy.

The next several days at sea were much like the first tanker mission except for the addition of a plethora of drills. All the ships in the task force had been through this before and the last mission was remarkable for the lack of enemy presence. So this time around, after the first day, drills were scheduled every day. These drills also included the tankers for the first time. Up until now the warships had been treating the tankers like non-combatants. But now the tankers would get to play at war too.

On the second day out, the Callaghan fired burst practice. All three types of guns were given a workout. The 5" guns fired 18 rounds while the 40mm mounts put up 147 rounds. The 20mm's only fired 80 rounds because most of the 5" bursts were too far away for their short range.

On the third day, the Callaghan provided the target bursts when it was the tankers turn to play war. Three bursts were fired at 20 minute intervals. After the tankers were through some of the crew observing aboard the Callaghan decided they had better provide a very good defense around the tankers!

Late on the evening of the fourth day a sound contact was obtained. Although the depth charges were manned, there was no particular excitement and no firing this time. After a few careful search sweeps it was determined that the sound contact was false. The Callaghan was developing a more professional approach to these sound contacts.

General quarters came bright and early the next morning at 5:30am. The formation course and disposition was changed. It was time to fuel up the escorts.

At 10 minutes to eleven o'clock, it was the Callaghan's turn. The Callaghan moved up alongside the tanker Lackawanna and steadied the prescribed short distance away from the side of the tanker.
Moments after the lines were thrown across and secured between the two ships, a sound contact was received. One can imagine what went through the minds of the two ship Captains at that moment. Both ships were sitting ducks if a submarine got a shot at them.

Immediately the lines were cast off. The second the lines were clear, Captain Johnson ordered full speed. The Callaghan's stern dug in as the 60,000 horsepower engines were opened up. Just as the Callaghan was getting up to a good attack speed, the contact was lost. The Callaghan continued the approach for a short distance and then turned back toward the tanker.

It took time to get the Callaghan back into position, approach the tanker again and resume the fueling station alongside the big tanker. Luckily for the crew who were now thinking about the lunch they were missing, the refueling was executed flawlessly. Over a thousand barrels of oil were transferred in 20 minutes.

The Callaghan cast off and accelerated to get back to its normal position in the screen of destroyers. Once there it slowed down to the relatively slow 12 knots that the destroyers were using that day. 30 minutes later there was another sound contact.

On this day the sonar operators were not popular. There were sailors still trying to eat their lunch when this contact was announced. Once again the Callaghan raced off to investigate. Once again the contact was declared to be a false one. Although the crew was not happy with these interruptions, a job was being done and this time, no ammunition was being wasted.

The rest of the day was uneventful. Night general quarters came and went. The supply task group continued to steam along on a straight westerly course. The enemy and its air bases lay to the west.

Most of the crew were in their bunks. The night watch was aware of the proximity of the task group to enemy territory. The Carolines including the Japanese bases at Truk and Yap were to the north. To the south was New Guinea which was divided roughly in two by Allied forces and the forces of Imperial Japan. To the west were islands associated with New Guinea that were occupied by Japanese troops. On several of these islands were Japanese airbases.

The Japanese knew something was up. Task force 58 had gone ahead to with the initial strikes against airbases in the Hollandia area. The Japanese commanders desperately wanted to strike back. First they had to find the American fleet that was attacking them. So they were searching. Searching with the only effective reconnaissance tool they had, aircraft.

At 20 minutes before 1:00am the SG radar got a contact at 6000 yards bearing 180 degrees from the Callaghan. Since it was moving at 130 knots it was obviously an aircraft. General quarters was sounded and the men went running to their stations. The contact was reported and soon the order came back from the task force commander to start the task group zigzagging.

Inexplicably, the contact never closed with the task group and kept on going. Soon it faded from the radar scope. The Callaghan stood down from general quarters and the men not on watch returned to their bunks. But this first contact was the beginning of real career of the Callaghan. Except for one midget, it was not submarines that would dominate the combat record of the Callaghan. Nor would the Callaghan ever fire her torpedoes at any enemy ship. It would be enemy aircraft that would constitute the score of the Callaghan and be the cause of all of her grief.

Morning general quarters came well before dawn. The Captain was being especially cautious as today was the day that the most important customers would come calling. Word was that the supply task group would rendezvous with Task Force 58.

The morning was uneventful. The task group changed course several times for no apparent reason. After lunch the crew was called to fire and rescue drill. Immediately after the drill was finished Task Force 58 showed up. The escorts from both formations were combined and a new giant screen formation was ordered into place. The Callaghan went racing off to its new assigned position.

Not long after the Callaghan achieved its appointed place in the new formation, it was ordered to a new position. In the time honored tradition of the military, the little guys were shuffled around until the Commander was satisfied.

The new position of the Callaghan really got the attention of the crew. They were sent out ahead of the now hugh task force to a station 8 miles ahead. Along with the USS Porterfield, they were serving as the point guards in front of the big guys. They were the eyes of the task force; looking for trouble that might come their way. The US Navy had learned from hard combat experience that it was very useful to have warships stationed as pickets in advance of an important task force. This allowed the all important radar to pick up oncoming trouble makers even earlier than usual. It also allowed the picket ships to investigate and identify visually any such early contacts if visibility permitted.

Evening general quarters came and went with no surprises. Soon the lights were out in the ship and off-duty personnel turned in. Sleep had been interrupted last night so most of the crew were trying to catch up on rest. The midnight watch came on duty with no sign of anything. It looked like it might be a quiet night.

At 2:45am the task force started zigzagging. No chances were being taken with the most important ships in all of the South Pacific. Then an hour later at 3:45, the Porterfield reported a radar contact bearing 325 degrees, range 48 miles!

The CIC (combat information center) immediately began trying to pick up the contact on their own radar screens. It took less than a minute.

"Bridge, CIC. SC radar contact bearing 325 degrees, range 41 miles. Bogey's course is 130 degrees. Speed about one-three zero knots, over."

"Roger CIC, bridge."
Captain to the bridge, sound general quarters!

The crew almost had a full night of sleep but here we go again. The gong making its obnoxious sound along with the quarter master on the bridge making his announcement on the public address system. "All hands man your battle stations. Repeat, all hands man your battle stations!"

The officer of the deck reported the confirming radar contact to Porterfield via the TBS (talk between ships). The Porterfield relayed the message to the task force commander even though the flagship had already heard it on their own TBS. In moments the flagship issued orders. All ships assume condition ZED (battle stations). The big carriers were ordered to launch night fighters immediately.

After the Callaghan was fully at battle stations a tense waiting period began. Would the bogey continue on toward the task force? Is it one of ours or one of theirs? If one of theirs would it attack? Would we open fire?

The Captain got on the phone with CIC and asked for steady reports on the range and position of the bogey. While he paced back and forth the bridge talker relayed the reports.

"Bogey bearing three two three degrees, range three-zero miles, speed one two zero knots."

"Bogey bearing three two two degrees, range two-zero miles, speed one two zero knots."

"Bogey bearing three two zero degrees, range one-zero miles, speed one two zero knots."

At range 5400 yards, word finally came from the Commodore aboard the Porterfield, "Permission to open fire." Word was relayed from CIC to fire control "Open fire." The gunnery officer gave the word to the sailor manning the pistol grip trigger connected electrically to the five main gun mounts.

BLAM! The five guns went off in unison. The crew had heard it before but this was NOT the same. It had all been drill until now. This was the real thing with a real enemy target. It was both thrilling and terrifying all at the same time.

The five guns continued to smash out salvo after salvo. The guns crashed followed by the sound of the empty brass shell cases bouncing off the steel deck after being ejected from the gun mounts. Salvo after salvo blasted away as each sailor not in a gun mount or otherwise employed by the gunnery department wondered what effect it was having. Lookouts strained to see the enemy plane against the black sky.

Just as suddenly as the firing began, it stopped. The "check fire" order had been given to allow time to make certain they were firing at the bogey and not friendlies. The night fighters were closing in and the Commodore wanted to make sure they were not about to blast a "friendly" out of the sky.

It only took ten seconds to check that they were indeed firing at the bogey. During this time the Callaghan turned right to course 330 degrees in order to uncover all of the guns. The bogey was moving in a position and direction that was about to make it impossible for the aft guns to fire at it because it would be behind the superstructure of the ship itself. Hence the turn to allow these guns to continue to participate in the effort to destroy the enemy plane.

BLAM! The five gun salvos began again. Sailors not on the gunnery net (telephone communications) jumped at the unexpected resumption of the main battery fire. A few more salvos were fired and then "cease fire" was ordered.

The very last salvo thundered out with an exciting result. The sailor manning the range finder in the main gun director above the bridge reported seeing the burst apparently hit next to the enemy aircraft. He said he saw an orange illumination as a result of the burst. Immediately a burning object was seen to fall off the plane and drop into the ocean. The brightly burning object was extinguished by the seawater. One of the observers who saw this was Captain Johnson himself who immediately reported this to the Porterfield.

The SC radar had lost the target when it flew within a couple of miles of the Callaghan but picked it up again as it flew out of range of the destroyer's guns. It watched with interest as several of the task forces night fighters closed in on the target. All of the planes faded from the radar screen at about 28 miles distance. That was the last they heard from the intruder.

It was late enough in the morning that the skipper simply kept the men at general quarters until dawn. Otherwise the men would have been dismissed only to return to general quarters in about an hour. The skipper was also mindful of the intruder that just visited and wanted to be ready in case the Japanese had decided to return, possibly with more planes. But that did not happen.

A very tired bunch of sailors shuffled off to the breakfast chow line that morning. At the same time the Porterfield and the Callaghan reversed direction to join up with the main body of the task force. Within a few minutes the task force itself reversed direction to head back to the east. Around 10:00

o'clock the Callaghan joined the outer screen of the task force. A slow march to the east went on into the afternoon when the big ships of Task Force 58 split off and left the slow Supply Task group behind. Soon afterwards another pair of tankers and its escorts joined up with them.

They immediately reversed course again and began zigzagging. This march back and forth across the same basic area of the ocean undoubtedly seemed pointless to some of the sailors but that was common for tanker groups. Their job was to be a gas station out in the ocean and they would be useless if they went wandering off too far away from the fleet.

That night they had another sound contact. The officers of the Callaghan demonstrated their new attitude about these nightly sound contacts. The contact was treated as if it was real until declared a "false" contact. But there was no longer the near panic that had occurred with every contact only a few weeks prior. This contact was also declared false and the Callaghan went back to station keeping in a mere five minutes. The depth charge crew lost a little sleep but no-one else did.

All night long the Supply Task group headed south. At dawn Manus island was sighted. The course was now changed several times as the Task group headed for LosNegros island. The superb anchorage called Seeadler harbor was located at LosNegros. When this part of the Admiralty islands had been captured by MacArthur's forces about 3 months back, the position of the Allies was vastly improved.

LosNegros was one of the kingpins in the ring around the Japanese fortress at Rabaul. Rabaul on New Britain island had ninety thousand Japanese troops ready to defend the fortress to the death. At first the Allies had planned to assault the fortress directly in what would have been a very costly campaign. Luckily planners realized that islands could be secured in a huge ring all around Rabaul which would isolate and by-pass the base. Most of these islands were taken with very little cost in casualties. Rabaul was now left with ninety thousand

Japanese troops which were totally useless to the Imperial Japanese government.

Seeadler harbor would now be the base for all naval operations against New Guinea and, later, islands to the north of New Guinea. Facilities were being constructed at a rapid pace even as the Supply Task group steamed up to the harbor entrance.

As usual the tankers entered first while the destroyers patrolled outside the harbor entrance. After all the big ships were inside the destroyers formed up and followed. At a quarter to 3:00 the Callaghan dropped anchor in 13 fathoms of water. The Callaghan was now anchored as far south as it would ever get.

The next couple of days were typical fleet anchorage days. Normal maintenance and resupply were the order of the day. For example, on the afternoon of the second day, the Callaghan received 100 rounds of 5" antiaircraft ammunition to replace usage during the long Supply Task group mission.

The only excitement was a couple of air raid scares that turned out to the usual friendly aircraft with no IFF (Identification Friend or Foe) signal showing for some unknown reason. The radar watch probably speculated about sleepy airman who forgot to turn their IFF on.

On the third day, the Callaghan pulled up its anchor and crossed over to the tanker USS Cahaba. The destroyer then moored alongside and topped off its fuel bunkers with 1037 barrels of black crude. After that was accomplished, it was time for the Callaghan to go to work again. Lines were cast off and the Callaghan steamed out of the anchorage to begin patrolling the east channel while Task Group 50.17 came to life again.

After a couple of hours, the big tankers had managed to plod out of Seadler harbor and assemble themselves into a Task Group. Once that was done the Callaghan quickly joined up to assume its assigned position in the destroyer screen. Though this was a complex task, it had now become routine. The Task

Group soon was steaming northwest, away from friendly territory.

The next day, the supply task group met Task Group 58.1 for a refueling rendezvous at sea. Once again they were giving the "big boys" and their escorts a drink. At 9:00am refueling was begun. Two hours later, general quarters was sounded because an unfriendly plane was reported on flying in toward the refueling formation. The Callaghan's radar picked it up at a very close 8 miles. Shortly thereafter, a message was flashed to all ships that the fighter cover had shot down the enemy plane, a twin engined "Betty" bomber.

After all this excitement passed, the destroyers settled back down to their assigned stations. Entertainment was provided for the top side crewmen as they watched some of the biggest aircraft carriers in the world join up with tankers for refueling.

Later in the afternoon when refueling was finished, the formation of ships was changed from the standard refueling formation to a cruising formation. For now, Task Group 50.17 was going to tag along with the "big boys." Callaghan's part of the formation change was to assume a new position in the outer screen.

Soon after the reshuffling of the ships was accomplished, they began to zigzag. It was comforting for the Callaghan to be finished with the slow straight-line refueling formation and to begin cruising in a proper submarine spoiling zigzag pattern.

For almost 24 hours, the supply Task Group remained with T.F. 58.1. At dawn the next day, they were detached from T.F. 58.1 in order to go join T.F.58.2 which was waiting nearby. Their services were needed by more of the big guys.

Not too long after refueling was begun for the ships of T.F. 38.2 another unidentified aircraft contact was received. Once again, general quarters was sounded and worried eyes scanned the horizon. This time it took 20 minutes for the combat air patrol to discover that the aircraft was friendly. Relieved skippers throughout the formation canceled the general quarters.

An hour and a half later it happened again. This was doubly annoying since the ships were in such a vulnerable position while conducting refueling. Shortly after the general quarters was canceled, the Callaghan got a break as it was ordered to escort the USS Cowpens, a light carrier, while it conducted flight operations.

This was a thrill for the Callaghan crew. During flight operations, every carrier was assigned a destroyer to perform what was called plane guard duty. This meant that the destroyer followed along behind the carrier at a distance of a thousand yards or so. Carrier flight operations was always hazardous to the planes involved. The destroyer's job was to pick up the crew of any planes that crashed while trying to land or take-off from the carrier.

This was the first time for Callaghan to perform this duty for one of the fleet carriers. This was a preview of the type of career that the Callaghan would soon take up and be concerned with for the rest of 1944 and part of '45.

Later that afternoon, the Callaghan left its position in the screen to steam over to the USS Bunker Hill, one of the large Essex-class fleet carriers. The mission this time had nothing to do with war but everything to do with morale. The Callaghan was picking up mail.

It actually took quite some time to cross the big formation, maneuver alongside the big carrier and then get the mail bags across on lines between the two ships. When it was over, the Callaghan left for new duty as one of the picket ships for the task force. The Callaghan went out approximately 24,000 yards or 12 miles from the center of the task force to join destroyer Marshall as the early warning ships of the force.

The Marshall and the Callaghan got to spend a relatively quiet night out in front of the task force. The only scare was a surface radar contact at 4:10am. In less than 20 minutes the contact was determined to be friendly ships. At 5:05, the formation changed course again back to the east and Task Group 50.17 was once again released from the cruising formation of fleet carriers. The Callaghan left the Marshall behind as it steamed at high speed to take its normal place in the destroyer screen around the tankers.

Minutes later dawn general quarters was sounded and a new day was under way. The supply Task Group changed course to due north. Not long after the Callaghan left the screen again to go find the USS Lexington, another Essex-class carrier. Once alongside, the bags of mail were transferred to it. The Callaghan then steamed to take position behind the Tanker group as refueling formation was assumed.

A few minutes before 11:00 that morning, the Callaghan was relieved by another destroyer in order to take it's turn at refueling. The Callaghan went alongside the USS Lackawanna. In less than 35 minutes, 807 barrels of fuel were transferred to the Callaghan's bunkers.

The Callaghan steamed away from the Lackawanna to take station of the starboard side of the tanker formation. It remained there while the tankers refueled Task group 58.1. At about 5:00pm the combined fleet formation changed course to the east. Two and a half hours later it changed course again to the northeast.

Shortly thereafter, the destroyer Meade reported a sound contact. This resulted in an order for an emergency course change for the giant formation. Since the joint formation was composed of both slow tankers and fast carriers that did not normally operate together, the course change was actually made in two relatively small course changes. This cautious maneuver helped prevent collisions and allowed the slow, ponderous tankers to make the course change without getting left behind by the much more agile warships.

Since nothing developed from the Meade's sound contact, the task group began stepping through course changes to resume the original heading. A half a dozen course changes were ordered over the next hour, perhaps to throw off any trailing submarines. After those maneuvers were over, the formation settled down to a straight course due east. They remained that way until after dawn general quarters the next day.

This day would be a replay of the previous. The course was changed a couple of times to bring the fleet heading south. Another sound contact was received before lunch but, once again, nothing came of it. More refueling was performed as there were yet more thirsty ships with bunkers to fill. For the Callaghan it was a good day because it was called upon twice to guard carriers as they left the formation to perform flight duties. This helped break up what would otherwise be tedious station keeping in the screen.

The night passed without event. In the early morning hours, the Callaghan registered a sound contact. As was now routine, the officer of the deck pursued the contact vigorously. Within seven minutes the contact was lost and the Callaghan simply returned to her place in the screen. Most of the crew not on watch never knew it happened.

The next morning refueling continued until 9:45am. At a quarter to noon, the Callaghan and other destroyers began patrolling while the big ships entered Seadler Harbor. Another strike mission was complete.

Once inside the harbor, the Callaghan steamed over to the USS Escambia and moored alongside. The fuel bunkers of the destroyer were then topped off leaving her ready for immediate action if called for. The Callaghan then left to find berth 323 where she would drop her anchor for a quiet day of post-sea maintenance.

The next day in mid-afternoon the Callaghan posted the sea detail and got underway. Before leaving the harbor this time, a little special maneuvering was required. It seems that some members of the crew were visiting the battleship Indiana. Captain Johnson brought the Callaghan alongside the Indiana but not for the usual mooring. The crew members were put into a gig and shuttled over between the two warships. In a few minutes they were aboard and the Callaghan was on its way.

The Callaghan made its way out of the harbor to take up anti-submarine patrol outside while waiting for the tanker group to come out. Presently it did and T.F. 50.17 was on its way out of the South Pacific. Course was set at 25 degrees for the beginning of the long voyage. The Callaghan was out on the starboard (right) front side of the formation.

Three hours later the Callaghan got a sound contact. Unlike the last couple of contacts, this one did not fade away. The depth-charge batteries were manned and the destroyer ran in to make the attack. A booming 10 charge pattern was dropped on the "enemy." When the Callaghan came around to investigate, something was seen. As the destroyer steamed back through the area of the attack, logs were seen on both sides of the ship. Not being sure if this was the source of the sound contact, the skipper continued the search. When nothing further developed, the Callaghan returned to the task group.

The night passed without further incident. An early pre-dawn general quarters was sounded at 5:00am. A few minutes later the Task Group rendezvoused again with Task Force 58. The supply Task Group split up into 3 parts. Callaghan, along with destroyers Morrison and Porterfield, joined tankers Cahaba and Neshanic to fuel T.G. 58.1. which had the carrier Hornet as the flagship.

The morning was spent screening the refueling operation. At 10:37 am the Callaghan got a sound contact which caused a little excitement. But after the usual charge to the position of the contact, it was determined that this was not a submarine. The Callaghan returned to its position in the screen.

At 11:15 the refueling operations were all completed and Task group 50.17 was released by the commander of Task Force 58. The fifth fleet was finished in the South Pacific and was now headed home to the central Pacific. It would not return again for many months.

The supply Task Group turned to a heading of due east for the next couple of days. One of the tankers was detached along with several DEs (a small, slower version of the destroyer) for duty in the South Pacific.

On the second day out, the Callaghan was detached temporarily to perform a little deception. While the Task Group continued its slow trek to the east, the Callaghan peeled off and headed back to the southwest at 20 knots speed. After steaming away for 3 hours, the Callaghan began broadcasting radio signals that were fake transmissions from the Task Group commander. These were designed to make the Japanese think that the Task Group was headed back to the Admiralties. After an hour and a half of this, the Callaghan shut down its radio and turned back around for a high speed dash back to the Task Group. They rejoined the formation just after dinner.

The following day was fueling day again. Something unusual was performed this time, however. The tankers paired up and certain tankers were emptied into other tankers. The purpose was probably to speed up the slowest tankers in the formation and also to provide some empty targets for the enemy if he should come calling. When the tanker transfers were completed, the escorts lined up for refueling. The Callaghan tanked off the Lackawanna this time.

The next day was the 3rd of May. This date was significant because they would have two May 3rds. The first was May 3rd, East Longitude. The second was May 3rd, West Longitude which occurred after they passed the International Date Line.

But first there was the matter of another sound contact. At 2:30 in the early morning, a contact was received and the depth charges were manned. 3 minutes later a full pattern of charges was dropped at shallow depth. After turning back, contact was regained. A few minutes later, an embarrassing barrage was dropped. 14 minutes after that, another full pattern was dropped at medium depth. At this point contact was lost and soon the Callaghan was ordered to rejoin.

The rejoin order was a good thing because the Callaghan had expended a total of 27 depth charges. The supply of depth charges aboard was suddenly very low. Luckily no more sound contacts were made that day. In fact, in a few hours the Task Group commander decided to detach the Callaghan and send her ahead to Majuro. There the Callaghan would pick up a new supply of depth charges as well as the mail for the Task Group. Course was set for 75 degrees and speed was increased to 24.5 knots.

The Callaghan made a high speed dash into Majuro arriving at 8:40 the next morning. They spent exactly eight hours there loading depth charges, mail and new personnel who were waiting to join ships of T.G. 50.17. They also refueled while they were at it to make up for the high speed run. Then they were on their way again, course 61 degrees to chase their task group down again.

On the 4th of May (West Longitude), they rejoined the T.G. at dawn. Their first duty was to rendezvous with each ship of the formation to pass over the mail that belonged to that ship. Hours later with that chore done, the Callaghan took a position in the screen.

Bound for Pearl Harbor, the only U.S. territory in the Pacific! The next four days plodded by as the men anticipated liberty in Pearl.

Of course, there were the usual training exercises ordered by Captain Johnson. There was no such thing as an idle day with Johnson as skipper. On the 6th, the gunnery department test fired 24 rounds of 5 inch ammunition with the new Mark 32 fuses. On the 7th at a minute past midnight, the Callaghan peeled off and steamed away at high speed to get out ahead of the formation. At 4:30am, they turned back heading for the formation which used the approaching destroyer for radar tracking practice.

Early on the morning of the 9th, the Callaghan was provided a target tow plane for anti-aircraft gunnery practice. Three passes were made and one sleeve was shot down. 25 rounds were fired in the process.

Then at 10:00am, the Callaghan stood patrol while the tankers began passing through the entrance to Pearl Harbor. At noon it was the Callaghan's turn. They moored next to the Morrison at berth X-7.

It was almost like being home. In fact, it was as close as the Callaghan would ever get.

Berth X-7 was a destroyer "nest" which meant a group of destroyers all moored together. In this case it also included a destroyer tender, the USS Piedmont. The Piedmont was a big ship compared to the destroyers. It was nearly 10,000 tons, a lot longer and much wider than the biggest destroyer in the fleet. It had a big crew too, around 800 men.

The Callaghan needed work so it was assigned a five day "availability" period next to the big tender. This meant that the Callaghan would be directly alongside the tender for the five days so that the repair and maintenance personnel from the tender could perform whatever work was required. All of the necessary equipment and supplies for such work was aboard the tender. The only thing the tender could not do was work on the bottom of the destroyer which, of course, was under water.

This meant that the Callaghan, for once, wasn't going anywhere. It did not mean, however, that the crew would get to goof off. A liberty section was released each morning to go ashore but this only amounted to about one third of the crew. The rest of the crew was stuck aboard with one work party after another to keep them sweating under the hot tropical sun.

There was also routine maintenance going on for certain departments of the ship. The black gang was kept busy working on the boilers and engineroom equipment. The torpedo gang was busy performing the never-ending maintenance on the complex torpedoes. Some of the sailors were spared working on their equipment because the tender personnel took over with special maintenance or calibration.

But having your regular equipment tied up was not necessarily a blessing. That just meant you were available for work parties. These went on all the time. One of the biggest ones occurred the first day: unloading ammunition. Nearly all of the 5" main gun rounds were unloaded so they could be refuzed by the Pearl Harbor ammunition depot. 1258 regular AA Common rounds were unloaded along with 218 AA rounds with the new Mark 32 fuses. Each of these rounds weighed 54 pounds so this was no easy task.

During this time another problem was solved for the Callaghan. The shortage of crew was handled by the Navy in a typical wartime fashion. A large group of brand new sailors, fresh out of boot camp, were sent directly from their training bases to the West coast. There they were loaded on a huge troopship which soon departed for Hawaii.

Upon arrival at Pearl Harbor, the new sailors were quickly debarked at the naval base. They were immediately divided up and assigned to various ships. Since the Navy was interested in doing this with speed rather than nicety, the sailors were divided up by starting at the top of the alphabet and working down. So a group of sailors whose last names started with "a" were sent off to the first ship and the next group of "a" sailors were sent off to the next ship. When the "a"s were gone, the group was filled with "b"s and so on.

This was all done quite late in the day at Pearl Harbor. Further it took quite some time to organize these groups and provide transport for them to their new homes, the various ships. So it was that at 11:00pm on May 9th, long after dinner had been served, a group of twenty tired and hungry new sailors arrived at the Callaghan. The duty officer was amazed at the names of these sailors: "Pitak, Pitts, Place, Plesky, Plofkin, Poissonier, Pokotdki, Policano, Polidori, Pollard, Pollock, Polenski,

Popeckie, Polonski, Popkin, Porsch, Potaczala, Pozzi, Prahl and Preitz."

So the legend of the "p" sailors of the Callaghan was begun.

Someone had to take care of these sailors who had completely missed dinner. The officer who took them under his wing was Ensign Frank Dunne, jack of all trades. Frank saw to it that they got sandwiches and were assigned a bunk. After more than three months in the Pacific, several missions and thousands of miles steamed, the Callaghan finally had a full crew.

While the Callaghan was having all of this work done on it and for it, Captain Johnson decided that now was the time to complete the task of finding a piece of equipment he dearly wanted. The mission to procure the metal bending machine was about to be fulfilled.

One day it arrived, was hoisted aboard and installed. The Captain was extremely pleased and proud. The Callaghan was probably the only Fletcher class destroyer in the world to have such a machine aboard.

At the end of the availability period new ammunition arrived to replace all the rounds that were unloaded the first day. Only this time there was even more: 1300 rounds of 5" Common and 277 5" Mark 32. The new sailors were finding duty in the Navy to be less than glamorous! Shortly thereafter the Callaghan took aboard 1950 barrels of fuel oil from the Pearl Harbor fuel depot. It was clear that they were getting ready for sea again.

The five days turned into less than four because the Navy was in a big hurry. Pearl Harbor was positively jumping with activity. It was obvious that a big operation was in the works. In addition to the usual warships including carriers and battleships on down, there were a huge number of amphibious ships of all kinds in various parts of the harbor with more coming in every day. There were new types of amphibious ships that had not been seen before. It did not take a genius to figure out that another invasion was planned for the near future. The rumor mill was working overtime!

Meanwhile, it was time for the Callaghan to leave its temporary mother (the USS Piedmont) and go stretch her legs. At dawn on the 15th the Callaghan got underway and headed down the channel for the sea. The assignment was to conduct training exercises as part of Task Group 52.14.2. This was the beginning of the Callaghan's new career.

This was half of Carrier Division 25 with Rear Admiral Bogan in command. The Callaghan was no longer a part of the logistics Navy. Although these carriers were the so-called "jeep" carriers converted from merchant ship or tanker hulls, they were warships. The Callaghan was now a part of the fighting Navy. No one aboard wanted to take the fight to the enemy more than Captain Johnson. He was determined to show what the Callaghan could do.

Task Group (T.G.) 52.14.2 consisted of the two escort carriers White Plains and Kalinin Bay along with destroyers Porterfield, Longshaw and the Callaghan. With only three destroyers for two carriers, the Callaghan was going to be very busy over the next few days.

Flight operations began the very first day at 11:00am. The Callaghan acted as either screen or plane guard for the White Plains. There were a total of four flight operation cycles that day which allowed for plenty of practice for everyone involved.

When not involved in flight operations duties, the Callaghan was occupying the starboard position in the anti-submarine screen formed by the destroyers. The crew noticed that the Task Group was steaming steadily to the south and east. The task group was headed for a safe training area just to the west of the big island of Hawaii.

The next day at dawn found the Callaghan screening the White Plains during flight operations. There were only two other flight cycles that day and the Callaghan switched over to screening the Kalinin Bay during these cycles. The rest of the day was passed with peaceful zigzagging back and forth in the appointed screen position.

Early on the 17th, just before dawn, the two task groups separated. The Callaghan assumed a new screen position out in front of the little task group. All day was spent at practicing formation maneuvers including changing courses, axis and positions. The Task Group was literally getting to know each other and its corporate capabilities.

The 18th was aircraft day and started in the early morning darkness more than two hours before dawn. The Callaghan screened Kalinin Bay while she launched aircraft. After breakfast the Callaghan stood plane guard duty for White Plains while she recovered aircraft. During this duty it became clear why a plane guard was so important.

All the crew topside loved to watch the planes as they came in, one by one, in the landing pattern that would take them to the carrier. The final turn in the landing pattern was made not far from the plane guard destroyer. Then the plane would line up on the carrier and slowly lose altitude until it was just above the rear edge of the flight deck. At that point it would either touch down or go around again under full power.

During this plane guard duty, the crew watched as one of the planes attempted to land but instead bounced off the flight deck right into the sea. Immediately the Callaghan responded. In headed over to the spot where the pilot departed from his sinking plane and stopped to lower a boat. Before the boat had even left the side of the Callaghan another plane that was launching from the other carrier, the Kalinin Bay, was observed to land in the water. The word was shouted to the boat that the Callaghan would return. It then quickly steamed over to the spot where the second plane had sunk it only 20 seconds. The other boat that the Callaghan carried was lowered and the pilot quickly picked up. The pilot was taken aboard but the boat was left behind.

The Callaghan then returned the second pilot to the Kalinin Bay. Once that was accomplished, the destroyer went back to recover both of its boats. The first pilot, Ensign L.R. Pool was taken aboard to experience the Callaghan treatment.

The Callaghan treatment of rescued pilots was in two steps. First they got examined by Doctor Parker. Doc. Parker almost always found the pilots to be in ok physical condition but required some treatment for the "experience" they had just been through. He always broke out the medical brandy that was a part of the medical supplies and gave the pilot a stiff shot of it. Since he believed strongly that a man should never drink alone, he always joined the aviator in knocking down some of the brandy.

Once Doc. Parker was through with the pilot, Captain Johnson insisted on seeing him in the Captain's quarters. After 20 minutes or so, the aviator would emerge to join one or more of the ships officers. It was noted that the aviators never wore their Navy issue watch after leaving the Captain's quarters. No one ever dared ask the Captain how he obtained the pilot's watch but the assumption was that he gave a speech about how the pilot could express his appreciation of his rescue. The watch ,of course, was the chosen expression of appreciation.

Occasionally these watches did not function after their experience in the sea while on the arm of the swimming or floating aviator. In that case, Captain Johnson soon had the chief engineer working on the watch to repair it. Apparently obtaining aviator watches had high priority.

The rest of the day and the morning of the next was spent in performing task group maneuvers. In mid afternoon of the 19th, the carriers followed by the destroyers entered Pearl Harbor once again. The Callaghan moored in the destroyer nest as usual.

The following two days were occupied with normal maintenance and supply matters. An additional 202 rounds of

5" were taken aboard. The fuel was topped off again with over sixty-six thousand gallons of fuel oil.

At dawn on the 22nd, the Callaghan and sister ship, Porterfield left their moorings to head out to another training area just to the west of Oahu. The commander of the squadron, COMDESRON 55, was along for the show in the Porterfield.

First on the agenda was torpedo rehearsal and firing runs. The Callaghan got to go first for four training runs and two live fire runs using the Porterfield as target. As mentioned before, these live fire runs in Hawaii were the only torpedo firings the Callaghan would ever make. But, of course, the crew and the Navy had no way of knowing that at the time. After the Callaghan was finished, the Porterfield had its turn at the same six torpedo runs using the Callaghan as target.

After that the destroyers waited for night fall for the next set of firing drills. At 8:00pm the two destroyers went to general quarters. About a half hour later the Callaghan practiced night spotting. It used up fifteen regular 5" rounds and eleven starshells in the process. Next was night battle practice. This time the main battery kicked out thirty regular rounds and only nine starshells. By 10:00pm it was all over for the night as the Callaghan took up station on the Port beam of the Porterfield for a slow night of cruising back and forth.

The next day provided realistic practice that was needed possibly more than any other kind. The Callaghan and Porterfield would have sound training exercises with a live submarine! The Navy had provided an old post-world war I type submarine, the S28, that was no longer useful for combat duties. But it was ideal for training inexperienced destroyer crews on the performance and sonar return of a submerged submarine.

The two destroyers worked with the submarine all morning and part of the afternoon. The Porterfield then left on assigned duty. The Callaghan steamed alone to the assigned night rendezvous point.

On the morning of the following day, the Callaghan cruised over to an assigned gunnery range and met the USS Lamberton. The Lamberton would be towing a target raft for the Callaghan's benefit. The two Captain's held a short conference to be sure each understood the schedule of events and to prevent any mistakes.

They began with the very important radar calibration exercises. This was accomplished at known ranges so that the radar could be calibrated to provide accurate ranges for firing the main 5" gun battery even when the target might not be visible. Radar directed fire at night or in bad weather was therefore possible. This was becoming increasingly important since Japanese aircraft were using night attack as a response to the US Navy's dominance of the daytime skies.

After the calibration was over, it was time for another round of day battle practice. The Callaghan then left the Lamberton behind to rendezvous with a tow plane for more antiaircraft practice. This was another heavy shooting session. The 5" guns put out 75 rounds and the 20mm guns put out 1288 rounds. But the real workout was by the 40mm guns. They put out 1405 rounds! When the tow plane left there was a lot of empty shell casings to pick up around the decks of the destroyer.

Late in the afternoon, the Callaghan left on a course due south to join up with the USS Irwin, another Fletcher class destroyer. COMDESRON 55 had transferred to the Irwin overnight so he was again present for the evening's show. About an hour or so after nightfall, the two destroyers practiced simulated torpedo attacks on each other. This continued until midnight. The Callaghan then took a screening position on the Irwin and remained there until after dawn.

The next morning the two destroyers formed a column in preparation for more antiaircraft drill. This time instead of firing at a sleeve pulled by a tow aircraft, they would be firing at a drone. This allowed a more realistic feel to the practice and could result in an actual shootdown.

The Callaghan put in two sessions with drones, one in the morning and one in the afternoon. The afternoon session was devoted to just the 5" main gun battery which put out 76 rounds and achieved a hit on the elusive drone. When the antiaircraft practice was over, the Callaghan set course for the Pearl Harbor entrance. They passed through the antisubmarine net gate guarding the entrance a few minutes before 5 o'clock.

The Callaghan moored at pier H-1 and proceeded to exchange two torpedoes. Later that evening the deck force got to wrestle with fuel hoses as the destroyer took on 1389 barrels of fuel oil from the dock. The Callaghan remained overnight at the pier which was unusual for a destroyer at this time in one of the busiest periods of activity that Pearl Harbor would ever see. What the crew could not know was that this was the last time the Callaghan would tie up to a pier in its short lifetime.

The next morning the Callaghan got underway to steam over to the destroyer nests and tie up at berth X-3. The next four days would be spent moored at this same spot. It was a time of final maintenance, resupply and training the new guys. Everyone knew that when they left Pearl the next time, it was going to be back out to the combat zone. No-one, including the Captain, knew where they were going or what the mission would be.

In the meantime, it was last chance for liberty. Though most of the guys had seen the sights of Honolulu by now, liberty was eagerly anticipated. It was a final opportunity to spend some of that pay in a civilized world that included real bars, civilians (though not enough) and whorehouses.

Since Hawaii had so many service men present and so few unattached females, the war department had quietly made arrangements for highly organized houses of prostitution. Back in those days it was considered to be an acceptable evil that was necessary to keep the "boys" under control. The authorities made sure that the houses were organized with fixed, cheap rates and ever present security. At times like these, before a major operation was to occur, the houses were visited by thousands of servicemen. As a result, there were always long lines of men waiting.

Some of the men found all of that very distasteful and avoided the whorehouses no matter what there friends were doing. Other more innocent forms of recreation were indulged in. There were organized sports all around Honolulu. There was even one sport unique to Hawaii at that time. Some of the sailors of the Callaghan tried out surfing.

Board surfing at that time was something that only the native population of the islands indulged in. What the sailors tried out was body surfing or surfing on common objects that would float like mattresses. Some were more successful than others but that did not matter. This was pure fun enjoyed by boys and young men in their twenties who did not get many such opportunities in the middle of a global war.

On the 29th of May the Callaghan took aboard 281 5" cartridges. More significantly they took aboard 2080 rounds of 40mm and 2700 rounds of 20mm. Suddenly the officers became real serious about getting supplies aboard. The word soon spread around the crew that this was their last day in port.

It was evident that this was the last day in port for a lot of other ships as well. The level of activity around Pearl was almost frantic. A fleet of slow amphibious ships had already left Pearl three days before. Now recreational activities nearly came to a halt as men were recalled to their ships or their units to help with the final preparations for what everyone knew was a big offensive that was finally beginning.

The next morning dawned with a flurry of last minute activity. Captain Johnson was particularly upset over the ammunition situation. The load of main gun 5" rounds was short by several hundred rounds. The officers were relieved when word came down that the Laws would provide 5" rounds. At 9:00am 350 5" rounds came over from the Laws and were stashed away in the ships magazines. Seven minutes later this activity was completed the ship got underway.

At 10:13am the Callaghan cleared the Pearl Harbor channel. Many of the men topside looked back as the familiar sights of Hospital point, the city of Honolulu and Diamond Head receded from view. They could not know that the Callaghan and some of her crew would never pass this way again.

CHAPTER FOUR: WAR

The Callaghan immediately took up her normal duty of anti-submarine screen for the task group that was leaving Pearl. However, this was a group of huge troop transport ships full of Marines, not the Escort Carrier group that she was assigned to. It was not until mid afternoon that she finally got to join her fellow warships in Task Unit 52.14.2 when the escort carriers came up to join the troop transports.

An odd thing was happening. Although they all knew they were going off to war on some big operation, they were going the wrong way. Course was set at 167 degrees which is south southeast. From Pearl Harbor this would take them to nothing but empty ocean. The officers knew that this was just a ploy to throw off any trailing Japanese submarines.

Sure enough, two hours after sunset, the formation turned around. Course was set at 245 degrees, west southwest. This was the direct course right back to the Marshall islands from which they had come over three weeks before. They would follow that general direction for a week and a half! This was a slow, slow invasion task force.

Absolutely nothing happened of any consequence the first two days. This was a great relief to everyone involved since the task group contained some of the most valuable and vulnerable ships of the war. If a Japanese submarine or two could find them and sink some of those troop transports, the whole invasion effort might fail. This would throw off the entire timetable in the Pacific war and act to prolong the war.

The task group was actually a double group with the troop transports in three columns within the first group followed closely by the second group which consisted of the Escort Carriers and accompanying destroyers. The Callaghan was staying with its own task unit, the carriers, for now.

Speed was a leisurely 14 knots. Zigzagging was standard procedure during the day and that with the 14 knot speed limit meant that they would take a long time to cross the ocean. During the early morning hours of the 1st of June they actually slowed to 12 knots. This had to be frustrating to the Captains of the big troop transports which were capable of much higher speeds.

In mid-morning of the 1st, the leisurely cruise was interrupted by a panic. One of the carriers, the Kalinin Bay, reported a torpedo passed in front of her from starboard to port. Since the Callaghan was the closest destroyer at the moment, orders were flashed to investigate. Captain Johnson had general quarters sounded and everyone ran to their battlestations. The experienced crewmembers were probably thinking "Here we go again." But for the new guys that had joined at Pearl Harbor, this was their first taste of the real thing and they were scared. More than one sailor told a new guy not to worry, we've been through this before.

What followed was a very thorough set of searches through the area where the torpedo was reported. Back and forth the Callaghan steamed. The sonarman strained to hear any echo that might come back from the sonar pings his equipment was sending out. Nothing. Nothing but sea for over two hours of searching. Finally, with the task group out of sight, orders came to rejoin. With great relief, the crew stood down from general quarters and the ship accelerated to 22 knots to chase down the task group.

Right after rejoining the task group, it was time for flight operations. After a fruitless two hour search, the Callaghan crew was pleased to take a place in the screen while the carriers turned into the wind. Now they could again enjoy the spectacle of the little planes making the transition from the freedom of the sky to the confinement of a narrow wooden flight deck.

Night came without incident. So ended another typical day at sea for a destroyer; the sheepdog of the fleet. Like a sheepdog, the destroyer must endlessly be on the lookout for predators that might threaten their charges. Like a sheepdog, the destroyer must often face the predator alone while the flock (convoy) moves to safety. Sometimes no predator can be found but if the master sends the sheepdog, it must dutifully put its nose to the ground to search.

The next morning after flight operations, the little carrier group changed its formation to a special disposition for firing exercises. The destroyers put in some burst practice. Although the Callaghan only fired 10 rounds of 5", this was a way to keep fresh everyone involved with the main battery: fire control, CIC, main director, turret crews. With such a slow march across the sea in progress, it would be a challenge to maintain their combat skills.

June 3rd brought some excitement to mid-morning flight operations. Once again the Callaghan observed first one plane crash into the sea and then a few minutes later, another! The Callaghan altered course for the second plane as it was much closer while the Longshaw went after the first pilot. A half hour later, an Ensign Billingsworth from the carrier White Plains was welcomed aboard the Callaghan. Although the log notes that he suffered no injuries, we know that Doc Parker took good care of him anyway.

The next day was but one minute old when the carrier task unit broke up. The Callaghan and two other destroyers made a new formation with the White Plains and proceeded ahead of the everyone else at a blistering 17 knots. That was near top speed for the White Plains.

Six hours and a half hours later came dawn. The USS Noa took station beside the White Plains for fueling. One by one, each destroyer took its turn to be fueled from the big ship. While the Callaghan was alongside the White Plains, it took the opportunity to transfer Ensign Billinsworth by breeches buoy. The young aviator was put into the "breeches buoy" which was like a half sack with leg holes which was then connected to a high line strung between the two ships. While the two ships were separated by 50 to 100 feet or so, the young man was then pulled across while he dangled from the high line over the sea which was rushing by at eight to ten knots. Although not recorded, it is assumed that the White Plains honored the tradition of sending back a five gallon can of ice cream in return for it's aviator.

When refueling was done the four ships returned to the other carrier and destroyers to reform the task group.

June 4th was unique in that the Callaghan changed the date to June 5th to be in synch with the rest of the world across the International Date Line. For the Callaghan, it would never be changed back again.

Therefore the next day was June 6th. The task group was approaching the Marshall islands. They were very close to the Callaghan's recent home away from home, Majuro. Being this close to a naval base presented an opportunity.

Once again the ships formed the special formation for gunnery practice. A target tow plane was sent out from Majuro for the use of the task group. This time the tow plane pulled a sleeve past for the benefit of the machine guns. For some reason, only the starboard guns had the pleasure of firing at the sleeve before practice was canceled. There must have been great disappointment on the port guns!

The usual flight operations were held without incident this time.

The next morning the great formation of ships began its journey through the Marshall islands. Not long after dawn, course was changed to 284 degrees. They were no longer heading west southwest, they were now heading west northwest. The task group was initially within site of Majuro. This course was designed to keep the task group and its very vulnerable troop ships near friendly islands and away from the few remaining enemy held islands in this area.

Flight operations went on as usual. At the mid-day cycle of operations, something unusual occurred. The carrier Kalinin

Bay lost a liferaft overboard. Either a plane or a piece of deck equipment knocked it loose. Since the Callaghan was in the general area of the liferaft, Captain Johnson maneuvered his destroyer to retrieve it for the carrier.

In the early evening came word via radio of the invasion of France at Normandy. Many of the sailors on the ships marveled at the great power of the Allied cause that while one great invasion was occurring, another one, a half a world away was in the making.

Late that night and again in the early morning hours, course changes were made to bring the task group closer to a northwestern heading. The formation was working its way right through the middle of the Marshall islands on its way to Eniwetok. The whole day was spent on a rather quiet cruise past one island after another.

At 7:00pm that evening, general quarters was sounded. An unidentified aircraft had been spotted on radar headed their way. Of course, as so often happened near friendly bases, the plane turned out to be one of "ours."

At dawn the next day, Task Unit 52.14.2 broke away from the troop ship formation and steamed away independently in order to enter Eniwetok lagoon first. The Callaghan patrolled for the next two hours while other ships steamed through the entrance to the lagoon. Finally at 8:40, it was the Callaghan's turn to go through the deep water entrance of the lagoon to find berth 241 and anchor. The longest ocean passage of its career was over.

Two hours later the Callaghan pulled up its anchor and steamed over to the tanker, USS Sangatack. Before it got there, an air raid alert was sounded and the destroyer went to general quarters. A few minutes later the alert was canceled but Captain Johnson decided to keep the crew at Condition II which was one step below general quarters. This high lighted the fact that Eniwetok was like a frontier fort for the US Navy. It was the closest fleet anchorage to the Marianas which was where the Japanese fleet had its headquarters for the central

Pacific. The Japanese regularly sent reconnaissance aircraft over Eniwetok and Majuro to try to figure out the next move of the US Navy.

The Callaghan tied up to the Sangatack and took on a full load of fuel, 2552 barrels of fuel. The destroyer was very low on fuel when it arrived that morning. It returned to berth 241 and spent the rest of the day and the next at anchor.

Routine maintenance and general last minute preparations for combat duty was performed all the next day. They got the word they were going to be leaving with the carriers for the big invasion tomorrow. A welcome addition was a late arrival of another 106 rounds of 5" ammunition. They had been told to expect the worst on this invasion and they didn't want to be caught short of ammunition.

Late that night another unidentified aircraft caused all the ships to go to general quarters. This only heightened the pervading sense that what was about to occur was a historic operation that would include very serious fighting. General quarters was canceled at 11:22pm.

Long before dawn, reveille was sounded. The tired sailors not on watch stumbled out of their bunks and got themselves ready for a long day. Just as a glow appeared in the eastern sky, the Callaghan pulled up its anchor and got underway. As dawn was breaking, the destroyer cleared the harbor and turned to take up its patrol station to the left of the sortie lane. It remained on patrol while the rest of the ships of the escort carrier task group steamed out of Eniwetok lagoon.

At 8:20am the Callaghan joined the screen of the task group and synchronized its course with that of the carriers. The initial course was south but that soon changed to a course of due west. The group slowed down to 13.5 knots to keep pace with the slower amphibious ships that were plodding along behind them.

At noon they changed course to a northwesterly heading. A thousand miles or so ahead of them lay the Marianas. This was to be the biggest invasion yet of the Pacific war and every sailor down to the lowliest ship's steward knew it. They also knew that these islands were going to be fiercely defended with every means the Japanese had.

Flight operations were carried out this first day out of Eniwetok and would be continued everyday until the escort carriers would be relieved long after the invasion. This was no longer practice. Torpedo planes took off on anti-submarine patrol and fighters took off on combat air patrol. Long range air patrol from the Marshall islands would give them warning of impending danger. After that the great amphibious fleet had to largely rely on its own resources for protection from any submarine or air attack.

The possibility of air attack was being reduced the very first day out. The mighty fleet carriers and battleships of Task Force 58 were already busy pounding the airbases and shore installations in the Marianas. In addition, one carrier task group was far to the north delivering the first attack on Iwo Jima. The invasion of the Marianas involved the most extensive fleet operations the US Navy had ever mounted.

The four days before the invasion were filled with constant vigilance and tension. The days were a blur of watches stood and flight operations guarded. Other than the usual maintenance problems, absolutely nothing happened. But still the quartermasters ticked off the nautical miles on the charts as the line representing the course of the Callaghan drew ever nearer the Marianas and the enemy.

Finally, just before midnight of the 14th of June the Escort Carrier Task Group arrived at its assigned operating area to the east of Saipan. Strange course changes began that had sailors on watch asking questions of each other. It quickly was confirmed that the Task Group was holding position by marching back and forth in this area east of Saipan.

The men were uneasy. They were aware that this was the biggest event in the Pacific war since the United States and its allies went on the offensive in the second half of 1942. There was a tremendous armada of ships both ahead and behind them. Saipan was too important to the enemy to ignore. There was going to be a fight and it was going to be bloody.

The sailors of the Callaghan knew that in the morning thousands of Marines would be hitting the beaches of Saipan. They also had been told that there were thousands of Japanese soldiers waiting on Saipan to stop the Marines. Many of the sailors reflected on what it would be like to be one of those Marines assaulting the beach. Probably to the man they were happy to be a sailor on this occasion and not a Marine.

The men were almost relieved to see the first faint hint of light heralding the dawn. Preparations could be seen aboard the escort carriers to launch aircraft. Planes were brought up to the flight deck, engines were started and warmed up and planes were spotted for take off. Suddenly orders went out on the TBS circuit that caused all of the ships of the task group to turn into the wind. Within minutes the little planes began roaring away from the flight decks. Task group 52.14.2 had joined the war.

While the planes were taking off, some of the men talked about what was going on at Saipan. The big gun ships, including the old battleships from the World War I era were firing on shore targets. The big 14" and 16" guns were firing to destroy enemy guns, to keep the Japanese troops down and to provide support for the frog men who were going in to clear obstacles from the landing beaches. The hope was that this bombardment plus the carrier strikes would keep the casualties to an acceptable level.

All day long the carrier task group marched back and forth in its assigned square of Pacific ocean. Flight operations were conducted on a regular basis. The destroyers all maintained a high state of alertness. Everyone expected some type of enemy reaction. All of the officers wanted to be ready. Nobody wanted to drop the ball now.

The afternoon dragged on. Men listened intently to every scrap of news that was radioed in about the invasion. They were glad that the invasion was apparently successful. But along with the news of the success was news of stiff Japanese resistance and heavy Marine casualties.

Some of the men began to think that the escort carrier group was out of the action. After all, they were east of Saipan, right? The Japanese planes wouldn't be looking here. They would go after the landing force. Sure they would, we'll be fine. Maybe soon we can all relax.

Suddenly, while some of the men were eating supper, general quarters was sounded. The men left their food behind and were running to their stations. Ok, maybe we're not out of it after all. What's the word?

A formation of unidentified aircraft had been spotted on radar and it was headed straight for them, 30 miles out. In three minutes all stations were manned and ready. The gun barrels of the machine guns were swinging back and forth as Gun Captains nervously checked out their mounts. Everyone was ready. This is what they trained for.

A division of four Wildcat fighters from the White Plains had been orbiting overhead at 10,000 feet. The were vectored out to intercept the incoming bogies. They found the bogies which turned out to be five Japanese Kates, single-engined torpedo bombers. In a running gun battle the fighters managed to shoot down four of the torpedo bombers.

Back at the Callaghan, the men in CIC (Combat Information Center) were monitoring the interception on the radio. At the same time the radar operators were watching as the blips representing the incoming planes steadily drew closer to the center of the screen. Up in the gun director they were getting word on the action from CIC. The sailor on the "gun circuit" was calling out the range as it steadily dropped. Bearing and range, bearing and range, the voices droned on.

121

Finally the lone Japanese survivor was within range. But he wasn't on the Callaghan's side of the formation! Ships on the other side opened up. The booming of the 5" guns was loud and rapid. They were certainly trying to get this guy.

But they weren't getting him. On he flew, low on the water. Word was flashed down to all the men on the firing circuit, a torpedo plane! Come on guys, SPLASH him! Instead the torpedo plane dropped his torpedo and abruptly turned and flew away apparently untouched. Luckily the carrier he was aiming at turned and easily avoided the torpedo.

A lot of keyed up men aboard the Callaghan were incredulous. What went wrong? How could a single torpedo plane make a lone attack against an alerted group of warships and get away? But it wasn't over.

A group of nine Wildcats had been launched from the carriers after the first alert. One of these pilots located the "Kate" with the nine lives by following the bursts of the anti-aircraft shells being thrown at the Japanese. He dove at full power through the bursts and opened up on the torpedo bomber. In a couple of firing runs he had the "Kate" on fire and slowing down. Flames spread all along the fuselage until the entire plane was one great flaming comet. It then smashed into the water and disappeared.

With that excitement over, the formation straightened up and waited for awhile to make sure no more bogies were on the way. After about 45 minutes or so, the carriers began to recover aircraft.

One of the aircraft trying to land didn't make it. A wildcat crashed over the side of one of the carriers. The Callaghan was in plane guard position so it went racing to the scene. Within five minutes the Callaghan's boat had been lowered to pick up Lt. (jg) S.W Bales, US Naval Reserve. He was not hurt so he got to spend the night aboard the Callaghan.

Nightfall followed the last round of landing operations and the first day of operation "Forger" was over. The escort carrier group spent a watchful but peaceful night east of Saipan. Everyone was aware though that it was anything but peaceful for the Marines ashore.

The next day was almost a repeat of the first day of the operation except that no Japanese aircraft came around to try to spoil things for the group. At noon the Callaghan transferred Lt. (jg) Bales back to the White Plains. The torpedo bombers from the escort carriers spent all day making bombing runs against targets on Saipan while the Wildcats flew along to make sure no Japanese planes could interfere.

The 17th of June dawned bright and clear with just a few puffy clouds in the sky. The first order of business was for the destroyers to get some fuel. The Callaghan left promptly at dawn to run over to a tanker group that had "parked" itself a few miles to the east of T.G. 52.14. The Callaghan went alongside the Neshanic and received a full load of 2202 barrels of fuel. It then hurried back to rejoin the carrier group.

The day was routine until around 6:00 pm. A large group of unidentified planes was spotted on radar 78 miles south of the group's position. All ships immediately sounded general quarters. The carriers began launching all fighters that could get into the air. By this time late in the day, the clouds had increased to big Cumulus clouds which were painted a beautiful rosette color by the sinking sun. It was a scenic backdrop to the deadly conflict about to unfold.

The formation was reoriented so that the destroyers could provide better anti-aircraft coverage and speed was increased. The Callaghan received the best seat in the house, 2000 yards directly to the south of the formation. Anticipation was high that this time they would not miss the action.

The fighter planes made their intercept of the enemy planes 32 miles away from the formation of ships. It was clear from what could be heard on the radio that this was a major shootout. 44 Wildcats were in the air against about 30 Japanese planes including the "Kate" torpedo bombers and the new "Judy" divebombers. The Wildcats fought tenaciously to bring down the torpedo planes and bombers that were trying to get to the carriers.

They were almost successful. Aboard the Callaghan men swept the skies to the south with every optic device that could be brought to bear. Again CIC put out the range that the radar boys were counting down. Suddenly some of the lookouts spotted puffs of anti-aircraft fire off to the southeast. The tanker group out in front of the carrier group was firing on an aircraft which was flying west between the two groups.

Permission was asked to open fire and quickly granted. The five main guns roared as one as salvo after salvo blasted out at the oncoming plane. Everyone topside felt their pulse quicken from a combination of concussion from the main guns and the realization that this was an enemy plane aimed straight at the Callaghan.

The enemy plane was believed to be a torpedo plane as someone said it was carrying a torpedo underneath. After 20 seconds of steady firing the plane suddenly disintegrated from a direct hit. Cheers broke out from some of the sailors who were witnessing their first "kill."

A second plane was spotted at about 3000 feet altitude and fire control switched to it. The plane, identified as a "Judy" dive bomber, was tracked for about ten seconds before the main guns opened up on it. The plane immediately went into a dive causing the gun boss to assume it had been hit. A cease fire was ordered and the guns quit again.

Many of the spectators began to realize that not all the planes out there were Japanese. Two Wildcats were observed following the Judy that the Callaghan had just fired on. Howard Gray, one of the quartermasters assigned to the aft navigation platform, wondered how the Wildcats could possibly come through all that gunfire without getting hit.

The Judy closed to about 2000 yards from the Callaghan and then reversed course with the two Wildcats right behind. At this point the forward 40mm mount on the starboard side opened fire on this plane and continued until the plane flew out of its arc of fire. The two Wildcats were observed at this moment to fire a final burst on the "Judy" and then zoom up out of the fight leaving it to the Callaghan. The midship 40mm (mount 43), the aft 40mm (mount 45) and the starboard 20mm's all opened up on the fleeing plane. Fifteen seconds later it burst into flame and crashed into the sea. Credit for this success went to the 40mm guns.

With scarcely time for a breather, a third aircraft was spotted by crewmen on the Port side of the ship and it was taken under fire by the Port mid ship 40mm (mount 41). Mount 41 stayed on this plane blazing away for 30 seconds when the plane suddenly crashed into the sea about 1500 yards away from the Callaghan.

At the same time this was happening, a Judy was spotted pulling out from a dive over the carrier Fanshaw Bay. The Judy was trailing a faint trail of smoke or oil and flew by between the carriers and the Callaghan. The 40mm mount 42 fired off four rounds but had to quit because the Judy flew in front of the White Plains. Mount 44 fired 12 rounds but had to stop for the same reason. The port 20mm guns then opened up on it because the short range 20mm rounds would fall into the sea before hitting the carrier over 2000 yards away. They pumped out 256 rounds before the plane winged over and crashed into the sea astern of the Callaghan.

Another ship opened fire on a plane that was about 3000 yards away and flying close to the water. Observing this mount 45 was quick to join the action and opened up as well. A little too quick as machine gun control recognized the plane as one of our Wildcats and had to do some yelling to get mount 45 to cease fire. Luckily only a dozen rounds went out toward the plane. 5" mount number five added a couple of its rounds as well under local control before it too was stopped.

It was over. After 15 minutes or so of tense scanning of the skies the men began to relax a little. The Callaghan men had

125

finally accomplished what all those months of training and pseudo combat had been aimed at. Along with the aggressive Wildcat pilots, they had defeated the enemy. The Callaghan was now a proud combat veteran with a record that would continue to build.

But first there was a problem to handle. The Fanshaw Bay had been hit by that Judy that dove on it. The hit was a serious one and the Fanshaw Bay was crippled. The job of guarding and assisting the Fanshaw Bay was given to the Callaghan.

Night had fallen while the rest of the task group steamed off, the Fanshaw Bay gradually slowed down and took on a list. Worried officers and men aboard the Callaghan watched both the carrier and the skies. If any Japanese planes returned to the scene of the action, the first thing they would do is attack the crippled carrier.

Captain Johnson gave orders which sent the Callaghan into a tight maneuver around the Fanshaw Bay. Meanwhile the Fanshaw Bay's Wildcats in the air had to be diverted to another carrier. As 40mm gun crews began to clear away empty shell casings from around their mounts, a discussion aboard the bridge of the Callaghan centered around what to do if the Fanshaw Bay needed direct assistance with fire fighting or the removal of wounded. The mood had changed rapidly from euphoria to one of tension and worry.

Damage control aboard the Fanshaw Bay went on for most of the night. Steering control was eventually restored and the list corrected. Fortunately for all the nervous sailors the carrier was quickly able to get back up to normal operating speed and rejoined the task group.

Meanwhile at 9:30pm a different kind of scare was thrown at the sailors. Radar picked up an unidentified surface target about 13 miles ahead of the formation. The Callaghan got the nod to run ahead and identify the unknown ship. 48 minutes later the mystery was solved. The Callaghan was amazed to find a fully lighted hospital ship steaming along as if there wasn't a war on. Of course, hospital ships, being the non-combatants they were, used running lights and illumination lights to show potential adversaries that they were a non-combatant.

So ended a very memorial evening and night. It would be awhile before the Callaghan would have such an action filled night as this one.

In fact it would be awhile before the Callaghan would see any action. Due to the damage to the Fanshaw Bay, aircraft loses and a need for reorganization of the task group, half of T.F. 52.14 was about to be withdrawn to Eniwetok. Luckily for the Callaghan it was to remain behind with the two carriers of T.F. 52.14 that would stay at Saipan. But they too would be pulled back for a couple of days along with the whole amphibious fleet.

The reason was simple. The Japanese Imperial Navy was on the way. Intelligence knew that the Japanese Navy meant to defend the Marianas with everything they had. The most potent weapon the Japanese Navy had was the carriers and battleships of the Combined Fleet. These ships had not been seen in action in fully a year and a half since the defeats the Japanese had suffered in the Solomons Islands. Now after rebuilding and reequipping they were coming out to fight.

Naval Intelligence had been tracking through various means the progress of the Japanese fleet as it left its anchorages in the East Indies and steamed across the bottom of the Philippines. The Navy never doubted what the destination of the Japanese fleet was. They knew it was Saipan. The only questions were what would the route be and how would the Japanese attack. Would it be a single massive attack or would it be a complex attack involving several phases and task forces? The latter was mode of operation in the first two big fleet actions of 1942: the Battle of the Coral Sea and Midway. It was demonstrated to a lesser extent in the few carrier actions near the Solomon Islands.

Admiral Raymond Spruance was in overall command of the operation "Forager." He had been in charge during the famous battle of Midway when three US carriers had defeated the entire Japanese Combined fleet. At Midway Spruance faced a vastly superior force. This time it was Spruance who had the superior force at his command.

But Spruance was a cautious commander who was mindful of his orders from Admiral Nimitz. His orders emphasized the protection of the amphibious fleet and the Marines ashore. Therefore he issued conservative orders designed to give the Japanese fleet little opportunity to damage to the invasion force.

Spruance ordered the invasion fleet withdrawn to a safe distance of a couple hundred miles from Saipan. At the same time Task Force 58 with all the fleet carriers and battleships would take position west of Saipan to intercept the oncoming Japanese fleet. The role of the escort carriers would be to "escort" the invasion fleet back to the safe area and provide air protection while they waited there.

As the Fanshaw Bay was leaving for Eniwetok, the escort carrier group was reorganizing itself. Although the greatest single air battle of the Pacific war was about to occur, the remaining escort carriers would only be involved in protecting the amphibious forces and bombing ground targets on islands in the Marianas.

The warships remaining with the invasion fleet in the safe area maintained a high state of alert. Everyone got the word that the Japanese fleet was on the way. Everyone was confident that Task Force 58 would defeat the enemy fleet but there was still concern for what might happen while the fleets were engaged.

The greatest worry was that some Japanese task force would make an end run around the Marianas and try to attack the invasion fleet while the big fleets were busy far to the west. In addition there was the constant fear of air attack. The Japanese still had several functioning air bases in the Marianas and it was well known that they were trying to stage significant numbers of aircraft through there to attack the Americans.

On the 19th of June the two greatest fleets in the world faced off across the ocean west of Saipan. So far there was no sign of any end run by a separate Japanese task force. Still vigilance was required as the ocean was vast. The Americans reconnaissance resources were still limited to a few seaplanes based at Saipan and whatever patrols the carriers could spare.

While the escort carriers launched protective patrols and the destroyers including the Callaghan steamed endlessly back and forth, the men listened anxiously for news. All day long on the 19th the radio waves were full of reports which indicated a big air battle was occurring to the west. It was not until the end of the day that it became clear that the carrier pilots of Task Force 58 had won a big victory in the air.

As the Kalinin Bay was leaving for Eniwetok, the Captain of the Kalinin Bay signaled to Admiral Bogan "Do not engage enemy until I return." Although it was a wishful thought it turned out to be very close to the actual events of the next few days. Task Force 58 turned west to pursue the Japanese fleet. The amphibious fleet was still steaming in circles far from Saipan and found things to be downright peaceful.

On the 20th the amphibious fleet got the go-ahead to return to Saipan. The escort carrier group returned first to the area just to the east of Saipan and remained there while its aircraft covered the return of the landing ships. There was more than the usual number of flight operations that day. At 2:30 in the afternoon they were joined by the other escort carrier group, T.U. 52.11.2. The two units formed one task group together.

At dawn the next day, Task Group 53.7 arrived to relieve T.U. 52.11.2. The Callaghan remained with T.U. 52.14.2 while aircraft were launched for strikes on Guam, Tinian and Rota. Now that the Japanese fleet was gone from the area, a vigorous effort would be made to suppress the nearby enemy airfields. This would be the only certain means that the Japanese would have to strike at the American fleet. Bombing airfields was a thankless task for the young escort carrier pilots but they would do it well.

For the Callaghan the next four days would be pretty much the same. Duty at Saipan quickly fell into a groove. Morning general quarters was followed by flight operations. During flight operations the destroyers would take turns at plane guard duty. The rest of the day would consist of steaming back and forth in the designated area broken up by the group turn into the wind for flight operations. At the end of the day came general quarters again along with the final flight operations as the last patrol planes were landed.

Once or twice the destroyers left to join a nearby tanker for fuel. But other than fuel, the destroyers did not need resupply. Ammunition was not a problem because the Japanese had not found the "jeep" carriers with their planes. There was no target practice as there were no extra planes available for towing a target sleeve.

Early on the morning of the 24th of June, the Kalinin Bay returned in record time from Eniwetok. She carried with her a full load of new planes. She went off on a quick errand to deliver some equipment but returned before the next day. With her back, T.U. 52.14.2 was nearly up to normal strength.

The 25th was a busy day of strikes, searches and patrols for the naval aviators from the "jeeps." For the Callaghan and the other destroyers it was just another day on station in the screen. However the combined group was larger now and, if anything, that required more vigilance.

In the afternoon of the 26th, the Callaghan left in company with the Porterfield to join a tanker unit for fueling. The Callaghan went alongside the Cimarron and took on 1270 barrels of fuel. More importantly, it took aboard some "miscellaneous provisions." Food, thank God, as the ships supply was getting down to the basics.

The need for vigilance was proven on the night of the 26th. At 10:55pm the task force was steaming due south when two enemy planes were picked up on radar. The two planes were flying very low to the water which resulted in a very late detection by the radar boys. The bearing and distance was relayed to the Callaghan but its radar was unable to find the planes for seven long minutes. Finally they were able to track the planes for about 2 minutes before one of the planes was close enough to open fire with the main battery. The five 5" guns roared out for ten seconds before a "check fire" was ordered. Apparently some officer was concerned that the planes might be friendly. Seconds later the Callaghan was given the "ok" to resume firing. By this time the plane was turning away from the formation. The Callaghan batted out a few more rounds before ceasing fire.

Only 27 rounds of 5" had been fired but it was enough to persuade the Japanese pilot that he didn't want to stay in that neighborhood. He flew off the radar screens and was not seen again.

Early the next morning the destroyer screen shifted stations with the Callaghan with the Callaghan at station 120 or right-rear of the formation. Flight operations began immediately after the reorientation of the screen. The carrier Sangamon and two destroyers left for refueling with the tanker group. Another mildly boring day was endured until 6:30pm when the Sangamon and two friends returned.

One minute later an unidentified plane was reported bearing 220 degrees at 26 miles distance. All ships went to general quarters. While the men were running to their battle stations, the destroyer screen pulled in to a closer ring of 3000 yards out from the center of the formation. At five minutes after 8:00pm, everyone canceled the general quarters.

At 9:18pm another unidentified plane was picked up at 225 degrees and 31 miles. It was back to general quarters again for the crew! The plane buzzed around out there until four minutes of 11:00. Then it closed in to around 21 miles. Seven minutes later an order was flashed to the Callaghan that had only been heard in training: "Lay smoke." All the destroyers started laying smoke from their smoke stacks. They continued to do so until five minutes before midnight when the plane disappeared. Everyone secured from general quarters and the most of the sailors stumbled off to their bunks.

The next day marked a significant change for the escort carrier group. They received orders to start operating during the day in an area west of Saipan. No more hiding off to the east of Saipan where the enemy planes seldom operated. They would be setting themselves up to be a target for planes coming in to bomb the landing ships anchored off the beaches to the west of Saipan.

Two of the carriers and three destroyers left that day making their group much smaller. There was some confusion as a result with the Callaghan switching stations and then switching right back again one hour later.

Just before 1:00am in the morning, an unidentified plane was reported at 150 degrees at only nine miles distance. Once again the circle of destroyers was tightened up. 30 minutes later the all clear was sounded. But 15 minutes after that another contact was made at 220 degrees and 20 miles out. The crew ran back to their general quarters stations that they had just left. This time they were at their battle stations for 40 minutes before the all clear was sounded. It was not a good night for sleep!

The next day at a little after noon, the commodore of the destroyer squadron transferred from the Porterfield to the Irwin. As soon as this was accomplished the Porterfield left on an assignment. Nothing much else of significance happened that day.

But that night the Callaghan had a real scare. Three torpedo wakes were reported to pass just in front of the destroyer. General quarters was sounded and an intensive search for the submarine responsible was begun. The Callaghan searched astern of the formation for almost an hour. At that point the search was called off and the men got to return to their bunks or regular watch station while the Callaghan hurried to rejoin.

In the wee hours of the morning the White Plains and a destroyer left the formation. The formation was becoming small again. They immediately headed south and soon were passing through between the islands of Rota and Aguijan, both of which were enemy held. Destination was their old operating area east of Saipan. Someone figured out that operating west of Saipan was not a very good idea after all!

After supper the White Plains and Ross rejoined the group along with a newcomer, the Cassin Young. The Cassin Young (DD793) was the sister ship of the Callaghan (DD 792). They were both built in the same shipyard, Bethlehem Steel at San Pedro.

At 8:06pm that evening, an unidentified aircraft was spotted 49 miles to the west. The ships went to general quarters. An hour later, the Callaghan left with the carrier Midway and the Longshaw to steam over to Saipan. A few minutes later the enemy aircraft left the area allowing the general quarters to be canceled. But at 9:45 another enemy aircraft showed up so the cycle began over again. 25 minutes later the alert was canceled.

At 10:45 yet another enemy aircraft appeared on radar screens! After this general quarters session had come and gone, the Callaghan set a condition of I "Easy." This meant that many of the anti-aircraft guns would be manned but the whole crew did not have to go to general quarters the next time an aircraft blip showed on the radar. Most of the tired crew dragged themselves off to sleep.

The escort carriers could now start anchoring just off Saipan for short periods. The threat from air attack was sufficiently diminished that even high value ships could remain at anchor for a few hours. This not only saved on fuel consumption but also allowed a break for more of the crewmen to rest. The watch while at anchor was much smaller than while underway. However, based on their first night's experience, some of the anti-aircraft guns would remain manned even while at anchor. It was obviously still important to be vigilant.

At 8:19am the anchor was released. The Callaghan was tethered to the earth for the first time since it left Eniwetok on June 11th. It had been a long time at sea constantly on the move, constantly on patrol. Now the crew could attend to a few mundane functions including resupply and performing maintenance that could not be done while underway. Mostly they just enjoyed the spectacle of all the anchored ships and sight-seeing with the nearby shore of Saipan.

Not long after anchoring another destroyer, the Patterson, came alongside to take 50 starshell rounds plus the 5" cartridges. The Callaghan didn't need them as long as they were protecting escort carriers. The Patterson, however, was doing some shore bombardment work for the benefit of the Marines and soldiers ashore. This included providing night illumination.

Just after lunch the Callaghan got underway again to steam over to the tanker Suamico. The deck crew got the Callaghan moored alongside and proceeded to hook up the hoses to take aboard the all important black crude. Only 1250 barrels were taken this time.

At 4:00pm the pleasant diversion at anchor was over. The Callaghan and White Plains got underway to return to the escort carrier task group. The Callaghan led the way until the two ships were near the task group. The Callaghan slipped in between two other destroyers and waited for the formation to reorient itself with the addition of the two arrivals.

Dusk general quarters was held, the formation reorganized itself and prepared for flight operations. Just as it was getting dark landing of the planes that had been on patrol was accomplished. The Callaghan was back in its element as night fell on the first day of July, 1944.

Over on Saipan vicious combat was going on nearly 24 hours a day between the US ground troops and the Japanese Imperial army and navy troops. Half a world away terrific fighting was occurring between Allied forces and the German army in Normandy. This was the beginning of the end for Germany and Japan in World War II.

After dark the Kalinin Bay and two destroyers left on an assignment. This still left four escort carriers in the group. The night was passed with zigzagging and various course changes but no disturbances from the enemy like the night before. A lot of sailors were deep asleep!

Morning general quarters came a little earlier than usual. There was a quick pre-dawn flight operation to launch an anti-submarine patrol. An hour or so later another flight operation was conducted to send off the morning strike against the enemy held islands. Right after the flight "op" was over another escort carrier, the Nahanta Bay, joined the task group.

This turned out to be one of the busiest days ever for flight operations. It seemed as if every hour or so another flight "op" was held. Around three o'clock in the afternoon the Kalinin Bay and its escorts returned to the group. This put the group back to full strength with six escort carriers. Since the big guys, Task Force 58, had left the Saipan area a couple of weeks ago, they were the only carriers operating in the Mariana's. This accounted for part of the reason for the heavy flight operation schedule.

At 6:53pm the warships "darkened ship" which meant they turned off all non-essential interior lights which would show from the outside. They then went to dusk general quarters. After dark two of the escort carriers with a couple of destroyers left on a mission. The rest of Task Group 52.14 spent the night quietly zigzagging back and forth over the sea.

The next morning started very early for the group as general quarters was held at 4:45am. The reason of course was a pre-dawn launch of some aircraft. After that the rest of the morning was routine until 10:15.

The destroyer Ross came alongside the Callaghan and delivered something they had not seen since leaving Eniwetok. Mail! Glorious mail from back home! Since it had been over 4 weeks from their last mail call, the crew was positively excited. Letters from loved ones, girlfriends, wives and parents were devoured eagerly. A few lucky men got packages from home including a wide variety of food and other items. A couple of unlucky men got dear-John letters. In this respect, life in the navy had not changed much in the last 75 to 80 years.

After lunch the ships got an unwelcome air alert because of an unidentified aircraft. Being the middle of the day it was no surprise that it turned out to be a friendly plane that was not displaying the proper IFF signal. For that mistake he was paid a visit by Wildcats from the combat air patrol who were spoiling for a fight. The alert was canceled while a chastened pilot got his IFF working again.

The rest of the day was full with a heavy schedule of flight operations. Dusk general quarters came and went and then a watchful peace settled over the group of warships. As usual the group spent the night steaming in a giant square.

The next day was the 4th of July. At home it was a holiday. Although fireworks had virtually disappeared because of war time needs it was still a day off with parades, picnics and family get-togethers. In the middle of the Pacific Ocean it was just another day of war. All day long flight operations were conducted as close as possible to an hourly schedule.

The hourly schedule was a new innovation being tried at Saipan. Since there were so many planes being launched for so many different missions, it was decided to provide order to the chaos of flight operations by launching and landing planes on the hour.

This way the pilots knew when they could get back aboard the carriers. If they were running low on fuel they could divert to Aslito airfield on Saipan to wait until the next landing cycle. In addition, it provided some welcome order to the routine for the destroyers in the screen. They were able to anticipate the course maneuvers necessary for the carriers to turn into the wind to recover aircraft. There was no reason to be caught unprepared by a sudden flight operation. The task group was now a well-oiled machine when it came to flight operations.

The next three days were nearly identical. Early general quarters were followed by a predawn flight operation. The Callaghan secured from general quarters at dawn which was followed by another flight operation. The rest of the day would be flight operations on the hour except for a two hour slot in mid-afternoon. Dusk general quarters was held in conjunction with the final flight operation of the day to land the anti-submarine patrol and the combat air patrol. The formation adjusted to night cruising and sailors not on watch slept. Sometime during the night a sudden general quarters would be held when the usual enemy snooper plane showed up on radar. It would not last long as the plane never showed any interest in the escort carriers and flew off.

The only real variation in this pattern was on the 7th when there were two night general quarters due to enemy snoopers. The second one closed to a distance of 9 miles before it flew off. There is no doubt that many officers and men in the task group wished that they could have night fighters aboard. The nightly interference was very annoying.

The routine was broken on the 8th. It was refueling day. Even the carriers were getting low on fuel again so a rendezvous with a tanker group was held. Each task unit of two carriers with associated destroyers was refueled in turn. The Callaghan went with the second unit to be refueled. The destroyer received 2209 barrels of crude from the Guadalupe. Unfortunately this time there was no food sent over. Since they had not been resupplied since the 26th, this was getting to be a real problem.

The two task units reformed together around 4:00pm and immediately held flight operations. Evening came and went peacefully. During the night the sailors were treated to a show. An enemy plane showed up to harass the troops on Saipan. It was not unusual for the sailors to be able to see anti-aircraft fire from the island. For the first time they saw it score. They watched as the tracers went skyward and the Japanese plane was hit. It flared up and they watched in fascination as it trailed flames all the way to the ground. Cheers rang out from sailors who were tired of the nightly G.Q.'s that interrupted their sleep. No enemy snoopers came near the task group that night.

The morning of the 9th started with the usual pre-dawn general quarters and flight operation. That finished the crew got the bad news. Starting on this date food was being rationed. This was a direct result of being at sea with little resupply for nearly a month. It took a lot of food to feed the approximately 330 men aboard the Callaghan. Anyone who grumbled was reminded that they could have joined the Marines or the soldiers who were living and dying in foxholes over on Saipan.

Just after lunch the Callaghan went alongside the carrier White Plains. Lines were passed between the two ships and then two special deliveries were made to the White Plains. One was the mail from the Callaghan with hundreds of letters and mailgrams for home. The other was Lt. Hoskins.

The Chief Engineer was leaving the Callaghan to the great regret of Captain Johnson. Lt. Hoskins was a great engineer but his health was not cooperating. He had severe problems with his arms and Doc. Parker couldn't provide a cure. Parker had finally told Captain Johnson that Hoskins would have to be transferred for treatment at a medical facility. Johnson tried to fight it but Parker insisted that the man's health was at stake and there was no other choice. Ensign Dunne had been doing the lion's share of engineering work lately. He now took over as the acting Chief Engineer.

Later that day the word came that the last Japanese troops on Saipan had surrendered. Saipan was finally secure about 10 days later than was originally planned. The United States commanders still were learning lessons about Japanese fanaticism.

At nightfall the White Plains and the Kalinin Bay along with their destroyers left for Eniwetok. The Callaghan stayed behind with the Midway and Nahanta Bay. Captain Johnson wanted to be in the war zone so he was happy to have the Callaghan remain behind. Low supplies and tired sailors were of no consequence.

The next three days were simply boring. The war was over on Saipan and the next operation on the next enemy held island would not start for a couple of weeks. The two remaining escort carriers were simply providing patrols and an occasional bombing strike against Tinian.

On the 11th an enlisted man was transferred to the escort carrier Midway for health reasons. Doc. Parker was seeing a lot of heat related health problems. It was very hot and humid in the central Pacific especially in the middle of the summer. There was no air conditioning aboard the Callaghan or any other surface warship. They did the best they could with fans and ventilation but it was not always adequate. Skin rashes were very common as well as foot problems. Sometimes it got out of control and the man affected had to the transferred for medical treatment.

At last at 7:00pm on the 13th Task Unit T.U. 52.14.4 set course for Eniwetok. The Midway, Nahanta Bay along with destroyers Longshaw, Mertz, Coningham and of course, the Callaghan, were heading back to a fleet anchorage. There was real relief felt by the weary sailors. The boring routine followed by hectic nights of general quarters and now the rationed food were taking their toll.

On the morning of the 14th the Longshaw transferred mail to each ship in the formation. The Callaghan got some but many of the men were disappointed. Most of the mail for the Callaghan had gotten lost somewhere. Although the navy did it's best, it was difficult to get mail out to a combat zone. The men could only hope that the mail would be waiting for them back at Eniwetok.

On the 15th while in route, a court martial was convened for one of the sailors. Now that the ship was out of the combat zone, attention was turned to more routine matters including naval discipline.

Finally at 4:30 in the afternoon, the Callaghan entered Eniwetok lagoon. On the way to its mooring site a rare mistake occurred. The Callaghan almost rammed a barge. Captain Johnson prevented the collision through quick action but he was instantly angry. The language from the bridge was explosive.

At 5:10 the Callaghan moored alongside a tanker. The deck crew got the hoses attached so the Callaghan could take on 2400 barrels of fuel. It was a long trip from Saipan!

As soon as the fueling was finished the Callaghan cast off and steamed over to its berth next to the USS Markab for the night. Ensign Pool reported back aboard. He had been at Pearl Harbor during the Saipan operation getting advanced gunnery and torpedo training.

The men spent their first quiet night in a peaceful anchorage without the sound of guns or a general quarters to disturb their sleep. Of course they were so used to the sound of the engines running and the wind roaring around the superstructure that the quiet seemed unnatural. It was also hot without that wind.

The next morning the lawyer reported back aboard. Lieutenant Hugh Owens was finally to assume his full duties. He had been at Pearl Harbor for C.I.C. school. His fellow officers would find this civilian turned warrior still remarkable for his ignorance of naval terms and traditions.

They received the depressing news from the naval personnel in charge of mail that the Callaghan's mail was lost. Apparently it had been forwarded to Saipan at the same time the Callaghan was returning to Eniwetok. Things like this made SNAFU a popular phrase among men in uniform.

Around lunchtime four sailors, Powell, Popkin, Adams and Cichy were transferred off the ship for medical treatment. Their fellow sailors along with Captain Johnson hated to see them go.

That afternoon the Callaghan received aboard 144 rounds of 5" ammunition and 704 rounds of 40mm. It was a reminder that they would not be in port long before going back to the war. The scuttlebutt was already going around the ship that tomorrow they were headed back out to sea.

In the morning they received 38 rounds of starshells. At 2:14pm the Callaghan got underway. Before they got too far, the Captain received word that they were to rendezvous with the destroyer Conyngham. Captain Johnson brought the Callaghan alongside the Conyngham and the deck gang brought over an additional 23 rounds of 5" AA common. After that the Callaghan steamed out the channel and proceeded to patrol the shipping lane while the carriers and cargo ships came out.

At 10 minutes of six, the Callaghan ceased patrolling and steamed over to join the screen of the combined formation of escort carriers and cargo ships. Course was set at 300 degrees. They were headed back to the Marianas.

The first night was uneventful. At 8:00 in the morning the escort carrier Midway left the formation to conduct flight operations. The Midway was designated the duty carrier and the Callaghan and Conyngham were designated as her duty destroyers to screen her during flight "ops."

The first day was positively leisurely in pace. The Midway only held four flight "ops." This was far fewer than the days at Saipan when they were held every hour all day long. Dusk general quarters was held a couple of minutes before 7:00pm. The formation plodded along at a slow 13.5 knots.

The next day was the same except that flight operations were not held by the Midway. Therefore the Callaghan had a completely boring day of simple zigzagging while in station in the destroyer screen.

Luckily the next day was the Midway's turn to do the flight operations for the day so the Callaghan was back in the business of guarding a carrier for flight "ops." At least this provided the show of the launching and landing of the planes.

Captain's mast was held in the morning. In the afternoon the Conyngham came alongside to deliver mail. Unfortunately it was mostly official mail. The men were not pleased.

Dusk came and went bringing the warm tropical night. Just after midnight the guys on watch got the word that the formation was getting close to Guam. Then, around 2:00am, some of the men saw the first starshell burst on the horizon. Warships up ahead were firing for the benefit of the troops on shore.

At a very early five minutes of five, the Callaghan's crew went to general quarters. At the same time the formation split with the two carriers and destroyers of T.U. 53.19.5 breaking off to starboard. The troop ships and cargo ships was continuing on to the west of Guam. The carrier group was steaming off to the east of Guam to conduct flight operations just as they had done during the invasion of Saipan.

The feeling of this invasion was much different for the Callaghan compared to Saipan. The Japanese fleet had been defeated at the "Turkey Shoot" on June 19-20. Saipan was now secure with a fine large airbase that provided land-based reconnaissance and combat air patrol. For these and other reasons, the danger to the escort carrier group was much reduced.

Flight operations would be held on a near continuous basis as before. But this time the concentration was almost entirely on strikes against land targets on Guam and the other Japanese held islands nearby. For the destroyers, watch was held just as before but the tension was gone. Nobody really expected any enemy air attacks now. There would be the occasional night time snooper to disturb sailors sleep. However there were night fighters available now to make snooping hazardous for these nocturnal guests.

There was the ever present danger of submarines, of course. That possibility would remain until the very end of the war. It was unlikely enough at this stage of the war that most of the men ceased worrying about it. Zigzagging and sonar were being conducted on a regular basis to deal with the submarine threat. Men on watch spent countless hours looking for periscopes that never appeared.

To illustrate the change in the situation from the invasion of Saipan, Captain Johnson held Captain's Mast the first day off Guam. No one, absolutely no one at all took the possibility of combat more seriously than Captain Johnson. If there was time for Captain's Mast in the middle of the day then things had changed indeed!

Two sailors were up for the usual infractions. One was for "disobedience to orders and shirking duty" and the other for "asleep on watch." What made this unusual was that these men both held the rank of Seamen first class. Captain Johnson was particularly annoyed since these men were suppose to be leaders and examples to the other enlisted men. The first was given 10 hours extra duty. The second was recommended for a general court martial.

The 23rd of July was the second day of operations at Guam. Dawn G.Q. came at about a quarter past five as the formation changed course to the east to conduct the usual pre-dawn flight "ops." Minutes later the rest of Task Group 52.14 showed up. Preparations were made to join the two groups of ships with a lot of maneuvering being required on the part of the destroyers. Just after breakfast the Porterfield came alongside the Callaghan. Greetings were made to the skipper of the Porterfield who was the former Executive Officer of the Callaghan. But far more important to the men of the Callaghan was what the Porterfield had brought. Mail bags were passed over. Big fat mail bags which the men were very careful not to drop in the water as they came over.

The mail was sorted as quickly as possible. When it was finally distributed there was quite a commotion as men gathered in groups to get their mail from their petty officers. A lot of good natured joking went on over who got what. Some men were ribbed for getting so much mail. In a few cases a couple of loud mouth types were ribbed for not getting mail. The later almost caused fights to break out.

Around supper time, a familiar looking destroyer joined the formation. The Callaghan found out that its sister ship, the USS Cassin Young, was back in her company. This was an unusual situation as many of squadron 55's ships were together for a change.

The following two days were duplicates in terms of the duties fulfilled by the ships of the escort carrier group. In fact a particular pattern developed. Not only did the flight operations occur at fairly predictable hours, they also caused course changes that were also very predictable.

The prevailing winds around the Marianas came in the same direction day after day. One would almost think they were designed by man. During the summer they always blew from the southeast. Since the carriers had to launch or recover their planes into the winds, the group always turned to the southeast whenever flight operations were held. In order to hold the same general position to the east of Guam, the group steamed to the northwest when they weren't conducting flight operations. With hourly flight operations being held all morning long, there was not time to steam off in some other direction except northwest and southeast.

Its a wonder that the Japanese never caught on to this regular pattern. One aggressive submarine could have caused havoc. Knowing that flight operations were going to start every day before dawn and continue every hour nearly all day added to the known direction of the prevailing wind would have made for an easy attack setup. It is a strong comment on the failure of the Japanese submarine force in World War II that such an attack never occurred.

On the 26th of July a break in the routine took place for the Callaghan. At 11:00 in the morning it left the group and steamed north to Saipan. Arriving in mid-afternoon, the Callaghan moored to the port side of the USS Whippet, a tanker. 2,238 barrels of oil were pumped into the bunkers of the Callaghan. This was now the accepted method of refueling in the Marianas. Saipan was secure enough to base tankers in the anchorage. At sea refueling was much more difficult and dangerous both to ship and crew members. Logistics would now be handled from Saipan.

Captain Johnson wasted no time leaving the side of the Whippet. While they were refueling, the whale boat had been sent off on a mission. The destroyer stopped in mid-channel to pick the boat back up. The Callaghan then steamed off to the south to rejoin its escort carrier group.

When the Callaghan joined up just after supper time, she found her old friends the White Plains and Midway were gone. They had been replaced by the Nehanta Bay, Gambier Bay and Kitkun Bay. These escort carriers were destined to become famous three months later in the battle of Leyte Gulf.

For the officers on the bridge of the Callaghan a little variety was thrown their way from the new SOP, Senior Officer Present. The formation was steaming in a new "special" cruising disposition called 5FB. The Callaghan was given station number 3 which was off to one side of the formation.

Dusk general quarters came and the carriers landed the last patrol planes for the day. Night came, the ship was darkened, the crew secured from G.Q. and tried to find a bearable place to sleep through the steamy tropical night. Many of the men had long ago taken to sleeping out on one of the decks of the destroyer.

It was too hot below especially with hundreds of men occupying bunks in close proximity.

The following three days were unremarkable except for one refueling at sea. Apparently the Navy decided to keep the task group intact due to a temporary shortage of destroyers. The carriers were needed off Guam for on-call air strikes. Therefore the destroyers were refueled right where they were, to the east off Guam. The Callaghan in her turn took on 665 barrels of Navy black oil. She didn't need much since she had been refueled at Saipan just a few days prior.

In mid-afternoon four of the destroyers of DesRon55 switched from escort carrier task unit 52.14.2 to unit 52.14.1. There was no longer a need to keep all of the available escort carriers off Guam so some of them were being sent to other duty. Because of the destroyer shortage, most of the escorts were retained to guard the two remaining carriers of 52.14.1, the Nehanta Bay and the Kitkun Bay.

Six more days of guard duty and flight operations dragged by. This was getting positively boring. There were no plane crashes for the Callaghan crew to get excited about. Just the standard flight operation which by now was losing its entertainment value. Luckily there was some shifting of assignments between task units so the Callaghan got a couple of high speed dashes which at least changed the tempo of the engines and the feel of the wind.

On the last evening of operations with the escort carrier unit off Guam, the Callaghan was relieved by the Harrison as screen escort. The Callaghan peeled off to join the Porterfield, Irwin and Cassin Young. The four destroyers were detached to the rear of the formation to practice some tactical exercises. A couple of hours later the Callaghan was ordered to replace the Harrison which was involved in a search for a submarine contact that had been reported by Navy patrol aircraft. The tactical exercises were forgotten as the Callaghan searched for another phantom submarine. When the search was over the Callaghan rejoined her three consorts steaming in a double column separate from the escort carrier formation.

August 4th dawned with the four destroyers headed into the channel of Tanapag harbor, Saipan. The Callaghan went to a temporary berth to await its turn to refuel from the Whippet, the resident tanker at Saipan. While waiting, two enlisted men and one officer were transferred to the hospital ship Relief for medical treatment. Then it was the Callaghan's turn at the side of the Whippet. 2170 barrels of fuel oil were pumped over which caused the Callaghan to sit a little over a foot lower in the water.

While moored alongside the Whippet, Lt. R.W. Willis was transferred off the destroyer. He had finally received his orders for flight school at Dallas, Texas. He was no doubt relieved to be out from under Captain Johnson's tight rein.

At noon the Callaghan left the side of the tanker and steamed over to moor alongside the repair ship Holland. Later in the afternoon some replacement 5" ammunition was received aboard, including 61 rounds of flashless powder. Apparently someone was expecting the Callaghan to be doing some night work.

The next morning at dawn the Callaghan got underway again to leave the Holland for an empty berth. Once there, the anchor was lowered and the Callaghan spent the rest of the day "swinging on its hook."

This day and a half period for the Callaghan crew was a welcome change from last several weeks spent constantly underway. It was nice to be able to hear things like waves breaking on the shore and birds screeching overhead. Natural things like these were a contrast to the incessant drone and hum of the machinery of a warship in motion.

Just before dusk the Callaghan and several other ships got underway to leave the harbor at Saipan. The Callaghan now temporarily joined Task Group 50.8 which was a cruiser task group. After almost three months with the escort carriers they were about to change partners. The destroyers of DesRon 55 had proven they could do the job. Now they were about to join the most powerful Task Group in the world. The Callaghan was off to join the cutting edge of the war in the Pacific.

On Sunday August 6th 1944 at 8:15 in the morning the main director sighted a battleship and several large carriers at a distance of 10 miles. It was Task Group 58.4 which had been busy pounding Guam for the last two weeks. The Callaghan's group joined with and became a part of T.G. 58.4. There was a sense of pride among the crew since they got the word that this was not temporary. The Callaghan had been reassigned as part of the screen of T.G. 58.4. No longer would they be plodding along with the slow and funny looking escort carriers. They were now a part of the fastest and most powerful carrier strike force in the world.

But first, even the biggest toughest warrior had to have fuel to keep going. The Callaghan put on speed to proceed to its new screening station in preparation for a refueling session. The orders were for the Callaghan took position off to one side of a battleship, their old friend, the USS Washington. No doubt Jake Heimark told some of the new men about his time aboard the Washington in 1941.

The Washington did not stay long. The escort screen was shuffled when the Washington was detached. The Callaghan, Porterfield and Irwin all moved to new stations. Just as they were carrying that out, an alert was flashed that a bogie had been sighted 54 miles out. The radar operators in CIC re-adjusted their sweeps to try to pick him up. But luckily before the situation called for general quarters the bogie was identified as friendly.

In mid-afternoon the refueling was completed and the Callaghan took station number three in the anti-submarine screen. At 4:00, the formation changed course into the wind and prepared for flight operations. Once again the guys topside would thrill to the sight of the fighters and torpedo bombers clawing their way into the air off the big carriers.

Flight operations were held two more times before the end of the day. At twenty minutes to seven, the ships went to dusk general quarters. Seven minutes later the formation started zigzagging and the day was over.

That night was marked by two events that demonstrated how the war was changing for US forces. Going back to the days of Guadalcanal, the day belonged to US forces while the night too often belonged to Japanese forces. This night off Guam belonged to US forces just as much as the day when the Army Air Force sent over Black Widow night fighters. The second event was generated by the carriers of T.F. 58.4.

In the darkness of the early morning hours the men of the Callaghan were surprised when the formation turned into the wind and flight operations were announced over the TBS. This was one capability that the escort carriers definitely did not have: night flying. It was comforting to know that night patrols could now protect the task group when it was most vulnerable.

More than an hour before dawn, flight operations were held again. It was a novelty with the big carriers that flight operations could occur twice BEFORE dawn general quarters! When the general quarters were held it was anti-climatic for the men on watch. When the opportunity came, they delighted in filling in the men who had been sleeping.

During the morning, the Cassin Young came alongside to deliver the mail. It seemed that the fortunes of the Callaghan had risen mightily in the last two days. They were not only a part of the big ship Navy, the Navy could even find them now!

The fighting in the Marianas was winding up. The Japanese troops on Guam had been pushed to the Southern most area of the island and were being pressed hard by the US forces. The carriers of Task Force 58.4 launched daily strikes against ground targets on Guam. These missions were now both boring and frustrating for the airmen. Seldom could the targets be seen. They were simply making milk runs in over a particular area and dropping their bombs where the ground controllers told them too.

Likewise it was boring for the escorting ships of the task group. The diminished likelihood of combat was now replaced by the tried and true navy tradition of drills. Captain Johnson was at it again. He conferred with his officers on what drills the Callaghan had not yet experienced. Soon they became apparent to the crew as various simulated emergencies were announced along with the drill to deal with it.

Anti-aircraft practice reappeared on the agenda. Towing planes were made available and dozens of rounds were fired at the sleeves they towed.

On the 9th of August the Callaghan went alongside the fleet carrier Essex for refueling. This brought out as many topside watchers as possible since they had never refueled from a fleet carrier before. It was fascinating to look over this big slab sided ship from just a little over a hundred feet away. The big carrier towered over the little destroyer like Goliath over little David. Only this time Goliath was on the same side.

The Essex passed 60,259 gallons of fuel oil to the Callaghan. As soon as the Callaghan pulled away from the side of the Essex, the whole formation turned into the wind. Shortly the carriers were performing the duty they were built for: flight operations.

Meanwhile the bosun's and line handlers aboard the Callaghan were having a very busy day. The Callaghan had received from the Essex the mail for every ship in the formation. As a result, the Callaghan visited every ship, came alongside, passed over lines, attached the mail bags and hauled em over. In between all this, the Callaghan provided screening during flight operations and worked in a short machine gun practice session.

The following day Captain Johnson got the word that this was their last day in the Marianas. He quickly asked for and got permission for another machine gun practice session. Only this time the amount of ammunition expended was virtually equal to the amount fired on the big air raid of the 17th of June. 311 rounds of 40mm and 527 rounds of 20mm were fired off. With or without an enemy threat Captain Johnson was determined that the Callaghan would maintain its proficiency.

In the late afternoon, the course of the formation was changed to 99 degrees. The grapevine quickly let every crewmen know that they were headed back. Visible relief showed on many faces as the endless time at sea off first Saipan and then Guam had worn the crew down.

Friday August 11th started out with the same routine as always, dawn general quarters and a round of flight operations. At the end of the morning it became clear why aviators received flight pay. At 11:30 the formation changed course to due south. A simulated air attack was commenced by some of the planes in the air.

Something went terribly wrong. One of the planes went straight into the water. The drill was immediately called off. The Callaghan received permission to pick up survivors. The destroyer immediately spun around, picked up speed and got to the site of the plane crash as quickly as possible. Unfortunately the plane had already sunk.

The pilot was spotted immediately. The Callaghan men with binoculars or scopes could see that he was in trouble. Orders were snapped to get the whaleboat into the water as fast as possible. Unfortunately the water was very rough that day. The deck crew did their best to get the whaleboat lowered and released but it took time because the destroyer was rolling so much in the heavy waves.

Meanwhile everyone could see that the pilot was head down in the water. Waves were washing over him. Urgency was heard from the men, "Hurry up, he'll never make it!"

The whaleboat finally got going and motored over to the pilot. Although it was difficult with the waves, they pulled him out of the water as fast as they could. The coxswain immediately opened up the throttle to head back to the Callaghan. But it was clear to the men in the whale boat that it was too late. When the body was removed from the boat and taken to sick bay, it was the first view of death for some of the young sailors of the Callaghan. The pilot was identified as W.C. Fryback and the carrier Essex was notified.

But the preparation for the war had to go on. The crew of the Callaghan went back to general quarters to do tracking drills while more planes from the carriers simulated air attacks on the formation. This time, thank God, there were no crashes.

Flight operations were held again to land the planes involved in the air raid drills. As soon as the last plane was landed, the Callaghan peeled off to steam over to the side of the Essex again.

The Callaghan was alongside the Essex again to transfer the pilot's body over to the big carrier. The carrier's crew would perform a burial at sea ceremony later on.

Just before supper, the Callaghan left its position in the screen of the formation to move out a small distance away from the other ships. When the Callaghan was safely away from the other ships, a test firing of one of the 5" guns was held. 24 rounds were fired with no difficulties, the gun was declared safe and the Callaghan returned to its normal position.

Final flight operations were performed for the day followed by dusk general quarters. When general quarters was over, the ship was darkened as the sun disappeared.

Another day went by on the steady march, course 99 degrees, speed 17 knots. Night came and, a couple of hours after dark, course was changed to 96 degrees. This was a positive sign that they were not far from base now.

Long before dawn, radar picked up a land mass ahead. Pre-dawn flight operations were held and then the ships rearranged themselves. Two columns of destroyers followed the cruiser San Diego. General quarters was sounded and anti-aircraft drill was announced. Soon along came two tow planes pulling target sleeves. One plane flew down along each column of ships. The Callaghan fired off a leisurely nine rounds of 5" and then it was all over.

General quarters was canceled and the formation was rearranged. The island of Eniwetok was now barely visible in the distance. The destroyers moved out to form screening lanes for the big ships which steamed majestically into the lagoon. After the last big ship entered, the destroyers lined up to follow.

The Callaghan steamed down the channel, into the lagoon and headed straight for the tanker Antona. Captain Johnson quickly conned the Callaghan to the side of the tanker and the two ships were tied together. Shortly the deck forces of the two ships had the hoses over to the Callaghan and fuel was flowing into the bunkers. The Callaghan was very low on fuel so the fueling took a long time. 1811 barrels later, the hoses were returned to the tanker.

The Callaghan got under way and steamed over to berth 581. The anchor went down and the engines were stopped. Minutes after anchoring, the Porterfield came alongside and moored to the starboard side. It had been a long month at sea!

The Callaghan and the other destroyers of DesRon 55 had put in many days at sea off the Marianas. The crews were tired and weary of the constant wind and hum of machinery. They were about to be rewarded with a long rest in the Eniwetok fleet anchorage. This was to be one of the longest rest periods for the Callaghan since she left the West Coast.

That was the good news. The bad news was that the rest period was to be spent at Eniwetok. This was one of the roughest forward bases that the Navy had. There wasn't much on Eniwetok. Everything had to be brought in via ship. Eniwetok was at the end of a very long Allied supply line. The Callaghan was to spend 18 days at this end of the war time pipeline.

Late that afternoon a Yeoman 2nd class, Raymond Cichy, reported aboard. That was a good start for a long boring stay in a fleet anchorage. The one constant thing in any branch of the military was the need to catch up with the paperwork. The paperwork was particularly heavy at this point in the Callaghan's life. The destroyer had been to sea for a month and a large number of men were about to be transferred either off or on the Callaghan. Each transfer involved paperwork, of course.

The next day, Monday August 14th, was a quiet day of routine maintenance and cleanup. That evening the first round of transfers occurred when 16 men, including five electricians and one quartermaster, went over to the transport General Hace. This was the first step in their journey back to civilization. One imagines that most of these men were very happy to be leaving the Callaghan at this stage in its career. It had Captain Johnson plus a long wait at anchor in Eniwetok.

Captain Johnson was not pleased. He had just lost 16 experienced crewmembers. The lose of five electricians was keenly felt as they were extremely valuable in keeping equipment running aboard ship. The only hope was that they would be replaced by new men who would quickly pick up the tricks of the trade in the sea-going navy.

The one advantage to being in a Navy anchorage was the availability of some entertainment, even though the delivery was crude. That night the movie "Tender Comrade" was played. The screen was makeshift and the seating was woefully inadequate but it was a real Hollywood movie. The crew had seen precious few shows of any kind since leaving the West Coast.

The following day a different kind of diversion in the form of swimming was allowed. This was a sure sign that this base was secure and that the ship would be here awhile. Swimming was never allowed when there was any real chance of enemy attack.

The rest of the days at Eniwetok were depressingly similar. Work routines every day which were poorly compensated for by simple entertainments such as sports and movies. One of Captain Johnson's famous Captain's inspections was carried out in the middle of this. But it simply meant more work for the crew. All in all, it was boring.

On the 19th, the Callaghan left its berth to cross over to the anchorage of a destroyer tender, the USS Markab. The Callaghan moored alongside the Markab where it was to spend several days.

That same day seven first class sailors were transferred off the Callaghan.

Two injuries occurred during the stay at Eniwetok. The first was caused by a fall down a ladder in the forward fireroom. The second happened during one of the liberties ashore. A first class named Ostrem was running backward during a baseball game. Unfortunately for him, this base was still under construction. He tripped and fell in the path of one of the construction tractors. The tractor did not stop in time and ran over the crewmen's leg breaking it. Ostrem was transferred to the USS Markab for treatment.

On the 26th, the last beer party ashore was held. A beer party was a liberty call in which the men involved piled into whatever boat was available and were transported to the beach. Once there the men lined up to be issued two cans of beer each. Generally the beer was warm as there were no adequate refrigeration facilities. Some of the men who were not fond of warm beer made good money on these liberties by selling their beer to other sailors.

Things happen when men are on recreation far from home. This time there was a serious casualty when a man from one of the other ships drowned while trying to swim out to a wrecked Japanese tanker.

Preparations for another big operation were in full swing. Supplies and ammunition were being loaded with a sense of urgency. The word was passed that the Callaghan and it's task group were leaving tomorrow. After 17 days at Eniwetok, the crew was more than ready to go.

Just before dusk the only destroyer in the "nest" with the Callaghan which did not belong to Squadron 55, left on assigned duty. That left four destroyers from the squadron: Porterfield, Morrison, Irwin and Callaghan. They were all given orders for departing in the morning with the carriers.

At 6:40am the Porterfield cast off, followed by the Morrison and then the Callaghan. It took until 9:00 before the Callaghan finally cleared Eniwetok atoll and took up patrolling station outside the entrance. Soon the big carriers started debauching from the entrance one by one.

This time the task group had a new name: Task Group 38.3. The significance of the change from 58 to 38 meant that the fleet had the famous Admiral Halsey in charge for this operation. When Halsey was in command it was the Third Fleet. When Admiral Spruance was in command it was the Fifth Fleet.

Task Group 38.3 was also more powerful than the "old" T.G. 58.3. It had the big 27,500 ton fleet carriers Essex and Lexington along with the 14,000 ton light carriers Princeton and Langley. These four carriers could field a maximum of over 250 planes.

Even more promising than the increase in power was the new leadership of T.G. 38.3., Rear Admiral Frederick Sherman. Unlike the previous Admiral, Sherman had a reputation as a fighter. He had a good rapport with his carrier pilots and they respected him.

Just before noon the first flight operations were held. True to form for the combat ready Pacific fleet, some planes were provided with target sleeves for scheduled antiaircraft practice by the escorts. In about an hour the destroyers were in formation with crews at general quarters.

However, in the tradition of hurry up and wait, the Callaghan had to wait until nearly four o'clock before it's turn came. In nine minutes of practice, 224 rounds of 40mm and 121 of 20mm were fired off. Since the Callaghan was last, general quarters was immediately canceled and the ships returned to the normal circular screen around the carriers.

Flight operations were held again to recover the aircraft launched at noon and to send up fresh planes for the anti-submarine patrol. These planes were recovered in the flight operation at dusk. The task group then settled down for a long night's cruise at 16 knots.

The next day was just a continuation of the cruise. There were more flight operations, a dry run anti-aircraft drill before lunch, then another live-fire exercise with the 40s and 20s. But at 5:00pm the routine abruptly changed for the Callaghan when it was called to go alongside the Lexington.

Once the Callaghan was 70 yards or so close to the Lexington and matched speed, lines were passed. A breeches buoy was hauled over to the Callaghan containing an officer. Once he was safely aboard, he handed orders to Captain Johnson. Orders were issued and the Callaghan increased speed and peeled off away from the Lexington.

A new course was set which had the Callaghan leaving the task group. Word was passed that the Callaghan had been selected for the special task of delivering a messenger to another task group several hours steaming behind task group 38.3.

Speed was set at 21 knots. Course was 115 degrees (southeast). The Callaghan steamed all night alone. Just after dawn the next day course was changed to 78 degrees and speed was reduced. The Callaghan was now trying to find Task Group 30.1.

At 9:00am radar contact was made and the Callaghan changed course toward the ships showing on the radar screen. A few minutes later the heavy masts of Battleships were spotted. 40 minutes after the first radar contact, the Callaghan was alongside the battleship New Jersey one of the Iowa class, the largest battleship in any Allied navy.

Admiral Halsey probably had a moments pause when he was told that the Callaghan had arrived. Admiral Halsey had sent Daniel Callaghan out on the fateful mission in which Admiral Callaghan died. Halsey had sent letters to both Callaghan's and Scott's widows in which he attributed his own promotion to four star Admiral on the basis of the heroism of the two junior Admirals who died for him at the battle of Guadalcanal.

Lines were passed just as they were 16 hours prior with the Lexington. The messenger, Lt. Weiner, was passed via breeches buoy to the New Jersey. He was delivering special documents to Admiral Halsey from T.G. 38.3.

After that task was accomplished, the Callaghan joined the screen of T.G. 30.1. After lunch the screen changed in preparation for anti-aircraft practice. No matter what group of ships the Callaghan was with, Captain Johnson made sure it got more than its share of target practice. Another 212 rounds of 40mm and 144 rounds of 20mm were fired from the Callaghan's guns.

Night came with the Callaghan in screen station #4, three and a half thousand yards out from the New Jersey. This was the way the Callaghan spent the final day of August 1944. The final months of 1944 would be full of action and danger for the Callaghan and the ships it would escort.

Sept. 1st dawned bright over the gunships of Halsey's task force. Before the sun was up the Callaghan had left the screen and maneuvered to the side of the New Jersey again. The special messenger, Lt. Weiner was transferred back to the Callaghan again. As soon as the dawn general quarters was canceled, the Callaghan was given permission to depart at 6:00am on its own to return to Task Group 38.3.

Halsey's ships would soon cross the equator and plans were made aboard most of the ships for another visit by King Neptune. The Callaghan did not have many pollywogs this time. With so many shellbacks and so few pollywogs, the preparations were begun early and were extensive.

While steaming to catch up to T.G. 38.3, the Callaghan held several surprise firing exercises. Captain Johnson was obviously concerned about the readiness of the Callaghan after such a long stay at the Eniwetok anchorage.

After breakfast the next morning, a torpedo exercise was conducted. Following that was another of the surprise firing exercises for the machine guns. At mid-day came the main event with the hapless pollywogs getting worked over by a ship full of shellbacks. All the while the Callaghan was closing in on its fellow ships of T.G. 38.3.

In the middle of the night, the course was changed to the northwest. The Callaghan was close to its Task Group. Long before dawn the gunnery department was called to its stations. Another torpedo exercise was run through. Neither the prospect of joining up with the big ships or the tired sailors in the crew was going to stop Captain Johnson from running through the drill until it was done to HIS satisfaction.

At 4:50am dawn general quarters was held. Two minutes later a torpedo bomber on anti-submarine patrol was sighted. This was a sure sign that the carriers were not far away. Eighteen minutes later there was large blips blossoming on the radar scopes. Identification was made using the IFF capabilities of the radar. The Callaghan was back among its brother warriors.

Permission was received to take the Callaghan directly alongside flagship Lexington. As soon as the Callaghan was stable alongside and within the proper distance of the Lexington, the lines were passed. Lt. Weiner was strapped into the breeches buoy once again and sent over to the "Lex".

While the transfer was being completed, the ships of the Task Group were preparing for refueling. A group of tankers was waiting out to one side of the carriers. The Callaghan received priority to refuel as she had been steaming at high speed on her trek between Task Groups.

The Callaghan went alongside the USS Tappahannock to refuel. The Callaghan's fuel bunkers were nearly empty. Fueling took well over an hour and a half. When through, the Callaghan had taken on a record 2780 barrels of fuel!

The destroyer immediately peeled off to take up station number nine in the screen. Minutes later her old friend Longshaw pulled up alongside to deliver some mail.

The rest of the day was spent wheeling back and forth as the carriers went through several cycles of flight operations. As usual the prevailing winds were from almost the opposite direction of the task groups track. This was a recurring problem for the Americans as they advanced west to attack each Japanese fortress in turn. Probably the only consolation was that the constant wheeling of the formations back and forth caused the ship Captains and their bosses to become the world's experts at formation maneuvering. It has been noted before that it is remarkable that there were so few collisions between US warships in the Pacific war.

Three days later it was time for the show to begin. First the destroyers refueled again. The Callaghan took on a mere 1035 barrels to top off the bunkers. Later that day the big carriers launched deck loads of planes into the air. The topside sailors watched them go knowing that the islands up ahead were in for a pounding. There was great relief knowing that once the strike was launched the enemy had lost its greatest chance to attack the formation. The swarm of American planes would diminish whatever capability the Japanese had in the Palaus.

This strike was led by an American commander who would become one of the most famous Naval aviators of all time, Commander David McCampbell of the USS Essex. He would lead 96 fighters in the initial sweep of the Palau airfields. There would be no air opposition this first day but plenty of ground targets to go around. The best targets were aircraft on the ground and barges in the waters around the islands. Both were worked over thoroughly by the deadly combination of .50 caliber machine guns and 5" rockets.

Later that day when the strike returned to the carriers the men aboard the Callaghan got the word of the lack of air opposition. This was both comforting and disquieting at the same time. What were the Japanese up to? Where were their planes? The same speculation was going on in Halsey's staff.

The next day the strikes were repeated with the same results. The Americans took advantage of the lack of air opposition by bringing in large numbers of torpedo bombers and dive bombers to hammer the ground targets on Peleliu. The pilots were really puzzled by the lack of any real effort by the Japanese to counter this attack on the former base of the Japanese Combined Fleet.

So far the carrier squadrons from Task Group 38.3 had been very lucky. There had been no losses from enemy opposition. Several planes had been damaged but managed to make it back to their carriers.

The third day of strikes were not quite so lucky for the carrier pilots. On the second strike a weather front prevented the US planes from getting to Peleliu. The leader of the divebombers diverted his force to Angaur island.

The anti-aircraft fire from Angaur was particularly heavy. One of the F6F Hellcats was hit while making a dive on a ground target. His plane caught fire immediately. Flames soon spread to cover the wings and part of the fuselage. Before he could bail out of his burning aircraft it spun out of control and crashed into the water. The pilot was not seen again.

Meanwhile a group of torpedo bombers was working over Peleliu. Two of them were mortally hit. One made a water landing with its crew being quickly rescued. The other bomber was seen to be on fire by wingmen who radioed for the crew to bail out. The pilot bailed out successfully but his two crewmen failed to get out before the bomber crashed. The pilot was picked up by a friendly submarine that was doing lifeguard duty for the carrier strikes.

In addition a Hellcat was hit after making strafing runs on anti-aircraft guns on one of the nearby islands. The Hellcat crashed into the sea taking its pilot with it.

For the Callaghan and its fellow destroyers of DesRon 55, these were hectic days full of constant maneuvering. Screening the fast big carriers was not like screening the slow escort carriers. The normal operating speed of the big carriers during the Palau operation was 18 knots. This was one knot higher than the fastest speed of the slowest escort carrier. In order to change positions while the big carriers were maneuvering at 18 knots, it was often necessary for the Callaghan to steam at 27 knots!

On the morning of the 8th, the cruisers and most of the destroyers of Task Group 38.3 left the formation to join up with the tankers again to refuel. This was a particularly busy day for the Callaghan as she was chosen to distribute the mail to all the ships of the task group.

Due to the lack of air opposition and the diminishing number of good ground targets in the Palaus, Admiral Halsey decided to take Task Force 38 on to the next major target. This target was a very important target both physically and psychologically. For the first time ever, US carrier planes would attack the Philippines.

On the afternoon of September 8th, the big task force steamed out of the Palau area and headed northwest toward the Philippines. The southern-most island of Mindanao was their destination.

The next morning general quarters was held before dawn. At 5:30 sharp, the great formation turned into the wind and increased speed. Within 5 minutes the planes started roaring off the decks of the four carriers within sight of the Callaghan. The planes rose into the air, circled and slowly joined up one by one into a great wheeling super squadron in the sky. Then they left for Mindanao. They would strike terror into the heart of the enemy. They would bring hope and courage to the long suffering people of the Philippines.

Back with the carriers, the Callaghan kept vigil along with the other ships. What would the Navy flyers run into? Would it be a trap? Surely the Japanese must fight this time.

It would be a long couple of hours before word would get back to the waiting ships about this first historic strike against Japanese bases on Mindanao. When the radio reports were intercepted it was good news. The strike had been a complete success. The Japanese had been caught flat-footed with their planes on the ground.

Lieutenant Commander Rigg's planes found one patrol plane in the air which they immediately shot down. When they arrived over the Japanese airfields, nothing. They dove down to the attack and found rows of planes unable or unwilling to take off. The strafing and bombing runs were devastating. It was just like Dec. 8th 1941, except this time our side used surprise to pulverize the other guy's air force on the ground.

When they were had done all the damage they could to the airfields, the strike flew off. It immediately found a Japanese convoy of 35 small ships and trawlers off the coast of Mindanao. The fighters and bombers went to work again sinking and burning much of the convoy.

Meanwhile, a second strike was going in against other airfields. It too worked over the convoy on the way out. All day long Task Force 38 sent out one strike after another to hit targets on or near Mindanao. The strikes were very successful and the air opposition surprisingly light.

The next day, September 10th, a dozen planes from the Essex joined a strike made up of Lexington planes. Again the targets were North Mindanao, Macajalar Bay, and several Mindanao airfields. In a virtual repeat of the previous day, the American fighter planes only encountered single Japanese planes flying alone. The outcome was predictable as each was shot down.

This strike and following strikes only hit facilities on land as no shipping was found this time. When the strikes were over, it seemed that the Japanese had abandoned the area. There was simply a lack of opposition, which figured prominently in the aviators' reports to Admiral Halsey.

Unlike the previous few days, this one involved some direct action on the part of the Callaghan. Two incidents occurred back to back. In the first, a torpedo plane went out of control causing the crew to bail out. The Callaghan hurried over to help pick up the crew. For some reason, the whaleboat of the USS Halsey Powell beat the Callaghan to it. Even stranger, it delivered the surviving crewman, a J.J. Zawisa, to the Callaghan for delivery back to the USS Langley, his home carrier. It is assumed that the Halsey Powell was occupied with other duties.

The second incident followed the first by barely half an hour. The USS Princeton reported a floating mine off her port beam. Six minutes later the Callaghan sighted the mine. Captain Johnson immediately instructed the machine gun mounts to prepare to destroy the mine by gunfire. Johnson then carefully maneuvered the Callaghan within easy shooting distance for the machine guns. 48 rounds of 40 MM and 189 rounds of 20MM were then fired before the mine blew up. It blew with a satisfyingly loud explosion that sent a great column of water into the air as high as the top of the mast. The explosion was so great that two pieces of shrapnel punched small holes in the Callaghan.

The fleet took a day off while it steamed off to a new location to be in position to attack the Visayan islands. Refueling was conducted during the morning and early afternoon. It was a good thing for the Callaghan as it was low on fuel by the time it was alongside the tanker Platte.

The next morning started out with a fighter sweep launched against airfields on Cebu and Mactan islands. This time the Japanese were not caught completely by surprise. The fighters from the carriers Essex and Lexington found dozens of

Japanese fighters on the airfields preparing to take off. Three strafing runs on the Cebu airfield flamed most of the Japanese planes there. But five miles away, at the main airfield on Mactan Island, dozens of Japanese planes were getting into the air.

What followed was a half hour of intense aerial combat. Luckily the Japanese fighters demonstrated no discipline or flight formations of any use. They fought individually which made them easy prey for the highly trained American pilots and their four plane flight sections. Japanese planes were soon crashing all around the two airfields.

It was a banner day for US Naval aviation. The fighters from the Essex alone downed twenty-seven Japanese planes. The strike that followed the fighter sweep caused a lot of damage to installations and shipping in the harbor. Three ships were sunk, a tanker was left on fire and several smaller vessels were sunk or damaged. At the end of the day there was virtually nothing left on Cebu worthy of a bomb.

The same afternoon, another strike worked over Negros Island. Few planes were in the air but a number were found under trees near the runway of the airfield. The torpedo bombers were loaded with 100-pound bombs, which they dropped on the hidden planes. They estimated that they had destroyed around 25 planes that way. As with Cebu Island, a number of small ships and other vessels were attacked in the harbor.

For the Callaghan, it was a mail day. After the usual morning formations revolving around flight operations, a couple of the other destroyers received orders to distribute the mail. First, a few minutes after 10am, the Callaghan went alongside the Longshaw to received mail for the Callaghan men. While the mail was being sorted out, the flight operations continued.

The earliest strikes against Cebu were coming back to the carriers. All through the mid-day, the task force wheeled back and forth, into and out of the wind that was out of the west.

These were high speed maneuvers that led to high fuel consumption.

Then just before 3:00pm, the Callaghan received orders to help distribute the mail. There was a lot of mail for all these ships and the task force staff wanted it to get to the men. Within a few minutes the Callaghan was alongside her sister ship, the Cassin Young. Mail bags were passed over and the Callaghan sped away. It took the Callaghan all of the rest of the remaining hours of daylight to distribute mail. This mail was going to the battleships and cruisers so there was a lot of it! Finally at dusk they were through.

It had been a busy day for the aviators and all the sailors of Task Force 38. Most were tired but pleased with the news that the carrier planes had achieved another victory over the Japanese air forces. Men off watch were looking forward to sack time. But, as usual, the Japanese had to get in a final word when a snooper aircraft caused general quarters about an hour after lights out.

Early the next morning, the task group turned into the west wind and flight operations were held as the first fighter sweep left for Cebu and Negros islands. For the Callaghan it was just another day of formation maneuvering for all the flight operations. During the first flight operation, the Callaghan did test fire a 300 pound depth charge to test the firing circuits. That was the only shooting the Callaghan would do.

But other ships in the formation got the chance to do some real shooting. At 6:45am a single Japanese plane, probably a Jill, was picked up on radar just outside the task group. It was flying very low and very fast. It dropped a single bomb near the Langley but missed. The Langley and the battleship Massachusetts took it under fire but it was not shot down. The Massachusetts claimed to have shot it down but some sailors thought they saw it fly away! In any case, the planes sent out by the Japanese that morning to attack the carriers never returned to base. Maybe the Massachusetts gunners damaged the plane enough that it could not make it back.

That afternoon the Callaghan received more mail from the destroyer Irwin. The task group was still trying to get the mountain of mail distributed.

Meanwhile, for the aviators in the fighter sweeps and strikes against Negros island, it was not a milk run. Altogether they found about 40 Japanese planes in the air or taking off. The combat hardened and disciplined Navy fighter pilots had no real difficulty in destroying or damaging most of the enemy's planes in the air. They did have some difficulty in destroying the planes on the ground however, apparently due to the fact that many of those planes had no gasoline in them. Therefore they did not burn.

Bacolod airfield was severely pounded. Aerial photos showed that after the morning strike only 11 planes were left. But other photos showed that Fabrica and Saravia airfields had more aircraft than on previous days (due to new planes being staged in). As a result, an additional strike was scheduled to attack those two airfields.

This strike, like the last several, was very successful. There was only one Japanese plane in the air so all of the action was against ground targets. Many planes were attacked. Some burned, a lot did not.

After the planes returned to the carriers, everything quieted down. The Japanese were so disorganized that they were having trouble getting routine patrols accomplished. As a result there was relative peace for the task group that night. Nothing of any consequence occurred to disturb the sailors rest.

The next day was more of the same for the aviators and their carriers. Again the air opposition was basically non-existent.

For the Callaghan, the most interesting thing that occurred was the staff meeting that the Admiral called. The Callaghan got the order to bring the participants who happened to be on other ships. That meant that the Callaghan left its position in the screen to go alongside several of the big ships in the formation.

Lines would be passed between the two ships involved and an officer would then come across via the breeches buoy. Needless to say, this was a slow process and it took the Callaghan all of the second half of the afternoon to get it done. The participants were then taken to the flagship: the carrier Lexington.

That evening during dusk general quarters, the Callaghan got orders to take the west picket station. That sent the Callaghan off to a position 12 miles from the center of the formation. The Callaghan spent the rest of the night in this position providing early warning with its radar of any enemy activity.

At 4:40am in the early morning darkness, the Callaghan left its picket station behind and rejoined the screen of destroyers surrounding the big carriers. There had been no alerts. The Japanese were still so disorganized in the Philippines that they were unable to put up effective night patrols to find the American task force that was causing them so much trouble.

Today was September 15th. The usual morning flight operations were held. Then came word that the invasion of Peleliu was going on about 250 miles to the south of the task groups' current location.

This was the reason for their mission. Nimitz's headquarters had decided that Japanese airpower in the Philippines had to be neutralized if the twin invasions of Peleliu and Morotai were to be successful. The Navy did not want to fight off waves of attacking Japanese planes that would certainly sink or damage some of the landing ships used in these invasions. It was decided, rightly so, that it would be easier and less costly to use Task Force 38 to attack these planes at their origin before the invasions started. It turned out to be one of the most brilliant campaign's of the US Navy.

This campaign against the Philippines had so impressed Admiral Halsey that he had made a bold proposal to Admiral Nimitz late on the night of Sept. 13th. He related the lack of any serious air opposition in the Philippines to Nimitz and suggested that the Japanese were much weaker than previously thought. His proposal was to abandon the invasion of Peleliu and move up the invasion of the Philippines to the first possible date.

Historians have largely confirmed the wisdom of Halsey's proposal. The Japanese were weak. More importantly, as the Marines were about to find out, the invasion of Peleliu was going to turn out to be terribly costly. Most historians now agree that Peleliu was not worth the cost. Peleliu was suppose to give the US airfields close to the Philippines which could be used to support the coming invasion of those islands. What the Pacific staff failed to realize was that Morotai would provide all the airfields the US would need to support the thrust into the Philippines. Morotai was roughly the same distance from the southern Philippines as Peleliu. Army bombers and Navy patrol planes would be able to sweep the Philippines from there just as easily as from Peleliu.

Nimitz's headquarters took note of Halsey's reports of the Japanese weakness and did adjust their plans. The invasion of the Philippines was moved up to mid-October. But the invasion of Peleliu was not canceled simply because the process had already begun. All day on September 13th, the "old" battleship force which had become such an efficient bombardment group worked over Peleliu. In addition, strikes from the escort carriers went in against targets on Peleliu and its neighboring islands. Minesweeping operations had also commenced in the waters around Peleliu.

Inertia won out. A great and bloody battle was begun which would cost the Marines almost as many casualties as it would cost the Japanese. Peleliu was one of the most natural fortress islands in the Pacific. The Japanese used the rocky terrain to great advantage in building an extensive complex of bunkers, caves and firing positions. It would not be until November that Peleliu would be declared secure. That, of course, was long after the invasion of the Philippines had begun.

On the 15th, Task Force 38 split up temporarily. The Callaghan and T.G. 38.3 including the Essex left behind the main body to go join the refueling group. It took two days for all of the ships to refuel and resupply. The Callaghan performed her usual duties in the screen during the first day of this effort.

Lt. Owens, the older Lieutenant who lacked seamanship skills, found his element this day. Captain Johnson put him in charge of a summary court martial. Perfect duty for a former lawyer!

On the 16th, it was the Callaghan's turn to refuel. Just before 10am, the Callaghan started taking on the black oil from the USS Neches. 2383 barrels later, they cast off. The Callaghan then proceeded to join another destroyer to receive that other essential supply, mail.

In the afternoon, Captain Johnson held Captain's mast. Although the task group was in enemy waters, it was obvious that the enemy was no threat and normal routine was returning. Both sailors were charged with refusing to obey orders and were given extra duty as their punishment.

Just about the time that the evening meal was finishing up, the Callaghan experienced some unwelcome excitement. The steering on the bridge failed! Imagine if you will, driving down a very wide freeway with other cars present but not very close and your steering wheel suddenly fails to operate. In this case, it is a 2100 hundred ton ship with 320 men aboard that suddenly can't control its direction! Luckily, as with all ships, there is a backup system. Steering was shifted to "aft steering" which was a cramped little room at the tail of the ship, adjacent to the mechanisms that actually turned the rudder. Steering this way was cumbersome as the bridge personnel had to relay steering orders via phones to the men in aft steering.

Engineering jumped on the problem. It took 45 minutes of intense work with Captain Johnson's frequent inquiries to add pressure. The steering gears connected to the wheel on the bridge had failed. The gears were temporarily repaired and the

Callaghan was once again under normal control. Ensign Dunne told the Captain that when possible the gears would have to be replaced.

The next morning was a busy morning. First the Callaghan went alongside the destroyer Yarnall to received more mail. Then the Callaghan went directly to the side of the new carrier, the USS Intrepid. The Intrepid passed over radar tubes via breeches buoy. The Callaghan then delivered these radar tubes to the USS Essex. After that exercise was finished, the Callaghan rejoined the screen. A little later, the Callaghan shifted back to aft steering again so that the bridge steering gears could be replaced. All that in one morning.

The rest of the day was quiet with only normal routine.

Two more days of quiet followed. Task Force 38 was supporting the invasion of Peleliu. As such it was on a tight leash that kept it within a radius of about 250 miles of Peleliu. The Japanese still had a formidable fleet with most of it based at Singapore. The Pacific fleet staff was fairly certain before the invasion that the Japanese fleet would sail to counter the invasion of Peleliu. After all, only 4 months before, the Palau islands had been the anchorage for the Japanese fleet.

But it didn't happen. What Pacific fleet headquarters was just beginning to realize was that the Japanese were weaker than had been thought. The Japanese Imperial staff knew that the Allies were going to invade the Philippines soon. They had decided to horde their precious resources for one last great battle with the US fleet. That battle would be triggered by the invasion of the Philippines.

On the 19th Task Force 38 was on the move again. Due to the lack of any significant Japanese response to the invasion of Peleliu, Nimitz's headquarters had turned Halsey loose again. This time the target was the main island of the Philippines, Luzon.

On the 19th, the ships refueled again. Although it was not sorely needed, it was standard practice to refuel if possible before going into battle. This was as far north and as close to Japan as Task Force 38 had ever been. Plus it was now known that the Japanese were concentrating their air forces around Manila on Luzon. Everyone was taking this raid very seriously.

Early on the 21st, the formation turned into the wind and dozens of planes began to launch from the big carriers. Once again Task Force 38 was delivering the "Sunday punch." At a little after 8am, Commander Campbell from the Essex led the first strike in against the Clark air base complex not far from Manila.

Despite this great air battle that raged over the heart of the Philippines, it was a routine day for the Callaghan. Lots of zigzagging and formation course changes were experienced. The only action the Callaghan had that day was to pick up a downed pilot from the Langley. Lt. (jg) Larson was returned to the Langley at the end of the day.

Everyone expected air attacks but none developed. The fact was the Japanese had been planning a heavy "surprise" air attack against the American carriers. But once again Task Force 38 beat them to the punch. Most of the planes scheduled for the attack were destroyed or damaged as they sat on the ground at the airfields around Manila. The Japanese attack was canceled.

Two days of air strikes were conducted against targets around Manila. The strikes decimated the Japanese air squadrons plus sunk or burned seventeen Japanese ships in Manila harbor. A convoy of seven ships including three escorts was discovered traveling north. It was wiped out. Many important ground installations were also heavily damaged. The air above Manila was thick with smoke from the numerous fires raging out of control.

On the 22nd, the Callaghan had the only combat experience it would get during the Philippine air raids. Early in the morning just before dawn, a single enemy aircraft flew directly toward the carriers. The Callaghan was in its path though so gunnery got permission to open fire. 14 rounds of 5" shells later the Japanese aircraft retired. It was certainly a scout plane tasked with reporting on the whereabouts of Task Force 38. He accomplished his mission and left.

Two hours later, another unidentified aircraft came towards the formation. This Japanese aircraft tried a new tactic. He was flying at very high altitude. Apparently the combat air patrol was not able to get to his altitude quickly enough and the Callaghan was again given permission to open fire. This time the firing lasted almost two minutes with 22 rounds of 5" fired. As before, there was no indication that the plane was damaged in any way but the intruder chose not to stay in such dangerous airspace!

The 23rd was a travel and refueling day as T.F. 38 headed away from Luzon back towards the Visaya islands. On the 24th, three big strikes went in against Cebu and its sister islands. There was no air opposition since all Japanese fighters were still on Luzon. However the anti-aircraft fire from both ground batteries and from ships was intense.

The navy pilots of Task Force 38 had become experts at destroying ships and ground installations. Despite the anti-aircraft fire, most of the selected ground targets were destroyed or heavily damaged. This even included smashing concrete piers with 2000 lb. bombs!

That night Task Force 38 retired to the Palaus islands, mission accomplished. Halsey's fleet had pounded the Japanese airpower and installations in the Philippines in preparation for the next invasion.

The original plan called for the invasion of Mindanao in mid October. That action would be followed approximately 2 months later by the invasion of Leyte. Leyte Island is located in the eastern area of the Philippines not far from the center. Since it is centrally located, Allied bases there could dominate the whole of the Philippines.

Halsey correctly assessed the weakness of the Japanese and realized that going directly to Leyte would shorten the war. He persuaded Pacific Fleet headquarters to cancel the planned invasion of Mindanao and go for Leyte instead. It would turn out to be one of the most important decisions of the war.

On the 27th at 8:30 in the morning, the Callaghan entered the anchorage in Kossol Roads near Peleliu where the Marines were fighting the entrenched Japanese. The long mission up and down the length of the Philippines was over. It had lasted nearly a month.

The Callaghan moored next to the Porterfield. Unfortunately for the crew, they didn't get to stay long. In mid-afternoon, the Callaghan got underway again. It was the Callaghan's turn to perform guard duty just outside the anchorage. This was important guard duty however, as most of Task Force 38, including all its valuable carriers, was inside the anchorage.

Everything was quiet until 9:30 that night. Suddenly there was a sound contact bearing 63 degrees at a distance of 2100 yards. The depth charge batteries were manned and Captain Johnson ordered an attack. On the first run in a full booming pattern of 10 depth charges was fired at shallow depth. On the second try only 3 charges were fired off to one side. After all that noise and disturbance, the sound contact disappeared. Whatever creature or thing had returned the sound echo had just been thoroughly hammered. The Callaghan returned to its silent patrol outside the entrance to the anchorage while the off-duty sailors went back to sleep.

The patrol duty lasted for 24 hours and then the Longshaw relieved the Callaghan. The Callaghan went back into the anchorage and proceeded to the tanker Caliente for fueling. Right after the Callaghan moored alongside the tanker, the destroyer Morrison came alongside to deliver ammunition. 69 rounds of 5" and 12 boxes of 40mm shells were passed over from the Morrison at the same time fuel was being taken on from the Caliente.

No time was being wasted for a very good reason. Word had been received that Task Force 38 was leaving. As soon as the Callaghan topped off with 560 barrels of fuel, the lines were cast off. Captain Johnson had the Callaghan headed out the channel in less than 5 minutes. The Callaghan joined the other destroyers outside the anchorage entrance just as the carriers started to leave.

At 7:30 that evening the Callaghan took its station in the screen of Task Group 38.3 once again. Course was set to the east for a few hours. Then in the middle of the night, the task group reversed course. The next morning the procedure was also reversed as the destroyers set up patrol while the carriers re-entered the anchorage. The Callaghan immediately went back alongside the Caliente to take on more fuel.

The fleet staff was taking no chances. Task Group 38.3 was putting to sea at night because the anchorage near Peleliu was not considered safe. The Japanese were still fighting desperately on Peleliu itself and there were Japanese held islands nearby. The entrances to the anchorage were wide not yet guarded by any anti-submarine nets. It would be all to easy for a Japanese submarine to slip through and cause havoc.

In fact, a safer fleet anchorage was being prepared at the same time. The Japanese had made the mistake of abandoning Ulithi atoll just before the Marines invaded Peleliu. The small force of Marines sent to Ulithi were happy to take it without firing a shot. The Americans immediately recognized that Ulithi was a better anchorage than Peleliu. The atoll provided a near complete circle around a deep lagoon that was big enough to hold the entire Pacific fleet! They quickly set about preparing Ulithi as the forward base for all future operations.

While at Peleliu, three men were transferred off the Callaghan. Western, G.L. and Connor T.H. were going back to the States for advanced fire control school. But the guy who would be missed the most was I.W. Jones, pharmacist. Doc. Parker and the medical team would all miss Jones. He had trained them all in the ways of the Navy medical system at sea. Parker no longer needed him because he had done the training so well. But he would still be missed.

One more time Task Group 38.3 would parade out of the Peleliu anchorage to stay at sea overnight and then anchor again the next day inside the anchorage. But finally, late on the afternoon of Oct. 1st, the task group sortied from Peleliu for the last time. The Callaghan would not return here again. Once clear of the island group, course was set due east.

All night long the task group steamed east. The crew got the word that they were headed to a new fleet anchorage called Ulithi. It turned out that the Japanese had made the serious mistake of abandoning Ulithi just before the invasion of Peleliu. Ulithi was actually much more valuable to the US Navy then Peleliu would ever be. Ulithi was one of the finest fleet anchorages in the entire world. The Ulithi lagoon was big enough to hold the entire US Pacific fleet.

In mid-afternoon on the 2nd, the topside sailors on the Callaghan got their first glimpse of Ulithi.

At first they were not impressed. It looked like just another low profile coral atoll. It was not until the Callaghan went through the channel and emerged inside the lagoon did they realize what made Ulithi so special. From the main deck with the naked eye, most could not see the other side! With a scope or binoculars they could make out the far side of the lagoon. This "lagoon" was like an inland sea!

At six minutes after 5:00, the Callaghan let go her anchor in Berth 113, Ulithi Atoll. The Callaghan would call Ulithi the closest thing to home for the next 4 months. The great invasion of the Philippines would be launched from here.

The Callaghan did not get to stay in the great lagoon very long on her first visit. The next morning, Task Force 38 left Ulithi with the destroyers going first, as usual. As at Peleliu, the Navy did not yet fully trust the security of these newly won forward bases. Task Force 38 did a giant lap in the sea south of

Ulithi for the next 24 hours. At the end of that time period, the mighty task force returned to Ulithi.

On Oct. 6th, Task Group 38.3, including the Callaghan, sortied from Ulithi once again. This time, however, it was no lap around the ocean that was on the Admiral's mind. They were headed north again but this time to the islands north of the Philippines and closer to Japan..

The next morning started with the usual flight operations well before dawn. One of the planes didn't make it. The Callaghan was ordered to search for the pilot. Unfortunately this time the search was in vain. No sign of the pilot was seen. He apparently went down with the plane.

Just before evening, the Callaghan picked up speed and moved out in front of the Task Group. Once again the Callaghan's had been selected to pull picket duty. When the destroyer was 12 miles out in front of the formation of ships, it settled down to cruising in a zigzag pattern. Maybe the Callaghan's reputation as a marksman anti-aircraft ship was still effecting its assignments.

The marksmanship was not needed, however, as the night passed quietly. The dawn came and the Callaghan rejoined the Task Group. Then the carrier group rendezvoused with a tanker group for a typical round of refueling.

The Callaghan joined up with the tanker USS Cache not long after dawn. 845 barrels of crude oil were taken aboard before casting off. Since it was a quiet day, Captain Johnson took the time for a Captain's mast. He awarded extra duty to two sailors for disobedience of orders. He was particularly severe with one of the black stewards named Penn. The charge was disrespectful language to an officer. Johnson busted Penn back to a lower rank.

The next day was the beginning of the tension that preceded an airstrike mission deep in enemy territory. The men knew the position of the task Group and knew that it was by-passing the Philippines and going even further north. American aircraft carriers had not been this close to Japan since the Doolittle strike in April of 1942.

The Callaghan served as plane guard for the light carrier Langley that morning. It was easy duty this time as no planes had the bad manners to go into the water. The rest of the day passed uneventfully.

At 3:19am on October 10th, general quarters was sounded. This unusually early GQ was called because the Task Group was getting ready for an airstrike on Okinawa. The Japanese had held Okinawa for well over a hundred years. During all that time it had never been attacked by any foreign power. Okinawa was an important staging area for the aircraft that were being sent down from Japan to the Philippines to counter the threat of an Allied invasion. It was considered crucial to try to damage this "pipeline" in preparation for the forthcoming Leyte operation.

About an hour before dawn the planes started launching. All morning long, at even intervals of about 2 hours, strikes were launched. Although enemy retaliation was expected especially in the form of air attacks against the carriers, nothing developed all day. The gunners aboard all the destroyers and cruisers simply stood by their guns with nothing to do. To the great amazement of nearly ever officer in the Task Force, the Japanese had been completely surprised.

As a result of the surprise factor, the air strikes had a devastating effect on their targets. The major airbases in central Okinawa were hammered until there was nothing left to attack. The relatively small number of enemy fighters that got into the air after the strikes had begun were quickly shot down. The real bonus on these strikes was the shipping that was sunk. Several freighters and small warships were sunk or damaged. Two of the freighters went up in a spectacular explosion that indicated that they were ammunition ships.

At the end of the day, the carrier pilots claimed a hundred Japanese planes destroyed in the air or on the ground. The US lost 21 carrier planes but almost all of the crews were rescued. It was a very one sided victory.

On Oct. 11th the Task Force split in two. The half that the Callaghan was attached to joined the tanker group again so that the big carriers could refuel. The other half of the Task Force went south to the Philippines to hit Aparri field on Luzon. This kept the Japanese guessing as to what was the real target and where the coming invasion was aimed.

The big target for this operation was not the Philippines. It was Formosa. Formosa, now called Taiwan, is off the coast of China. It is a huge island about a hundred miles long. At that time Japan had 24 airbases on the island. It had more Japanese aircraft than any other location outside Japan itself. Admiral Halsey wanted to do something about all those aircraft. So he brought Task Force 38 to do the job.

Early on the 12th, Commander McCampbell from the Essex led the first strike in against Formosa.. This time the Japanese were not surprised. The Japanese had the 2nd Air Fleet on Formosa and they used it. Hundreds of fighters from airbases all over Formosa rose to challenge the Navy flyers. This was going to be the biggest air battle since the Marianas Turkey Shoot.

The results of the air battle over Formosa on the 12th was similar to the famous Turkey shoot. 160 Japanese planes were shot down. Although 43 US Navy planes were lost, this included planes lost to antiaircraft fire on strikes against land targets. The Japanese were suffering from a lack of combat experienced pilots. The US Navy carriers in Task Force 38, in contrast, had the most combat experienced pilots of any navy in the world. Even the inexperienced pilots were much better than the Japanese due to a superior training system the US had evolved since the beginning of the war.

The Japanese pilots made one glaring mistake time after time. They left their flight formations to attempt combat alone. The US pilots maintained tight formation discipline. This difference alone accounted for a great deal of the advantage that the US pilots experienced.

For the Callaghan, it was a tense and busy day. Flight operations were held frequently. Reports came in via the radio shack about the great air battle being fought over Formosa. The Callaghan sailors had every expectation that the Navy pilots would once again devastate the enemy and they were not disappointed.

When the last group of aircraft from the last strike was recovered followed by the air combat patrol, the task force settled down to await any night time enemy reaction. The wait was very short. Moments later an alert was flashed that large formations of enemy aircraft had been detected in two directions. Planes were expected from the north and northeast. The task force was already at dusk general quarters so it simply turned southeast and picked up speed to 25 knots.

At 7:00pm, flares were sighted off to one side of the task group. These were being dropped by an enemy plane that was trying to illuminate the American ships for a Japanese attack. Soon anti-aircraft fire was spotted in the same general direction.

The Japanese had sent out their famous "T" force to attack the American carriers. The "T" force was a group of torpedo bombers with a successful history. They had been partly responsible for sinking the Prince of Wales and the Repulse in Dec. 1941. But this was not 1941 and their opponent was not two unprotected British battleships. Task Force 38 was up to taking on the very best the enemy had. "T" force lost several planes that night. Not a single American carrier was even scratched.

No planes were spotted near the Callaghan during the first round and general quarters was canceled just before 11:00pm. 45 minutes later another bogie came in to snoop the American formation and the tired sailors of the Callaghan were back at their battle stations. This time they would not have to simply watch as distant ships fired at the snoopers. One of them came right at the Callaghan. Flares were dropped immediately behind the Callaghan. Since these flares were endangering the Callaghan and all the ships around her, it was decided to try to knock out the flares with the main battery. Seventeen rounds blasted out at a very low angle directly aft of the ship.

This low angle firing had very serious consequences for the men stationed at the three 20 mm guns on the stern of the ship. Many of them had their eyes burned and at least three of them were knocked out by the concussion. Several sailors stationed nearby ran to assist them. Tom Raabe carried two of the gunners to safety in the passageways of the aft superstructure. While carrying the second one, he was thrown to the deck from water that came boiling up over the side. The Callaghan was maneuvering at very high speed and the huge wake from the big propellers combined with the hard lean of the ship away from the turn was putting a lot of water on the deck. Tom was barely able to keep the man he had been carrying from washing over the side.

The second round was long as the Japanese aircraft persisted in their attempts to locate and attack the American carriers. General quarters was canceled and called again as the Japanese planes came in and out of range of the American ships. Three minutes before 2:00am, the destroyers were ordered to make smoke. A couple of minutes later, the Callaghan again opened fire on one of the Japanese planes. 65 rounds of 5" ammunition were used this time as this intruder showed much more determination. A Callaghan sailor named Vallino in turret number 5 was injured by a hot shell.

One more time general quarters was canceled only to be reinstated in less than an hour. At 3:31am the Callaghan opened up again on a snooper. 24 rounds were fired and then the plane was out of range. At 4:30 in the morning, general quarters was canceled for the final time. It didn't matter much since the whole night was dedicated to the Japanese planes that had tried and failed to attack Task Force 38.

The weary sailors not on watch shuffled off to get one hour of sleep. Then it was time for dawn general quarters and another busy day. Probably the only saving grace was the youth of most of these sailors and the fact that they were already experts at falling asleep instantly whenever the opportunity arose.

The 13th was another day of flight operations. Strong airstrikes were sent in against Formosa and the nearby Pescadore islands. But this time the results were very disappointing. In complete contrast to the previous days showing by the Japanese airforces, only three planes were spotted in the air and they fled. The Japanese airmen had new orders to stay away from the deadly Navy fighter pilots of T.F. 38. The Japanese Admiral in charge was planning a mass attack the next day and he wanted to make sure he had aircraft available to attack with. The other reason for the disappointing results had to do with the poor weather. A front had moved in and there was clouds everywhere. The Navy planes had to find holes in the clouds to attack their targets.

Meanwhile most of the weary sailors of the Callaghan not on duty were catching some sleep. Many of them skipped breakfast in order to get more sack time. For those on duty, attention was paid to shutting down boilers or other equipment that was not immediately needed. The high speed operations all day and all night would take a toll in both fuel consumption and equipment breakdowns. It was decided to operate with just two boilers most of the day.

There were contacts with bogies throughout the day but none resulted in any action. General quarters were held just before 6:00pm as the final flight operations were being completed. 30 minutes later a bogie was reported closing fast. The plane was spotted at about 200 degrees relative (the back, left side of the ship). The main battery opened up and fired 33 rounds with no result. The plane apparently escaped. At 10 minutes after 7:00pm another plane showed up and the Callaghan briefly fired at it as well. But it was dark, the sea was rough and the planes were moving fast. No hits were made.

Other Japanese planes were operating that night. The Callaghan heard later that the Heavy Cruiser Canberra had been hit by a Japanese torpedo launched from a plane. Formosa was turning out to be a more dangerous target than any of the previous targets during the last several months.

After general quarters was canceled, the entire night was spent at Condition I Easy. This meant that a high state of alert was maintained with most of the guns manned but the rest of the off-watch crew was allowed to sleep. This was a very wise decision on the part of the officers because it helped keep the crew from becoming totally exhausted. A dead tired crew was not going to be very efficient in combat.

Oct. 14th dawned with stormy seas. It was time for the destroyers to fuel. The high speed running both day and night had drained the bunkers down to a low level. The Callaghan got orders to go alongside the Battleship South Dakota for refueling. This was a lucky break because the big 40,000 plus ton Battleship would partially compensate for the rough weather. The Admiral would try to have the fueling formation cruise in a direction in which the bulk of the big ships could block the waves away from the destroyers while they were refueling. The Callaghan took 1533 barrels of oil from the big warship in only 31 minutes. It was a very successful operation especially for so early in the morning.

That was a good thing because this was going to be a fateful day for both Task Force 38 and for the Callaghan. After such a very long run of luck and successful combat against the enemy, both were going to take casualties this day.

At two minutes past three in the afternoon, general quarters was called. The word went quickly around the ship's talk circuit: enemy planes coming in. About 13 minutes later an enemy plane was spotted coming in. It was low and clearly making an attack. In seconds the order to open fire was given. The main battery of 5" guns opened up as usual. Unlike the night attacks though, the 40mm guns got to join in. The Japanese plane flew extremely close to the Callaghan, as little as 100 yards away. But the cease fire was called fairly quickly as the plane flew between ships and the Callaghan was in danger of hitting those ships.

A second plane came in low directly toward the stern of the ship. That reduced the number of 5" guns that could fire at it as the forward guns could not bear on the target. It didn't matter. As the plane was nearing, the number 5 gun planted a 5" round right in front of the plane. It burst into flame and flew into the water.

There was little time for cheering. More planes bore in obviously intent on striking the big ships in the formation. It was time for the sharpshooters on the starboard 40mm mount to demonstrate how anti-aircraft gunnery was done. First a torpedo plane came in alongside heading for the cruiser Reno which was just ahead of the Callaghan. The starboard mount hit the plane hard when it was just short of the Reno. Unfortunately the plane had enough momentum that it was able to continue on just long enough to crash into the stern on the Reno.

Within a minute or so another Jap torpedo plane came along virtually the same route. This time the starboard 40mm had its measure. 40mm rounds were firing in a steady stream reaching out to the plane. When the stream and the plane met, fire and smoke were the result. This plane also dove into the water.

Suddenly the call went out for the medics. After the guns ceased fire it was discovered that one of the 20mm gunners was hit. Carlo Nuccio, seaman first class was hit by a 20mm shell in the calf and ankle. There was instantly some confusion. Was he hit by the guns of the Japanese plane? Or was he hit by a US 20mm shell fired from one of the other ships in the formation?

About 40 minutes after the attack flight operations were held. More fighters took off to protect the fleet. The task force staff was certain that more attacks would be forthcoming. As if on cue, a little past 5:00 that afternoon a large number of torpedo bombers came in again.

The Callaghan went to general quarters again. In just a few minutes the torpedo planes were spotted and the main battery went into action. 129 rounds were fired from the Callaghan in a furious air-ship battle. Then, as suddenly as it had started, it was all over.

This time the Japanese had hit a Light Cruiser, the Houston. As with the Canberra, it had taken a single torpedo which caused a lot of damage but the cruiser was not in danger of sinking. Both cruisers were taken into tow and protected by cruisers and destroyers which were detached for that purpose.

The Callaghan stayed with the carriers. As the sun set, the sailors prepared for another long night of waiting for enemy attacks. The Captain ordered condition II set so that most of the men could get some sleep. Unfortunately it was not to be.

Four times that night the sailors were called to general quarters. Japanese planes were actively snooping the task force all night long. Whenever a contact got too close to the carriers, general quarters would be sounded again. The fourth and last time that G.Q. was called, the director and some of the sailors with binoculars could see a flame in the distance. It was finally reported over the radio that this was the wreck of a Japanese plane burning on the water.

The next day dawned with tension throughout the task force. Two cruisers were severely damaged and being towed away from Formosa. The task force was headed back home but not fast enough for most of the sailors. What the men didn't know was that Halsey and his staff had decided to come up with a plan to get the Japanese. The word was that the Japanese fleet was only a few hundred miles distant. Halsey decided to use the crippled cruisers as bait.

The two cruisers under tow were put in a small protective force of destroyers and cruisers. Since the top speed while under tow was not more than 8 knots, this little task group was leaving the area at a painfully slow pace. Meanwhile, Halsey made sure that the rest of T.F. 38 was further out from Formosa but within easy striking distance if the Japanese fleet decided to show up.

The Japanese never unleashed their warships. At this point in the conflict the Japanese were already anticipating the next major Allied invasion. They were fairly certain that it would come to the Philippines. If not there, it would have to be Formosa. Either way, their plans were to conserve all ships and planes to counter the invasion in one massive all-out counter-attack. That is why Halsey was disappointed that his bait of two crippled cruisers was never taken. The Japanese wisely decided that there were more important battles to wait for.

All of that did nothing to help the sailors aboard the Callaghan and fellow ships who were worried about covering the crippled cruiser task force. They even made up a nick-name for the little group of ships: Crip Div 1. It was a play on the usual name for a cruiser division: Cru Div 1 (or whatever number).

Refueling was scheduled for this day after the big battle. The Callaghan refueled from the oiler USS Tomahawk. The destroyer took aboard less than 1000 barrels but it also received a very precious commodity: mail. The Callaghan steamed immediately to go alongside the destroyer Dortch to pass the first allotment of mail.

Next stop was the battleship Massachusetts. Mail and a patient were transferred this time. Seaman First Class Nuccio was transferred over to the battleship for treatment of his shattered leg. Battleships were very well equipped with full medical operating facilities and a surgeon on the staff. The Callaghan's first direct combat casualty left the ship for good.

Most of the rest of the day was consumed with the task of delivering the mail to various ships of the task group. The Callaghan then resumed its station in the screen while the last of the ships to refuel were finishing up. The tanker group then cleared the formation and each group assumed its normal disposition.

The formation of ships assumed one of the typical wide circular dispositions for night cruising. The destroyer Pritchett left to take up picket duty out front of the task group. After all the mayhem of the previous two nights, this one was quiet as the ships slowly drew away from Formosa.

The next morning, general quarters was called well before dawn. After G.Q. was canceled, the formation met up with one of the support groups again. This time the Callaghan went alongside a fast cargo ship. Word went around the ship like lightning: a very important passenger was coming aboard. Commander C.M. Bertholf was reporting aboard as the replacement Captain for the Callaghan.

The rumor-mill went into overtime as the curiosity level of everyone aboard was sky high. What was this guy going to be like? He couldn't possibly be any tougher than Johnson, could he? He's got to be better, right?

When they saw him standing on the deck of the USS Cotton they knew he had to be different. This guy was a lot younger, a little taller and a lot slimmer. A good looking guy, too! But first they had to get him over to the ship. He was strapped into the breeches buoy and then they started pulling on the lines to bring him over. As he got to the middle, a little extra slack was allowed to play out and the officer hung perilously over the sea dipped down almost to the water. Years later, Bertholf would always tell everyone that this was the bosun mate's way of letting him know that he depended on the crew for his well being.

CHANGE OF COMMAND PICTURES
Ulithi, October 1944

Captain Bertholf on the left; Captain Johnson on the right

CREW PICTURES FROM OKINAWA, 1945

The Junior Officers

The Chiefs

Top row: CY Mertz , CWT Brag, CBM Simonton, CMM Soderlund
Middle row: CCS Smith, CQM Guernsey, CPM ?, CWT Reamer, CRM Block.
Bottom row: GMC Maiwald, CEM Ecker, FCC Berger, TMC Williams, MMC Hand

Deck Division

Cooks and Bakers

Sailors replenishing the 5 inch main gun ammo.

The Callaghan's score board on the main director

PICTURES OF THE USS CALLAGHAN

Callaghan at anchor, Bow view

Transferring a pilot via breeches buoy to USS Wasp

Transferring Arleigh Burke, future CNO of the Navy,
via breeches buoy

USS Callaghan overtaking the aircraft carrier, USS Wasp

Callaghan underway at 20 knots

When the trip between the ships was over, Captain Johnson formally welcomed Bertholf aboard the ship. He assigned a sailor to show Bertholf to the Captain's quarters while he finished with the business of transferring mail and supplies from the Cotton. Johnson never delegated the conning of the ship to anyone else while they were alongside another ship at sea. He would never take the chance of suffering an embarrassing collision which would instantly become known to the other skippers in the task group.

Within just a few minutes Bertholf joined Johnson on the bridge. From that moment on, the two men spent nearly every waking moment together. These men were very different in age and temperament but they shared the same mission of turning over command of one of the finest warships in the US Navy. Johnson probably knew that he was relinquishing his one and only sea command. He was determined to carry out his duty to the Nth degree. Bertholf, of course, was curious to learn everything he could from the previous skipper.

There would be a lot for Bertholf to observe on his first day aboard the Callaghan. The Callaghan left the side of the USS Cotton with mail for several of her fellow ships. That morning she went alongside the destroyers Preston, Porterfield, Cassin Young and the cruiser Reno. The mail was delayed going to the Porterfield. The deck force was just about to put the lines over when an enemy plane was spotted and all ships went to general quarters.

The Callaghan swung out away from the Porterfield. The main battery roared into action and 15 rounds of 5" antiaircraft were pumped out toward the distant enemy plane. The plane departed the area with the assistance of explosions following right behind it. The future commanding officer of the Callaghan was impressed both by the seamanship demonstrated in tricky maneuvering close to other warships and with the ability to quickly get the main guns into action with little warning.

The rest of the day was filled with delivering the mail and the usual flight operations. Evening general quarters came and went. To demonstrate the uncertainties of their mission an air alert was called 45 minutes after dusk G.Q. was over. It was quickly canceled when the "bogie" was discovered to be one of the carrier planes.

The task force spent most the night traveling around the perimeter of a giant box. They were still providing cover for "Crip Div 1", the task group bringing the two torpedoed cruisers to safety. Flight operations were held early the next morning to send protective fighters back over the damaged cruisers.

If someone decided to script another demonstration day for the prospective commanding officer of a destroyer, this next day might have been it. In mid-morning, the Callaghan went alongside the Battleship South Dakota to refuel. Then, after lunch, the destroyer went alongside the flagship carrier the USS Lexington. Mail was passed over and six passengers were passed over! Passing over one man via breeches buoy was always a show that everyone topside watched. This time there were six.

The Callaghan peeled off from the Lexington and steamed over to another of the huge Essex class carriers, the Hancock. Two war correspondents named Butchett and McGaffin were passed over to the Hancock. Then it was off to the carrier Intrepid. Two officers and two more war correspondents were sent over to the Intrepid to finish off the transfer of passengers for the day. The Callaghan proceeded to the side of the biggest Battleship in the US Navy, the New Jersey, which also happened to be Halsey's flagship. Mail was passed over with a potentially very important audience.

The Callaghan left to rejoin its own task group, T.G. 38.3. While enroute, Captain Johnson held mast. This gave Commander Bertholf a chance to observe the discipline administered aboard ship.

When the Callaghan rejoin its own group, it went alongside the Lexington to pass mail. When finished with this chore, the Callaghan sped away from the formation. It was on its way to the night picket station way out in front of the formation. Bertholf was getting to see a lot and it was just beginning!

The night passed quietly. At dawn the Callaghan rejoined the escort screen. T.F. 38.3 again joined up with a group of tankers. The Callaghan had other duties first and steamed over to join up with the USS Princeton, a light carrier which we will hear more about shortly. Four Navy personnel were transferred over to the Callaghan for transport to another ship. The Callaghan was getting the call for a lot of this taxi service.

Next stop was the USS Essex. Six more navy personnel were transferred aboard including a Navy Captain! The Callaghan then proceeded to go alongside the USS Barnes. Four of the passengers were transferred to the Barnes and four more picked up. The Callaghan then went to the USS Escambia for refueling. Only 599 barrels were taken aboard since it had not been long since the last fill-up.

Then it was back to the Essex. Apparently someone had been overlooked on the last trip so the task group staff simply sent the Callaghan back. Finally the Callaghan had all aboard and went alongside the Lexington to deliver them. That done, the destroyer rejoined the escort screen for its usual routine.

The next day was completely boring. The task group ran mostly to the northeast as it headed for a position near Cape Idlefonso to attack airfields in the central Philippine islands. This was actually the calm before the storm. At the same time, hundreds of ships in several task forces were converging on a point in the Eastern Philippines. Tomorrow would be the long awaited invasion to take the Philippines back from the Japanese.

Flight operations began early on the 20th as strikes were sent against the Japanese airfields. Meanwhile to the south, the bombardment force of old battleships and cruisers were pounding Leyte island. At the appointed hour, hundreds of landing craft went in to deliver American soldiers to the beach. The liberation of the Philippines had begun. Amazingly, the resistance on the beaches of Leyte was relatively light. Only one Japanese army division was being used to defend Leyte island. The Japanese were planning to make their main defensive effort with the army on the main island of Luzon.

Admiral Sherman's Task group 38.3 took the day off. Its air strength was being saved for the days following the invasion when the Japanese air effort against the invasion was expected to grow. The Americans had long experience with Japanese tactics against invasions. The first day was usually quiet in the air as the Japanese sent out reconnaissance planes and prepared their counter-strikes.

On the 21st, T.F. 38.3 came to life as a series of air strikes were flown off to strike those central Philippine airfields. T.F. 38.3 would operate alone for the next three days in its role as the suppresser of the Japanese air strength on Luzon. The other carrier groups were either directly supporting the invasion by attacking ground targets or striking the Southern Japanese airfields.

Several airfields were attacked with mixed results. The truth was that the air strength in the Philippines was still a shell of its former self due to the earlier attacks by US carrier planes. Three cargo ships were found and attacked, one being sunk.

For the Callaghan, the first four days of the Leyte invasion were a time of normal activity with no interruptions caused by the enemy. It was abnormally quiet. The most significant things to occur was the return of Lt. Pomeroy for duty and the temporary loss of Chief Gunners Mate Gene Maiwald. Lt. Pomeroy had been off for school for several months and was now returning to the ship. Maiwald had been down with an illness that Doc. Parker could not treat. Maiwald was being transferred to the Lexington for diagnosis.

Toward the end of this interlude, the word started around that the Japanese fleet was on the way. This got the guys excited because everyone had been itching for a fight with the enemy fleet ever since the Marianas Turkey Shoot. Right or wrong, the perception was that the Japanese fleet had been allowed to slip away after the Turkey Shoot. Every sailor in Task Force 38 was convinced, rightfully so, that the American carriers and its pilots could defeat anything the Japanese could bring to a fight. The Japanese battleship force was largely intact and many of the Japanese carriers were still afloat so it seemed like the opportunity was long overdue.

In fact the Japanese fleet was on its way. For the first time since the attack on Pearl Harbor, the Japanese Navy was committing everything it had. Separate task forces were on their way from Singapore, China and from Japan itself. Four task forces were to operate independently in a very complex scheme designed to fool the Americans and overcome the superiority of the US fleet. The strange thing is that the plan almost worked!

The opening of the great Naval battle of Leyte Gulf began on Oct. 23rd. Two US submarines ambushed the main Japanese task force of battleships and cruisers. By this time in the war the American submarines were the most effective and skilled undersea force in the world. These two subs sank two heavy cruisers and severely damaged a third in just a matter of minutes. It was a shocking blow to this Japanese task force and its Admiral. Admiral Kurita was using one of these cruisers for his flag ship so he was forced to abandon ship and transfer to the Battleship Yamato. This was a very humiliating start to a battle that was suppose to turn the tide and win the war for the Japanese!

In the meantime, Admiral Halsey was receiving intelligence reports of the location of the various groups of Japanese warships that were on their way to Leyte. As a result, late in the day his staff issued orders for the carrier task groups of Task Force 38 to concentrate again into one force. Most of the groups were clustered around the Leyte landing site. These groups would move north to join T.F. 38.3 the next day.

The 24th of October dawned windy with a cloud cover over most of the sky. The Japanese command in the Philippines had decided that this was the day for the great air counter-strike against the American carriers. This would lay the ground work for the naval task forces that were closing in to annihilate the American forces. This air attack, launched from the airfields of Luzon would be aimed directly at the nearest US carrier group which at that time was due east of Luzon. Those carriers belonged to Task Group 38.3, which was guarded by a group of experienced and determined destroyers.

The Japanese air strikes like Admiral Kurita's task force, got off to a bad start. The fighters took off first and were followed by waves of dive bombers and torpedo planes. Unfortunately for them, each following wave was late taking off. This meant that the ideal coordinated strike with all types of aircraft represented was blown from the very beginning. In addition, about 50 miles off the coast, the first elements ran smack into a group of US carrier fighter planes. The ensuing melee not only caused the loss of some of the Japanese planes, but put the attack further behind schedule.

Finally the Japanese planes joined up and headed out again toward Task Group 38.3. Commander McCampbell took off from the Essex with five other planes and met this force as it was approaching. In a now famous air battle, Commander McCampbell and his wingman took on the largest group of Japanese fighters high over the Pacific. In an unbelievable display of aerial gunnery, McCampbell, using short, careful bursts, downed nine Japanese Zeros. His wingman downed six. Between the two flyers, they shot down nearly a whole squadron of Japanese fighters. It was a feat worthy of a John Wayne movie!

Meanwhile, every carrier in T.F. 38.3 had all flyable fighters flown off to deal with the huge number of Japanese planes that could be seen on radar. The combat air patrol from each floating airfield was desperately trying to close with and fight off the Japanese attackers. This was proving to be difficult due to the confusion of several different groups of attackers in different parts of the sky using their own unique tactics. In addition, the cloud cover was making it difficult to find and stay with these Japanese planes.

Despite the difficulties, the American fighters were successful and the Japanese planes were driven off. All but one. One very intelligent Japanese dive bomber pilot stayed high above the American carriers and used the clouds to hide in. He could see through holes in the clouds that the carriers were maneuvering in wide circles. He waited until the battle was over and all of the other planes from both sides were out of sight.

Far below, the USS Princeton was recovering its combat air patrol. The last plane landed just as the lone dive bomber above made its attack. Witnesses on several ships, including the Callaghan noted that the plane dove steeply down, released a single bomb, pulled up and flew away. The Princeton's 40mm and 20mm guns opened up in a desperate attempt to stop the attack but it was too late. The bomb went straight down to the middle of the Princeton's flight deck, crashed through and exploded in the carriers hanger deck.

The Princeton was instantly in big trouble. The bomb blew open and set on fire several torpedo planes on the Princeton's hanger deck. Ammunition in the area started going off. A raging fire was fed by the aviation gasoline that was pouring out of the shattered aircraft. The mortal blow came an hour or so later when torpedoes stored adjacent to the hanger deck started going off. The torpedo warheads had about 500 pounds of volatile torpex in them. The damage caused by these explosions made it impossible to save the ship.

The destroyer Morrison and Irwin were assigned to assist the Princeton in its fire fighting efforts and to remove the wounded. An incredible struggle began as the storm squalls of the morning led to increasingly stormy seas. As each destroyer in turn moved in to assist the Princeton, it found that the simple process of getting alongside the Princeton was extremely dangerous. First the Morrison was seriously damaged when it got trapped under the over-hanging flight deck of the Princeton. It's radar antennas were destroyed and a lot of other equipment was severely damaged. Virtually the same thing happened to the Irwin when it replaced the Morrison alongside the crippled carrier.

Meanwhile the Callaghan and the remaining destroyers were performing the usual task of guarding the other carriers of the task group. Maneuvering was complicated because the admiral kept the task group within sight of the Princeton for quite some time. Coupled with the need to turn into the wind to launch aircraft, this caused some unusual twisting and turning of the task group.

Everyone was on full alert for any more Japanese planes that might try to attack at this vulnerable time. The other carriers refueled and rearmed their fighters as fast as they could and put many of them back up in the air to provide cover over the Princeton and the ships assisting it.

At one o'clock the Japanese were back. The ships all went to general quarters and the combat air patrol tried to intercept the intruders. It took awhile before the attackers found the ships of the task group. The ones that broke through found the guns of the task group firing furiously. The Callaghan opened up with everything she had. 57 rounds of 5", 80 rounds of 40mm and 110 rounds of 20mm were fired off in a short but sharp fight with the diving enemy planes. Then it was suddenly over as the few surviving Japanese planes flew away. There were no more attacks that day.

But there was more tragedy for T.G. 38.3. First a reconnaissance plane ditched near the Callaghan. The Callaghan stopped to lower a boat but only the gunner was rescued. The pilot was not found. Worst, the fight to save the Princeton was about to get extremely bloody.

Most of the fires aboard the Princeton had been put out. The only area that still had a stubborn fire that couldn't be put out was the stern. Just before 3:00 in the afternoon, the cruiser Birmingham was ordered alongside the Princeton. The Birmingham was assigned the role of both firefighter and tow for the Princeton. To accomplish these roles hundreds of sailors were out on the decks of the Birmingham handling hoses, putting lines over to the Princeton or preparing the towing gear. In addition, there were many sailors helping the wounded that were sent over from the Princeton.

At about 3:25, the fire in the stern of the Princeton got to the aft ammunition magazine. The magazine blew up in a huge explosion which literally fragmented the stern of the Princeton into a million flying pieces. Tens of thousands of these pieces of flying metal pierced the side of the Birmingham and the bodies of the sailors that were crowded around the decks.

The decks of the Birmingham ran red with blood. Over 220 officers and sailors were killed. Another two hundred were seriously wounded. An additional smaller number of officers and sailors aboard the Princeton were casualties. In terms of casualties it was the worst single incident to occur to Task Force 38 in 1944.

The damage to the Princeton was fatal and she was abandoned. Just before sunset, the destroyer Irwin tried to torpedo the Princeton to put her out of her misery. Since the torpedo equipment had been badly damaged in her collision with the Princeton, it refused to operate properly. 6 torpedoes were fired but only one hit a minor blow. The Irwin was pulled out and the cruiser Reno stepped in to do the job. Two torpedoes hit the Princeton and it disintegrated. The tired and bloody ships which had been standing by left the scene to rejoin T.F. 38.3.

Other than two Japanese snoopers which disturbed the sleep of the sailors, the night passed quietly for the ships of the task force. However, far to the south at Surigao Straits, an epic battle was being fought between the battleships, cruisers and destroyers of the U.S. bombardment force and the Southern attack force of the Japanese Imperial Fleet. It would be the last time in history that battleships would fire on other battleships in combat. It resulted in a completely one sided victory in which both of the enemy battleships and all but one cruiser was sunk.

The battle and the pursuit of the surviving Japanese ships went on through the night until dawn the next day. At that time, the next phase of the great Leyte Gulf battle opened both to the south and to the north of where the Callaghan patrolled.

North of the island of Leyte was the San Bernardino strait. The powerful Central Japanese task force of 5 battleships and 9 cruisers had been given orders to go through the strait to attack the Leyte landing forces on the 25th. The central force had spent much of the 24th fighting off air attacks from Halsey's other carrier task groups. In the process it had lost one of its battleships, the Musashi, and one of its largest cruisers. After briefly reversing course to the west it had resumed its advance toward San Bernardino strait.

One of the great controversies of World War II revolves around the fact that Halsey assumed that the central force when it changed course to the west was retreating and therefore out of the fight. Halsey had been searching for the Japanese carriers which had not put in an appearance yet. He finally found them in mid-afternoon on the 24th. He was far more concerned about these carriers than he was about a group of battleships and cruisers limited to the range of their guns. The Pacific war had been primarily a carrier war and this wasn't going to change. The Japanese carriers had to be eliminated.

So the combination of the near simultaneous news of the discovery of the Japanese carriers way to the north and the apparent retreat of the central battleship force determined Halsey's next move. He ordered the concentration of his carrier task groups and preparations for attacks on the Japanese carrier force in the morning. The three available task groups joined up in the middle of the night and steamed north.

Due to a misunderstanding resulting from a radio message of Halsey's to Pacific Fleet Headquarters, Nimitz and nearly everyone else outside of Task Force 38 thought that Halsey was leaving a force of surface ships to guard San Bernardino Strait. In fact, Halsey had all 67 ships heading north with the sole intention of attacking the Japanese carrier force with every available means, including his surface ships.

At dawn on the 25th, two separate battles began. To the north, Halsey's carriers started launching air strikes to attack the Japanese carriers. To the south, Admiral Kurita's central force of battleships and cruisers had come out of San Bernardino Strait, turned south and ran smack into the northernmost escort carrier task group which was operating in support of the troops ashore.

Both battles were mismatches. Halsey's carrier forces were far stronger than the Japanese carrier force. The Japanese carriers had left Japan with only about 116 planes total. They now had fewer due to the abortive attack on the 24th against T.F. 38.3. Halsey's carriers had well over 500 aircraft with veteran aircrews. The American Hellcat fighters quickly destroyed or damaged most of the meager combat air patrol that the Japanese carriers were able to put up. That made the way clear for the American dive bombers and torpedo planes to attack the carriers at will.

Kurita's force of battleships and cruisers were a far more powerful force than the puny escort carrier group they had stumbled upon. Kurita still had 4 battleships and 8 cruisers left despite the air attacks of the day before. Admiral Sprague's "Taffy 3" force consisted of four escort carriers, two destroyers and three even smaller destroyer escorts. It is important to note that the four escort carriers were old friends of the Callaghan. These were the same carriers which it had served with in T.F. 52.14 back in the Marianas campaign.

Since there had been no warning of possible attack from Japanese ships, the escort carriers did not even have their small force of torpedo planes armed with the small supply of aerial torpedoes they had aboard. Instead, the torpedo planes were armed with 500 pound bombs intended for ground targets.

There was no time for the torpedo planes to go through the long process of changing from bombs to torpedoes. With the much faster Japanese ships bearing down on them, Sprague ordered the torpedo planes into the air with what they had. He launched all his planes including fighters and then proceeded to attempt a hopeless race away from the Japanese ships. This epic battle is worthy of a whole book itself but since it does not directly involve the Callaghan, it will not be dealt with here.

Far to the north, the Callaghan watched as Halsey's battleships and most of the cruisers were detached from the carrier task groups and formed into a separate task group called T.G. 34.1. It then steamed ahead of the carriers with the intent of smashing any Japanese ships that either were foolish enough to come south or were crippled by the air strikes. This task group was the one that Nimitz and all the other Naval commanders thought was being left behind to guard San Bernardino Strait.

The Callaghan stayed with the carriers. All morning and early afternoon waves of planes took off from the carriers to form up and head north. Finally at 2:40 in the afternoon came an order that electrified the officers and crew. The Callaghan along with the Porterfield were ordered to leave the carriers to join Destroyer squadron 50. They were being called north to join the hunt for damaged Japanese ships!

The destroyers took off at maximum speed. Frank Dunne was told by the Captain to get all the speed he could out of the powerplant. They were soon doing 33 knots; all that the Callaghan could do. Just before 5:00 the crew went to general quarters. Smoke was sighted on the horizon. Word went around that it was from a Japanese carrier that was sinking up ahead. By the time the destroyers arrived on the scene the carrier had gone down. What the crew saw will never be forgotten. In addition to the usual debris floating on the water, there were about 200 Japanese sailors swimming in the water.

The men were so keyed up by the combat of the last few weeks that some of them went running for the small arms (rifles and pistols) that were kept aboard. The destroyers temporarily slowed down but a quick consensus was reached that nothing could be done. If they stopped to pick up survivors, they would miss the impending action up ahead. No combat hungry destroyer skipper would ever pass up an opportunity to join a fight. Therefore, the decision was made to leave the Japanese behind and the destroyers went to "flank" speed again.

The reactions of the men aboard the Callaghan are typical of how most American men serving in the Pacific felt at the time. One torpedoman stood up and shook his fist. Many of the men were yelling obscenities at the swimmers. One quick thinking sailor at the stern ran over to the Ensign (American flag) that always flew while underway. He grabbed it and held it out so that any swimmer who looked up could see it.

About 40 minutes after they passed the site of the sunken carrier, the destroyers rendezvoused with the cruisers and destroyers that they had been chasing. The combined force then took off after the last Japanese target left in the area. What was thought to be a Japanese light cruiser was up ahead. The force sped after it for about an hour.

Finally, the target was just ahead. Destroyer Division 100, which now included the Callaghan, was ordered to make a torpedo attack. At the same time, the cruisers were firing their main guns at this target. The Callaghan formed up behind the Porterfield and the destroyers proceeded to make a torpedo run on the target.

This was what the torpedomen had been trained to do for over a year. All that training and all the many drills were finally going to culminate in this one chance to fire the two ton monsters at a live target. The torpedo directors were trained on the target which could be seen burning up ahead. The men on each torpedo mount followed along with their pointers and gyro repeaters. Just as they reached the point of firing, the men who could see the target realized that something was happening to the target.

In fact, it was all over. The target, actually the destroyer Hatsutsuki, had capsized (rolled over). The officers quickly came to the conclusion that there was no point in wasting torpedoes on a doomed metal hulk with no chance of survival. The attack was called off to the bitter disappointment of the torpedomen. This was the closest that the Callaghan would ever come to firing its torpedoes in combat. It was the only time that the destroyer would come this close to an enemy surface warship.

The other two Japanese ships that the cruiser/destroyer task group was after were now too far away to close within a reasonable length of time. Besides, the destroyers were now getting low on fuel. So they turned around and headed back south to join the carrier task groups that they had left behind.

By dawn on the 26th it was becoming apparent that the great battle was pretty much over. A few Japanese ships were far enough behind that air strikes were able to get to them. A cruiser and a couple of destroyers were sunk in this way. Halsey tried for a few hours to catch the fleeing Japanese ships but was unable to. Low fuel and the need to protect the landing forces from possible attack prevented him from going too far afield.

For the Callaghan, it was a day of refueling and getting back to the normal routine. A radioman was passed over to the Lexington but that was about all that happened. After being up nearly all night long, the men off watch tried to get some extra sleep. It had been an exciting few days even though the Callaghan had not been involved with the surface combat that many of the other destroyers had seen.

There was still some excitement left though, when a submarine was spotted on the 27th by an aircraft. The Callaghan and sister ship, Cassin Young, gave chase. The sub contact was quite a distance away from the task group's original position.

When the task group steamed off in the opposite direction that the two destroyers were going while chasing the sub, the separation distance grew. A couple of hours later, word was received that Japanese cruisers were coming out to intercept the two destroyers. They immediately turned about and steamed at "flank" speed for several hours to rejoin the carrier group they had left.

Two days later, the Callaghan and Task Group 38.3 were finally able to return to Ulithi for rest, recovery and repair. It was the first time at anchor for the Callaghan in weeks. The destroyer tender Prairie was present to provide for the destroyers needs. Maintenance support was a high priority after weeks of hard charging and combat.

On the 31st came an event that had not been experienced before on the Callaghan. It was time for a very formal ceremony in the life of the sea-going Navy. It was time for the change-of-command ceremony.

Over two weeks after coming aboard, it was finally Commander Bertholf's hour. All of the men and officers not on watch were gathered on the focscle to witness the solemn occasion. Captain Johnson read his orders detaching him from the Callaghan and sending him back to the States. Bertholf read his orders which assigned him to the Callaghan as commanding officer. There was a new Captain, and it was a new era aboard the Callaghan.

It is important to note what Commander Bertholf said about Captain Johnson years later. When Johnson turned over the ship to Bertholf, he gave the new skipper a ship and crew in top condition. All Bertholf had to do was "pull the trigger." Whatever he needed done in the normal life of a destroyer would be done. Johnson had been a tough task master but there was no doubt about the ability of the crew he had trained so hard and led so vigorously.

The first day of November opened with three transfers aboard: Donofrio, Biggs and Harold Smith. Of note, too, was the single transfer off the ship this day. Leonard Konabroski, ship's baker, was leaving the Callaghan. Here was a sailor who would be sorely missed. He not only provided good basic food for the sailors but also was able to take all the good-natured griping about the food. And of course, he had been a real source of pride for his ability with his fists in the ring. The men hated losing the bragging rights of having the former fleet champion aboard.

Two passengers were brought aboard in the early afternoon, and then it was time to leave. Smoke was rising all over the anchorage, as Task Group 38.3 was getting ready to move out again. This time it was scheduled to be a trip south to Manus for some rest and recreation. The Callaghan had not been to Manus since April.

As always, the destroyers got under way first. The Callaghan was steaming away from its anchorage by 3:30pm. The destroyer patrol line was established outside the giant atoll. Soon the cruisers and carriers were on their way out of the entrance. The formation turned south once it was well clear of the atoll.

After less than two hours steaming away from Ulithi, the formation abruptly turned around. Word had come back from Leyte that the other carrier task groups were under pressure from the Japanese airforces, in particular, the Kamikaze threat. In addition, intelligence thought that the Japanese were going to try to send another battleship and cruiser task force to try to attack the American landing ships. As a result it was decided that Task Group 38.3 was needed again to help subdue the threat. That night a fast cruising pace was set for the ships on their way back to the Philippines.

Refueling was done on the 3rd to get all the ships fully tanked up before the final run into the Philippines. The Callaghan got its black oil from the Nantahoba that day. 1177 barrels were pumped into the bunkers. A radio electrician, Williams, E.J. was transferred over to the Nantahoba as the first step on his transfer to another assignment, probably stateside. The

Callaghan then cast off all lines and steamed back out to take its usual place in the escort screen.

At 4:00 in the afternoon, the Callaghan left the screen again to go alongside the USS Owens. It was time to get rid of the two passengers who had been picked up at Ulithi. Once the two officers were passed over, the Callaghan steamed once more to its place in the screen.

Dusk general quarters came and went without incident. The task group was steaming steadily toward Leyte when an attack came totally without warning. At 11:30, an explosion shook the anti-aircraft cruiser Reno. It was not clear immediately, but the Reno had taken a torpedo. A couple of sailors were blown into the sea from the blast. The Reno was seriously damaged with no steering control and half its power plant out of commission.

The Callaghan went to general quarters again and was ordered with three other destroyers to protect the Reno while it struggled to clear the area. For an hour and a half the four destroyers circled the Reno. Finally at 1:00am the Callaghan secured from G.Q. and was ordered to rejoin the task group.
The Reno with her escorts steamed slowly away to return to Ulithi.

After that serious matter, the Callaghan got a much lighter assignment. She was ordered to steam independently toward Task Group 38.1 and maintain station in the middle between the two formations. The purpose was to get the mail. As early as possible, the Callaghan would join T.G. 38.1 and find the carrier Wasp.

An hour before dawn, the Callaghan found T.G. 38.1. Just as dawn was breaking, the destroyer was alongside the Wasp, and lines were put over to the Callaghan. It only took 15 minutes to get the mail bags across, and then it was off to the races. In less than two hours the Callaghan was back with its own formation and alongside the Essex. After passing mail to the big carrier, the Callaghan proceeded to join up with four destroyers, plus the battleship Massachusetts, to pass along each ships' mail respectively.

The rest of the day was spent in the usual flight operations.

Sometime during the first two days at sea, after the new Captain took over, he decided to make an announcement to the crew. It was an announcement that most crewmembers would remember decades later. Many of the surviving sailors remember it to this day. It was an announcement that defined the new era that had come to the life of the Callaghan. Although the announcement was not recorded, there is remarkable agreement among the sailors as to the core of what was said.

Bertholf noted that the Callaghan was in the middle of a great war. "None of us know whether or not we will return to our homes and our loved ones." He said that things were going to change aboard the ship. From now on, if crewmembers decided that they wanted to grow a beard, it was ok. Further, if someone had something important to say to the Captain, he would try to accommodate them.

A cheer rang out from the crew. This announcement was the beginning of a bond that would develop between Captain Bertholf and the crew that would last forever. It would last through war, peacetime, tragedy and the many reunions that would be held decades later. No Captain could have wished for more respect and admiration from a crew. No crew would ever have more devotion to their Captain. They would follow him anywhere. In fact, they were bound together for trials of endurance, storm, the terrors of war and survival itself.

On of the fun events in the life of the ship grew out of that announcement by Captain Bertholf. Some of the sailors were bragging about how fast they could grow a beard. Several soon sported some version of a beard. There were many goatees and mustaches, and even a few full beards with a weeks growth before being trimmed. Two of the torpedomen kidding around one day made a bet as to who could grow the best looking beard. They vowed they wouldn't shave or trim their beard until orders came to return to the states. These two men, Ed Mello and Al Foster, kept their bet until July 28, 1945, when orders came to return stateside. During this time each grew beards to a length that when a strand was stretched full out, it was over 14 inches long. Foster even wrote home and had his mother send a bar of beeswax so he could shape and maintain a handlebar mustache. Who won the contest was never very clear. But Wilford Wallace remembers Foster's very well, so perhaps he had the winning beard. In fact Wilford remembers that one day a shipmate asked him when he thought the ship would return to the states. He replied, with a chuckle, probably not until Foster had to part his beard to unbutton his fly. It was a diversion during a long difficult time in the war zone far away from any civilization.

Nov. 5th would begin the new round of air strikes against the Philippines by T.G. 38.3. It was going to be another tense day of planes coming and going with the ever present danger of a sneak attack by enemy planes. If the Callaghan crew knew what was in store for the task group for the rest of the month, they might have asked to trade their Navy life for an army foxhole.

It had become apparent by now to the Navy brass that the Japanese were trying a sinister new tactic against the Pacific fleet. Since the last day of the Leyte Gulf battle, Japanese planes had come roaring in over 7th and 3rd Fleet ships and, instead of dropping bombs or torpedoes, they dove on the selected target in attempts to deliberately crash it. These suicide attacks were becoming increasingly common with each week that went by. Several warships including some of the big fleet carriers had been hit. One destroyer had already been sunk.

These desperation tactics were borne out of the realization that the Japanese planes were no longer any match for the superb US Navy fighters and the well trained anti-aircraft crews aboard the US warships. Admiral Ohnishi had been sent to the

Philippines before the Allied invasion arrived to work a miracle with the defeated Japanese air forces there. The miracle he came up with was the Kamikaze.

Kamikaze means divine wind in Japanese. It comes from a legend revolving around the attempted invasion of Japan by Genghis Khan's hordes in the 13th century. The legend is that a divinely inspired storm was the instrument of the Chinese hordes' defeat. The storm struck the Chinese fleet as it was approaching Japan and caused countless ships to sink and thousands of soldiers to drown. Now the Japanese were counting on the same divine intervention to save their empire.

All day on the 5th, the airmen from the carriers struck at the airfields, shot down the Japanese aircraft they could find, and attacked shipping in Manila harbor. In return, the Japanese sent out a combination force of bombers and Kamikazes. It was during this attack that the carrier Lexington was hit by a Kamikaze that dove into its "island." The Lexington was set on fire and suffered 187 casualties. But due to superb damage control, the great carrier was able to get back to normal operations in half an hour.

The Callaghan did not participate in any of the shooting this time as the enemy planes were not attacking anywhere near it. But the destroyer was given a unique mission late that day. It was sent out to act as a communications link between T.F. 38.3 and the other task groups of Task Force 38. It returned to the formation just before dark.

Two days later an unusual odyssey began for the Callaghan. It began with a routine mission that the destroyer had performed many times before. The Callaghan went alongside the Essex and received 11 pilots via the high line and breeches buoy. These pilots were supposed to be transferred to the USS Esperance, an escort carrier, in order to get replacement planes for the fleet carriers. Among these pilots was Wayne Morris, a movie actor in his former civilian life. Wayne was now a very successful fighter pilot from the same air group that Commander McCampbell was in charge of.

It took the Callaghan about three hours to steam between T.G. 38.3 and the little group of ships which included the USS Esperance. By that time it was dark, and the transfer was postponed until the next day. The next day was spent cruising with the Esperance and its escorts in what seemed like a very slow pace to the men of the Callaghan. They had almost forgotten the huge speed difference between the fleet carriers and the slow escort carriers. The weather had turned bad during the night, and all day on the 8th it was extremely rough. All of the pilots on board were sick.

At the end of the day the Callaghan was detached to rejoin T.G. 38.3. The 11 pilots had to be very unhappy with the turn of events. It was bad enough being passed between two heaving ships on a high line. This followed by a storm while aboard a pitching and rolling "tin can" made life unbearable for these hot shots. Finally they were faced with the fact that it was all for nothing as the Callaghan headed back.

T.G. 38.3 and the Esperance had been headed in opposite directions all this time, so now the Callaghan had quite a trek to rejoin her home Task Group. The first day found a couple of large sea-going Navy tugs in the way so the Callaghan joined up for a short while. Bertholf brought the ship within shouting distance of one of the AT's to discuss some Navy news. Then the Callaghan peeled off to renew its journey back to its home task group.

The destroyer steamed for two days and still was not in sight of 38.3. The first reported position of their Task Group turned out to be wrong. T.G. 38.3 had left to pursue a report of some Japanese heavy warships near Luzon. The Callaghan arrived to find them gone and had to find out the new position by radio.

It had been months since the Callaghan had operated alone this way. Gunnery practice was suggested to the new skipper who readily agreed. The main battery was manned and a target burst was fired for the other guns to aim at. When the gunnery practice was over, a couple of other drills were announced. But this was different than the drudgery and pressure of the incessant drills the crew experienced earlier under the previous administration. This was more like showing off to the new guy. The few drills were polished off with skill and Bertholf complimented the crew.

Finally at about dawn on the 12th, the Callaghan made contact with task group 30.7, a tanker group. This was a big relief to Captain Bertholf as he knew that 30.7 was traveling with T.G. 38.3. He received permission to have the Callaghan first in line for refueling. All that steaming between task groups and chasing down it's home group had depleted the fuel bunkers.

The Callaghan lined up alongside the tanker USS Tappahannock.. While the refueling proceeded, the 11 pilots from the Essex were transferred over to the tanker. They were all greatly relieved. Although the Callaghan crew had been as hospitable as possible to the pilots, a 2100 ton destroyer was not the same as a 27,000 ton fleet carrier. Most of the pilots had actually experienced sea sickness when the storm that prevented their transfer to the escort carrier tossed the Callaghan around like a cork. They were used to a big heavy carrier that rode out a storm with a lot more grace!

The Callaghan received orders to go visit the Cassin Young as soon as it was finished refueling. Mail was waiting aboard the Cassin Young and it was eagerly received. Then it was time to rejoin the escort screen to resume the destroyer's normal function. It was a good feeling to be steaming among old friends again.

On November 13th T.G. 38.3 was steaming in a 13 ship circular formation. This did not make the sailors, who tended to be superstitious, very comfortable. Flight operations were held throughout most of the day as strikes were continued against airfields on Luzon. The enemy made trouble for T.G. 38.3 as Japanese planes were spotted on radar several times. The Callaghan was in and out of general quarters all day. It was a tense day, but no actual fighting resulted for the Callaghan.

In early evening, the master gyro compass was taken off-line while repairs were made. This was the critical instrument in the navigation of the ship. Without it, the course that the ship took would be suspect. Luckily the repairs were accomplished in record time and the gyro compass was back on line.

The next day was more of the same. In general the crews of T.G. 38.3 were getting punchy. With the exception of the 3 days at Ulithi at the very end of October, they had been in the combat zone off or near the Philippines for 6 weeks straight. Admiral Halsey was very concerned for the safety of his ships and sailors. The possibility of an accident or, worse, failure to react correctly to an enemy attack, was increasing.

Consequently, on the 15th, T.G. 38.3 was detached and turned once again toward Ulithi. With the exception of occasional flight operations, the course was held on a direct line to the giant forward Naval base. The only non-routine activities that the Callaghan indulged in were test firings of certain ammunition and target practice. The trip was short and unremarkable.

At about 7:30am on the morning of the 17th, the Callaghan entered Ulithi lagoon, stopping to pick up some navigational charts of the area from an LCI being used for that purpose. The destroyer then went alongside the USS Rainier to perform an unusual task. The Callaghan swapped nearly its entire 5" ammunition supply for new rounds from the Rainier. Apparently the ammo load was being updated with a new improved type of 5" round.

After that chore was performed, the Callaghan steamed over to the tanker Malvera to take on a new record amount of fuel oil: 2865 barrels! Now it was finally time to find a berth and settle down. The Callaghan ended up moored alongside fellow DesRon 55 destroyer Pritchett in a nest with the destroyer tender Praire. Only 1 boiler remained lit to provide power and hot water while moored. With the day nearly gone, most of the sailors not on watch wrote letters or simply sacked out. It was time for a well deserved and long-overdue rest!

The next day began a five day stay at Ulithi. Watertender Sykes and Radarman Harmon were both transferred off the ship, the first for medical reasons, the second for advanced training. Liberty parties were soon organized so that the men could spend some time at the "recreation" area on Mog-Mog island. Mog-Mog was very spartan with just the minimal ball fields, horse-shoe pits and other sport related activities. Warm beer was provided with each sailor getting two cans. Many of the men elected to sell their ration of the warm beer at a premium to their mates.

It was at Ulithi and Mog Mog island that the Callaghan solidified its reputation as a fighting ship with a fighting crew. It's not certain if the great "beer" fight occurred during this stay or a later one. But every Callaghan man present at the time remembers it.

There was, typically, liberty parties from several ships on Mog Mog on any given day during this period of the war. One day the Callaghan had a large liberty party ashore at the same time a destroyer tender had a much larger party ashore. Being a larger liberty party, the tender group had a bigger ration of beer. They got very involved in one of the team sports that was going on and neglected to keep a guard on their beer. The beer was usually keep in large ammunition cans.

One of the Callaghan crew realized that a couple of 40 mm ammunition cans contained the beer from another ship. He quietly got a few buddies from the Callaghan to help him "borrow" the cans. In no time at all, the Callaghan crew had polished off most of the "borrowed" beer.

Unfortunately the tender crew came looking for their beer. It did not take a genius to figure out that the happy group of sailors with the extra ammunition cans were the culprits. An ugly confrontation ensued. That's when one of the tender sailors made the serious mistake of physically threatening one of the Callaghan sailors. A punch resulted, followed closely by a general brawl by all hands.

Although the Callaghan had lost Konabroski, it still had more than it's share of skilled boxers and former street fighters. The fight was fast and furious with a lot of team action by the Callaghan crew. The months of tough discipline that the destroyer crew had endured made for a outstanding combat team in more ways than one. The big fighters were out front smashing faces while the little guys found weapons and tripped up the unfortunate tender sailors. The tender party had an Ensign along as chaperone who made the mistake of trying to stop the fight by firing his .45 caliber pistol into the air. It had no effect on the Callaghan sailors who really had their blood up now. Out of the melee a fist found the Ensign and he went down.

The fight ended when the tender party fell back defeated. The Callaghan party soon left aboard their liberty boat to return to their ship.

The next day Commander Bertholf was summoned to the destroyer tender in question. The destroyer tender was a much larger ship with a much larger crew. As a result it rated a skipper with a higher rank than the Callaghan, probably a four stripe Captain. Bertholf was shown the line of sailors at sick bay and was severely dressed down by the tender skipper.

When he finally had the opportunity to defend his ship and himself, Bertholf simply pointed out the great disparity in the size of the tender crew versus the crew of the Callaghan. Bertholf suggested that if he was the Captain of the tender, he would not want it to get around the fleet that a much smaller destroyer crew had roundly beaten the crew of the tender.

When Bertholf returned to the Callaghan he called together the sailors who were in the liberty party the previous day. He asked them what happened and got a very reluctant partial description out of the men. He then explained to the men that he was not going to do anything to them. He said he was proud to be skipper of such a fighting crew. But he did tell them to never, ever, hit an officer again.

Once again Bertholf had won the respect and admiration of the crew. They knew now the depth of the change that had occurred in their leadership. The feeling of absolute loyalty was instilled, to remain throughout the years.

On the 22nd, T.G. 38.3 moved out again. It was headed back to the Philippines. As usual the destroyers sortied first, followed by the big ships.

At 3:00pm the Callaghan held gunnery exercises. For well over an hour and a half, the various guns got a chance to shoot at sleeves. 62 rounds of 5", 160 rounds of 40mm and 360 rounds of 20mm were fired off. It was a good exercise that was needed to shake off the cob webs from lack of activity.

Early on the 24th, flight operations were held to launch the dawn patrol. One of the planes had trouble on takeoff and ended up in the water. The Callaghan got the rescue mission. It turned out sharply and steamed over to the sinking plane. The boat was lowered and Lt. J. S. Taylor was pulled out of the water. After the boat and pilot were aboard, the Callaghan sped away to join up with the light carrier USS Langley, Taylor's carrier. A flawless transfer was executed and a pilot was reunited with his shipmates.

The show opened early on the 25th. Once again T.G. 38.3 was east of the Philippines preparing to launch a strike against enemy airfields. Long before dawn an unidentified plane was spotted about 20 miles out. All ships immediately went to general quarters. The plane was apparently chased off by night fighters, as it never came near the ships. At the first hint of dawn it could be seen that the carrier decks were full of Hellcats, Avengers and Helldivers. Flight operations were brisk and business-like. Two major strikes were flown off that morning.

At about 10:00am enemy planes were reported closing the formation. Crews raced to battle stations again, while the formation wheeled around to head east at high speed. This course change sent the ships steaming away from the reported position of the enemy planes and also put the nose of the carriers into the wind so they could launch extra fighters. Every advantage, no matter how slight, was being sought against the deadly threat of the Kamikaze.

In a few minutes the enemy planes were upon the formation. Emergency turns by all ships were begun to throw off the aim of the enemy pilots. This time the action was on the far side of the formation so the Callaghan crew got to watch as gunners from their fellow ships tried to down diving Japanese planes. Fortunately, this time, the attack was carried out by amateurs who missed their targets.

Everyone in the formation was edgy after this attack. There were a couple of distant contacts but no further attacks developed.

The next six days was more of the same. Frequent flight operations were the norm as Task Force 38 continued to pound the Japanese airfields throughout the Philippines. The Callaghan held anti-aircraft gunnery exercises three times as the gunnery department wanted to keep everyone sharp. The Callaghan crew was not about to let some Japanese flyer who was ready to die for his emperor get lucky while they were on duty.

Toward the end of this stint off the Philippines, Captain Bertholf held Captain's mast for three of the stewards' mates. The stewards were all black as was common practice in the Navy during this segregated era. The three all got 5 extra hours of duty for showing disrespect to the chief steward's mate.

On Dec. 2nd, the Callaghan and T.G. 38.3 returned to Ulithi. This time the Callaghan was to have a stay of nine days. This was almost too long, considering the fact that the facilities were so primitive.

On Dec. 10th, Task Force 38 moved out again. General MacArthur was going to invade another island in the Philippines called Mindoro. The whole idea to securing this island was to provide airbases for army aircraft that could support the later invasion of Luzon. Luzon was the big prize but it was known to be heavily defended. It was felt that only with the help of army aircraft could adequate air coverage be provided without the huge risk of losing valuable units of Task Force 38.

In fact, the Kamikaze threat had changed several things. No longer would total reliance be put on Task Force 38 unless it was flat impossible to get army aircraft over the target. In addition, Task Force 38 was reorganized into three Task Groups instead of four. Each of the three task groups was much stronger than the old model with four or five carriers instead of three or four and a much larger number of escort vessels. In addition, each of the big Essex class carriers reduced the number of dive bombers and torpedo bombers and substituted fighters. The total maximum number of fighters was now 73 on each of those carriers.

On Dec. 10, Task Force 38 and Task Group 30.4, it's replenishment group that would support it left Ulithi. They all headed back to the Philippines. This would hopefully be the last time that Task Force 38 had to expend its power pounding airfields in the Philippines. Admiral Halsey was not eager to perform this task again. He had richer targets in mind further afield. But for now, the air threat had to be dealt with.

On the 13th T.F. 38 met with T. G. 30.4 to refuel. Most of the ships were just topping off as they had only been steaming for 3 days. The next day T.F. 38 positioned itself 200 miles to the northeast of Manila. For three days planes from T.F. 38 ranged over most of Luzon and adjacent islands preventing Japanese airpower from having any effect on the invasion of Mindoro.

That invasion went in on time on the 15th. The army was quick to consolidate its gains. Meanwhile the carrier planes of T.F. 38 were suffering losses from three days of strikes against ground targets all over the Philippines. Not one plane was known to be lost to an enemy fighter plane. Despite this, 54 planes were lost to antiaircraft fire, accidents and simply running out of fuel. Admiral Halsey was very aware of this and was anxious to replace his losses.

During the evening of Dec. 16th, T.F. 38 turned southeast to steam to the designated rendezvous with T.G. 30.4 for refueling and replacement planes. T.G. 30.4 was over two hundred miles distant. The previous three days of flight operations had seriously depleted the fuel of the escorting destroyers. A few of the destroyers were down to only 15% fuel capacity. Unfortunately due to the distance involved and necessary maneuvering of the two formations of ships, refueling could not be started until mid-morning the following day.

At 11:00am refueling was begun by tankers of T.G. 30.4. At the same time, Halsey's battleships were attempting to refuel destroyers who were critically low on fuel. Halsey's flag ship, the USS New Jersey attempted to refuel the Fletcher class destroyer USS Spence. By this time the cross chop of the waves and the rising winds made refueling extremely difficult.

The Spence should have had it easier than most, as the New Jersey was the largest ship available to refuel from. The New Jersey's large mass and high freeboard meant that it had a better chance of creating a lee for the Spence from the increasing winds. Despite this, the Spence was in for a wild ride. Halsey himself observed the Spence while he had lunch in the flag mess. The pitching and rolling of the Spence was so great that many aboard the New Jersey thought that the Spence would collide with the great battleship.

In the end the Spence was only able to take aboard 6000 gallons of fuel, a very small amount for a fleet destroyer. Most of the other destroyers trying to refuel that day experienced the same thing. Some of them even tried to refuel from astern of their assigned tankers. This method proved no more successful that the along-side method. There simply was too much wind and unfavorable waves to allow refueling on that date at that particular location in the ocean.

The Callaghan meanwhile had been standing by, waiting. It was scheduled to go in next as soon as the destroyer currently refueling from its assigned tanker was finished. The Callaghan never got the chance. At 3:30 in the afternoon refueling operations were canceled. Admiral Halsey set a new rendezvous point for refueling to commence first thing in the morning of the 18th. On advice from his meteorologist, he ordered a northwesterly course for the fleet. It was decided that there was a tropical storm to the southeast of the fleet and that a northwesterly course would have the best chance of taking the fleet away from the track of the storm.

Aboard the Callaghan, Captain Bertholf requested that the officers see to it that everything be tied down or otherwise secured in preparation for rough weather. There had already been a great deal of severe pitching and rolling experienced. The officers and Chiefs began taking precautions throughout the ship to prevent damage to equipment and increase the safety of the crew.

That evening the bunks of the crew were triced which means they were tied or hung at an angle to help prevent the sailor in the bunk from falling out. It had to be uncomfortable but the ship was being tossed about so much that it probably didn't matter. Sailors on watch topside were required to wear life jackets. Lifelines were rigged on the weather deck so the men would have something to hold on to while going back and forth from the aft end of the ship to the forward.

During the night, Captain Bertholf was awakened by a sudden roll the ship took. He decided that refueling in the morning was going to be impossible. He made what was perhaps the most intelligent decision of his career. He called up the Chief Engineer, Frank Dunne, and told him to ballast the ship with seawater.

Warships such as the Callaghan had large bunkers to hold the fuel oil that gave them long endurance at sea. It was normal practice to keep the bunkers reserved for fuel oil only. Sea water could be let into the bunkers but most Naval officers were reluctant to do so for fear of contaminating the fuel. If sea water got into the feed lines that ran to the boilers, the fires could go out and the source of power suddenly lost. But the bunkers were located low in the ship's hull and therefore were low in relation to the center of gravity of the ship.

If the bunkers were empty the ship would ride high in the water. The higher the ship rode in the water, the easier it would be for wind and waves to push the ship over. Normally a destroyer was subject to a lot of roll compared to larger warships. If the ship rode too high and the wind/wave action combined to produce an extremely powerful push against the side of the light ship it could roll the side away from the wind down into the sea itself. If the ship was unable to right itself, it would capsize and eventually sink.

The next morning, Task Force 38 once again rendezvoused with the supply task group. Both groups had to turn to a course of 60 degrees True (northeast) to attempt refueling. Any maneuvering of any kind was becoming increasingly difficult due to the monster waves that were threatening all ships. These waves were estimated to be as high as 40 to 50 feet at dawn and they were getting bigger as each hour passed!

On the Callaghan, sailors continued to take what precautions they could to prevent damage to the ship and crew from the storm. Captain Bertholf was convinced that refueling attempts would be useless and he informed the escort commander by radio that the Callaghan was not immediately available for refueling. The Callaghan stood by while other destroyers fought to get into position to refuel.

An hour and ten minutes later, Admiral Halsey realized that the situation was hopeless and that the fleet was going to have to put all of its effort into fighting the storm. The fleet was ordered to change course to due south. Each task group came around to the new heading with extreme difficulty. Destroyers and other escort vessels were unable to retain their assigned positions in each group.

The fact was that each task group was losing its integrity. The largest ships were able to maintain position and heading but only with difficulty. Smaller ships including many cruisers and light carriers were not able to maintain position for very long. Destroyers found themselves out of position and completely unable to increase speed enough to compensate. The wind and waves pounded the destroyers with great force even when the ship was moving at low speeds. Higher speeds meant serious instability, severe pounding and increasing amounts of damage.

The Callaghan was in for the fight of its life. All watches were canceled except those absolutely necessary for the operation of the ship. Everyone else was told to stay below and avoid any exposed deck. Many of the men were advised by their chiefs to stay in their bunks. Normal routine such as meals was canceled. Many of the men could not eat anyway. Simple movement became dangerous, as at any time the ship could lurch so severely that a sailor would be thrown against equipment before he could catch himself. There were many minor injuries among the crew.

On the bridge it was up to Captain Bertholf and the helmsman to save the ship. The helmsman clung to the ship's wheel, which made it difficult to operate it properly. How do you spin a wheel rapidly when you are clinging to it? Captain Bertholf had to hang on to various pieces of equipment to keep from losing his feet. It was made more difficult for Bertholf, due to the fact that he had a tall, skinny frame. During the worst times, he had to wrap his arms around something to hold on. In the meantime the task was ship handling at its very worst.

After Halsey gave up on refueling, the fleet course was set to due south. The wind and the waves were coming from the northeast. The southerly course put the wind a little behind the port (left) side of the ship. Further the direction of the storm was slowly changing as the center of the storm drew closer and closer to the fleet. Eventually Halsey told every ship to steer its own best course while trying to avoid collision with other units of the fleet.

The wind and waves pushed the ship over to starboard. Therefore the rolling movement to starboard was more severe than the opposite rolls to port. The helmsman found it increasingly difficult to keep course. The rudder movements required to correct the course of the ship became larger. The force of the wind and waves was becoming more powerful than the rudder. Aggravating the situation was the fact that the rudder was far less effective when the ship was rolled way over.

As the size of the waves and the depth of the valleys in-between grew throughout the day, strange things occurred that were never seen before on the Callaghan. Some waves buried the ship in water up to the level of the bridge. Anyone standing out on the main deck or the weather deck (above the main deck) would have been instantly crushed or washed overboard. Conversely, there were times when the aft end of the ship came so far out of the water that the rudder became useless and the helmsman noticed that all feeling went out of the wheel on the bridge. At the same time the propellers spun madly since there was no water resistance to slow them down to normal speed. Maneuvering became almost impossible.

At times a sailor or two would find a protected place topside where they could watch the raging storm. What they saw was awe inspiring. The sight of the waves towering as high as the top of the mast was both thrilling and terrifying. Other ships close enough to be in sight despite the low visibility would disappear completely when the Callaghan was in a trough between the waves. Coupled with the extreme difficulty that most of the ships were having with maneuvering, the danger of collision was added to the list of possible disasters.

The destroyer took a fearful pounding. Any object inside the ship that was not tied down or fastened in some way was either smashed or became a missile for the sailors to dodge. It became a burden to grab such objects and tie them down but it often had to be done for the safety of the men. But it was not at all safe for the poor sailor who got the nod to capture and hog-tie the offending object. It was risky to simply try to stand on the pitching deck. To let go with even one hand to try to grab something was tempting fate!

The slamming and the terrible body blows the waves made against the top and sides of the ship did take their toll. Certain pyrotechnic and depth charge equipment was damaged or smashed over the side. In retrospect, it is a wonder that more damage was not done. Larger ships including four light carriers and four escort carriers suffered more severe damage.

The men grew exhausted. It was next to impossible to sleep. To stay in a bunk required hanging on with a death grip. As soon as a man would let go, he would be thrown up against the bunk overhead or out of the bunk altogether. At least one sailor tried to tie himself into his bunk.

At the height of the storm, the Callaghan's rolling took on a terrifying new edge. When the rolling went past 60 degrees off the vertical, the ship would hang in the rolled over state for long frightening moments. The crew began to wonder if the ship would fail to roll back. The horrible prospect of capsizing in the middle of a typhoon became suddenly real to the crew. They all knew that such a catastrophe would mean certain death for most of the men.

In the meantime, Frank Dunne's black gang were faced with a diminishing fuel supply. Just after the peak of the storm, it became clear that the fuel oil was going to run out. Frank and his chiefs made plans to switch the fuel lines over to the diesel oil tank. Every modern warship carried diesel fuel to run an auxiliary generator in case the normal generators tied in to the power plant failed. In the Callaghan's case, there was about 7000 gallons of diesel oil aboard for this use. 7000 gallons wasn't much for a warship with a capacity of over 160,000 gallons of fuel oil. But it might be just enough to last until they could finally refuel from a tanker. In any case, it was the last card they had to play.

Finally, at about 3:00pm in the afternoon on the 18th things started to improve. The weather was still bad but the rolling was no longer threatening to push the Callaghan over to never return. However, the rolling was still dangerous to the bodies of the sailors inside the ship!

There was now time to pay attention to the radio messages coming through from other ships in the fleet. Many were reporting men overboard. There was still no hope of rescuing such men but the chief bosun was directed to post a couple of sailors so that they could throw life rings to anyone they saw in the water. The lucky sailors were lashed down near the aft end of the ship where they could carry out this duty.

What the crew of the Callaghan did not know was that three destroyers had been sunk by the storm. In fact, no-one in Task Force 38 knew of the disaster until the morning of the 19th. Although radio messages had been received from two of those destroyers indicating trouble, no message had been received indicating the ships were sinking. One can only guess that the ability to transmit radio communications was lost at the same time the ships started sinking.

The day after the great typhoon devastated T.F. 38, the Callaghan prepared to finally refuel. The Callaghan waited for its turn and then went alongside the tanker Marias (AO57).

With some urgency, the deck crew under the watchful eyes of the Bosuns took the hoses aboard and connected them to the fuel bunkers. Since the bunkers were empty, this was the greatest load of fuel oil the Callaghan would ever take aboard; at total of 2988 barrels of crude. In addition, for the first time at sea, the Callaghan took aboard a couple of thousand gallons of diesel fuel to replace the diesel that had been used when the normal fuel oil had run out.

On the 19th, Halsey sent most of the damaged ships back to Ulithi. After it was realized that three destroyers were missing, an extensive search for survivors began. The waves were still higher than normal which hampered efforts to find men floating on the sea. In the end, only 255 men were rescued from the three warships. A total of over 700 men were lost as a result of the typhoon.

On the 20th, Halsey made an attempt to go back on station for further strikes against the Philippines. But poor weather and the discovery of additional damage on some ships caused the proposed strikes to be canceled. Halsey had to give up the attempt, and radioed a message to General McArthur that he was unable to provide any more support to the army at that time. Task Force 38 turned back to return to Ulithi.

T.G. 38.3 and the Callaghan arrived back in Ulithi on the morning of Christmas eve, 1944. After entering the great lagoon, the Callaghan steamed over to the side of the tanker Manater. Once moored alongside, the Callaghan proceeded to top off with 936 barrels of fuel, a pittance compared to the huge amount taken on the 19th. Next the destroyer was off to find the ammunition ship Nitro. From the Nitro came replacement ammunition for the rounds fired off in gunnery practice.

The Callaghan received word that it would receive an availability in one of the floating drydocks the next day, Christmas day. It was ordered to prepare for this event immediately.

The Navy was putting small ships through the drydock in just 24 hours. Such would be the Callaghan's experience. With only minor damage from the typhoon and normal maintenance required on the bottom of the hull, the Callaghan would be given just Christmas day. Then the drydock would be made available to the next ship in need.

Because of the short time allowed, Captain Bertholf made it clear that every man aboard would be required to help with the maintenance duties. That included officers. Officers would be supervisors where needed and pitch in with the manual labor if a supervisor was not needed.

On Christmas morning the Callaghan got under way. It steamed slowly across the Ulithi anchorage to the destroyer tender Dixie and its destroyer nest. The Callaghan moored alongside its fellow Fletcher class DD, the Dortch. A sailor was sent over for confinement aboard the Dixie. Another was sent a couple of hours later for medical treatment.

At 3:30 in the afternoon the Callaghan got underway from alongside the Dortch. For the first time since commissioning, the Callaghan was under tow. Two tugs towed the Callaghan over to the floating drydock. It was considered safer for these experienced tugs to put the Callaghan into the drydock. At 4:05pm, the bow of the Callaghan eased over the sill of the drydock and the first lines were thrown over.

With lines between the ship and the drydock, it became an easy matter to put the Callaghan in the precise position required exactly over the submerged wooden blocks that would hold the ship up once all the water was pumped out. Thirty minutes later the pumping was begun to empty out the drydock. At the same time, the remaining fires were put out beneath the only boiler still operating on the Callaghan. Electrical lines and water lines were connected from the drydock to provide life to the ship.

Work began as soon as the water was out of the drydock. Lines were rigged and platforms put over the side of the ship. One of the most distasteful tasks in the US Navy was about to begin. The ship was to be chipped and scraped to remove the old paint and rust from the steel plates of the hull.

Scaffolding was draped all around both sides of the ship. Sailors were soon hard at work with hammer, chisels and scrapers of various kinds. As each area within reach was prepared, the planks would be moved. The sailors found the chipping and scrapping to be hard, dirty work.

Even though the Callaghan had only been commissioned thirteen months ago, the hull had picked up an incredible number of barnacles. These little sea creatures that resemble

231

shellfish, fasten themselves to anything in the sea. Thousands of them will fasten to any ship in just a few short months. Since the thousands of little shells on the surface of the hull increase the drag of the water against that hull, they decrease the speed of the ship.

It's difficult to describe or imagine how hard it was to chip and scrape the hull. The sailors had no power tools. All of the work was done by hand. It was probably like preparing a house for painting, except that this house is all metal, covered with barnacles, and you have to finish the whole job in just a few hours.

Once the chipping and scraping was finished, the painting began. The standard Navy grey paint was provided in dozens of 5 gallon buckets. Large paint brushes replaced the hammers and chisels used earlier. The object here was not to do a "neat" job. The object was to do a thorough job but as quickly as possible. As a result, it was very messy.

Sailors soon had paint all over themselves and anyone else who was in the area. Even the first Lieutenant, "Buzz" Buzzetti had paint spilled on him from an over-zealous sailor. But the result was a 376 foot long hull with a shiny new paint job in just a few hours.

The crew was probably too beat to care, but Captain Bertholf was pleased. No Captain wants to command a "rust bucket." The Callaghan was once again looking like the fast "In Harm's Way" kind of warship that she really was!

Over the next 3 days, more routine maintenance and resupply was taken care of. One of the surprises that showed up during this time was cold weather clothing. The crew had not seen cold weather gear since the Callaghan had left the west coast in Feb. of '44. Speculation was rampant on what this meant. Some sailors even insisted they would be going to Japan!

On the morning of December 30, the Callaghan, along with all the other ships of Task Force 38 prepared to leave on what promised to be a really big mission. As had been mentioned before, all of the carriers had been changing their air groups to increase the numbers of fighters aboard. For the first time since early 1943, a new fighter type was coming aboard the big carriers. The vaunted Hellcat was no longer going to be the only day fighter flying from the fleet carriers. The famous F4U Corsair was joining the fleet!

There were a couple of reasons for putting Corsair fighters on the big carriers along with the Hellcats. First, since the decision to put 72 fighters aboard each Essex class carrier was nearly double the number previously shipped, the Navy was having a hard time coming up with enough combat ready Hellcat squadrons to fill the need. Equally as important as the potential shortfall was the fact that the Navy was looking for a faster fighter. The one drawback to the Hellcat was the fact that it was one of the slowest of the second generation World War II fighters that the US was using. With the recent use by Japan of fighter planes converted for Kamikaze use, it was essential to have fast interceptions. Stopping a Zero fighter equipped with a bomb required much more speed than stopping a slow torpedo bomber loaded with a one ton torpedo.

The Corsair was almost 60 knots faster than a Hellcat. It became famous for speed before Pearl Harbor when it set the record as the first US single engined fighter to exceed 400 mph in level flight. It had also earned a reputation for being a hard hitter when flown by the Marines in the Solomon Islands campaign. The Corsair had not been used on US Navy carriers due to the high number of landing accidents experienced with the plane in early carrier qualification tests. It had also been decided to stick with one fighter for the big carriers in order to simplify logistics and maintenance.

Now the need for speed and more fighters overcame the initial objections of the Navy's air bosses. One of the first big carriers to receive the Corsair was the Callaghan's old friend, the Essex. Air Group 4, which was now aboard the Essex, had its fighter strength increased with the addition of two squadrons of Corsairs. Not only were these two squadrons equipped with a new fighter but they were also manned by pilots new to the fleet. The pilots were all Marines!

Task Force 38 headed north toward Formosa. In prepartion for the coming big invasion of Luzon, it was imperative that the airfields on Formosa be neutralised. The threat of Kamakazes was so great that a special joint effort was planned against Formosa. Along with the carrier planes from T.F. 38, the Army Air Force was going to send in planes from China as well.

New Year's eve came with the Callaghan on the job screening the big ships from whatever danger might be ahead. This New Year's eve was much different than the last one spent pierside on the West coast of the States.

Instead of being a brand new ship with a raw, green crew, the Callaghan was now a well broken in ship with a highly experienced, combat sharpened , veteran crew. Although the crew was vigilant while performing their duty, there was a relaxed atmosphere around the ship that was due to Captain Berholf's firm but friendly leadership style. Lastly, the war had changed dramatically in one year. It was now clear to the world that Germany and Japan were losing the war. The only question now was how long they could hold out.

Captain Bertholf's relaxation of the rules led directly to a most interesting log entry for the first watch of 1945. For the first and last time, the entry was in prose!

Old Year Out, the New Year In,
This is the thought - where do we begin?

Steering as before - Task Group 38.3
ComScreen and 55 in the PORTERFIELD together
Steaming along in the beautiful weather.
Our station is one, we're just passing through
But look who's on deck - its the best he can do.

Fourteen tin cans holding down circle nine
origin 180 degrees - C. K. BRONSON behind.
ComScreen has left with some engine trouble
but we expect by dawn she'll be back "on the double".

Formation axis is one double O
(the reason for entry I do not know).
Base course 295 pgc and true.
Checks 289 - whichmeans psc to you.
Our speed is 25, but I'm not very sure.
For the hoist has been read by our signalman MUHR.
On the main steam line, two boilers are steaming,
that, I presume if the firemen aren't dreaming.
The fires burn bright under boilers one and three.
Material "Baker" set -- that's what they tell me.
The formation is darkened and so are we.
With condition three set in each battery.
To be in the states this year is the OOD's wish,
and leave this simple rhyme to the digestion of fish.
At 0025 we changed course and speed,
It's now three zero five -- we're in the lead.
It checks 297 - speed now 22,
We may stay on station -- if the helmsman steers true.

R.B. Sheffield
Ensign, USNR

This first mission of 1945 against Formosa was the beginning of a long, nightmarish campaign to prepare for the twin invasions of Luzon in the Philippines and Iwo Jima in the Bonin island group. This campaign was extremely important to the war effort against Japan. First and foremost, it would keep the Kamikaze threat from delaying these invasions. It would also disrupt the Japanese convoy system linking Japan's remaining possessions and conquered territory with Japan itself.

The campaign was a nightmare for the ships of T.F. 38 for several reasons. To begin with, there was the ever present fear of the kamikazes. The whole fleet knew that the first priority of the kamikazes was to hit the American fleet carriers. This meant that the maximum effort would be aimed directly at T.F. 38.

Next was the absysmal weather. Although the typhoon in December was more dangerous, it had lasted only about two days. The first two months of 1945 saw endless weeks of poor weather in the Western Pacific ocean area. This period of duty became somewhat like the duty in the North Atlantic where long lasting stormy weather was expected. Such weather was very fatigiung for the crews of the smaller escort vessels which were so prone to violent rolling and pitching.

Another stress factor for this campaign was the fact that T.F. 38 steamed all the way from Japan in the far north to Saigon, Vietnam in the far south. These distant forays took the ships of TF 38 far from their supporting bases. If something broke or a ship suffered damage by enemy action, there was not simply an option of detaching the troubled ship for a one or two day trip back to the fleet anchorage at Ulithi. Steaming time back to Ulithi was around four days for most of this campaign.

The task force was totally dependent on the at-sea service task group, ServRon 6, to provide support. The ships became very self reliant out of sheer necessity. A mechanical breakdown meant, for the smaller ships, the possibility of being left behind thousands of miles from friendly territory.

What made this tiring duty more difficult was the nature of the fighting. There was no feeling of the fair fight enjoyed during the Saipan campaign. There the Japanese planes flew in during daylight and fair weather to try to bomb the American ships. Here the Kamikazes were trying to sneak in under bad weather or by hiding behind returning US carrier planes to make a sudden high-speed dive into the side of one of the carriers.

It is much easier to fight against a slow flying torpedo plane of a high flying dive bomber than a fast fighter plane with bomb strapped underneath. The fighter (usually a zero) was likely to burst out of a cloud bank to dive at full speed with no intention to pull out. This meant that the ship's gunners basically had one chance with much less time to gun down the speeding plane. Merely hitting the plane was not enough. The kamikaze pilot intended to die anyway, so mere damage to his plane would have no effect. If he retained any control of his plane at all, he would continue the dive straight into his target.

One of the precautions taken to try to reduce the kamikaze threat was to man part of each ship's anti-aircraft guns during all daylight hours. This was, of course, in addition to the time spent at general quarters when all guns were manned. As a result, gunners were spending long hours at their guns, day after day, week after week. This was boring duty for the gunners and meant that they had less time to fulfill their regular duties. Since these duties were necessary (the unnecessary ones having been done away with long ago), other sailors usually had to take these on. Everyone's work load was increased to compensate.

From this point on in the war, there was considerable concern from the lowest ranks all the way up to the Chief of Naval Operations over the exhaustion factor with the surface navy in the combat zones. A lot of suggestions were made regarding various manning schemes. For the Callaghan, as for most destroyers, the emphasis was put on doing required activities while letting the optional or infrequent activities slide.

One of the shifts in emphasis for destroyer gunnery departments was to the put the manpower in support of the anti-aircraft guns. The torpedo gang found themselves reassigned to the 20mm or 40mm guns. Only the torpedo directors remained manned during alerts but, in reality, these positions were used as communication posts now. Since the torpedos were no longer manned, there was no point in setting up firing solutions on non-existant targets. The torpedo gang were now reassigned as loaders for the 20mm guns. Frequent gunnery drills were held to make sure that everyone knew their new tasks.

On the night of January 2nd, Task Force 38 began a high speed run to close the distance with Formosa.

This was the standard tactic to try to surprise the enemy and prevent spoiling attacks by Japanese bombers. The Callaghan put all four boilers on line and steamed 26 knots all night long.

Early the next morning the various task groups turned into the wind. The big carriers started launching the planes for the first strike. The sailors on the Callaghan noticed that there were only fighters taking off. But most of the fighters were armed with either rockets or a bomb so they would be directly attacking Japanese airfields and shipping.

Setting the pattern for most of the rest of this mission, the weather did not cooperate. The strikes had to fly through cloud fronts, often relying on their instruments to navigate. The Japanese fighter forces on Luzon did put up resistance. The American Hellcat fighters had their usual one-sided victory in downing at least ten Japanese fighters for the loss of only one of their own.

There was no followup that afternoon as the weather turned worse. Reconnaissance flights were flown both to check the weather and to assess damage from the morning strikes. At dusk, the great task force steamed away from Formosa for a few hours while the air staff planned strikes for the next morning.

Within minutes after the formation turned to a heading away from Formosa, the Callaghan crew received a scare they weren't expecting in these open waters. A mine was spotted floating dead ahead.

There was no time for any manevering, as a turn would have caused the destroyer to swing its stern directly in the path of the mine. Fortunately the bow wave seemed to push the mine away, and it just barely missed striking the stern. The Callaghan made a sharp turn, once clear of the mine, with the intention of destroying it with gunfire. But the mine was lost in the increasing darkness of the evening and the Callaghan was ordered to return to the formation.

Just before 1:00am, a bogie closed in on the Callaghan's formation, T.G. 38.3. The Callaghan went to General Quarters. The ships remained at G.Q. for 50 minutes until the night fighters finally chased the Japanese plane away. Sleep was thoroughly interrupted and the remainder of the night was too short to make it up.

The next morning new strikes were flown off against Formosa again. These strikes had even less success than the previous day's strikes, due to the absymal weather. When the morning strikes were evaluated, it was decided to give up on Formosa for now and head back to the Philippines.

But while that evaluation was going on, things got exciting aboard the Callaghan. At 11:42am, a mine was sighted off to the right of the ship. The Callaghan left formation to destroy the mine. One minute later, while the Callaghan was still turning toward the mine, an enemy bomber was sighted directly over the formation of ships. All ships went to General Quarters.

The combat air patrol was on the job and Hellcat fighters pounced on the enemy bomber. It was last seen fleeing at top speed with fighters on its tail. Consequently, the Callaghan was free to deal with the mine. Captain Bertholf skillfully maneuvered the Callaghan to within easy shooting range but not too close. The 40mm guns opened up and blew up the mine after firing only 39 rounds. The Callaghan still had its gunnery skill honed to a fine edge.

Less than an hour later, Task Force 38 turned away and headed southeast. The rest of the day was spent in watchful vigilance while the ships steamed away from Formosa at high cruising speed. The seas got progressively rougher as evening drew close. Word came that six mines had been spotted by other ships. There was tension among the topside sailors as the officers and chiefs made sure the lookouts stayed sharp. Even the officers were frequently seen scanning the sea and sky with binoculars.

The evening and the night were uneventful. Early in the morning preparations began for refueling as the formation rendezvoused with the tanker support group. In mid-morning the Callaghan refueled from the Merrimac and took aboard 1798 barrels of oil. Mail was also received from the destroyer Preston later in the day.

At about 7:00pm that evening, the Callaghan put all four boilers on line to prepare for the high speed run toward Luzon. After steaming southeast for most of the last 24 hours, the formation now headed almost due west. They had made an end run around the northern end of Luzon and were now steaming in to be within strike range of the Clark air field complex and Manila area by dawn.

The approach was flawless as no enemy aircraft or submarines were detected anywhere near the carrier groups. On the morning of the 6th, the now standard heavy fighter sweeps were launched against the Japanese airfields. However, once again the weather prevented the fighters from instituting the "big blue blanket" over all the enemy airfields.

The cloud layers were thick and low; in one area as low as 200 feet. Some action was generated with 14 enemy planes claimed as shot down and another 18 claimed on the ground. But this was nothing compared to the air battles of the last 4 months of 1944. The weather forced the Navy planes so low that one F6F returned after a strafing mission near Manila with mud splattered on its undersides!

The poor weather apparently kept the enemy planes from finding the American fleet as no significant contacts were made all day. It was an unexpected break since the carrier groups were so close to enemy bases.

The seventh brought better visibility over Luzon but Mother nature balanced this with rough seas and high wind in the area where the carriers were operating. Eighteen Navy planes were lost in accidents that day. It would have been a perfect time for the enemy to retaliate against the carriers but they failed to show up. One possible reason why was that the "big blue blanket" was working again. Only 4 enemy planes were shot out of the air. Most of the enemy planes never got off the ground due to the American planes flying overhead.

Back on the Callaghan, Captain Bertholf was getting bold. Though they were operating in enemy waters not far from dozens of enemy airbases, the Captain called an abandon ship drill in the middle of the morning! Perhaps the Captain wanted to know what he was supposed to do if the worst occurred.

A little before one in the afternoon, the Callaghan steamed alongside its old friend the Battleship Washington to prepare to refuel. The two ships never got the chance to transfer anything. The seas were moderately rough. On this campaign, the bosuns had the deck crew wear both lifejackets and life-belts as a precaution against a mishap. Thank God for their foresight. As the crew struggled to get lines across between the ships, the bow wave from the big battleship hit the Callaghan just at the wrong moment. The Callaghan had just taken one of those downward pitches that destroyers were so prone to. The combination of the downward pitch of the destroyer combined with the arrival of the bow wave from the battlewagon sent three men over the side and into the sea.

One of the men, Witkowski, was washed back up alongside the ship with the next wave and grabbed by fellow sailors. In the process he received a broken arm and leg. He was carried off to sick bay.

Meanwhile, Captain Bertholf reacted immediately. He signaled a break away to the big Battleship and then turned the destroyer on its heel to go back to rescue his crewmen still in the water. Luckily the floating men were visible most of the time. When the Callaghan had completed its loop and was coming up on the men, life rings on ropes were prepared to throw to the men.

Captain Bertholf stopped the Callaghan just short of the men in the water. The life rings were thrown to the sailors in the water repeatedly with no success. The men were struggling with the wind and waves. They were either not able to hold on to the life rings or were not able to swim the short distance to grab one.

Bosun Jacobson sized up the situation and decided that action was called for. There was a harness available that was sometimes used for such situations. He put it on the harness, which was then tied to a line connected to a winch. He then took off his shoes and jumped in. He attempted to swim to the two sailors who were clinging together in the water but before he got there he found that the line tied around him pulled him up short. He yelled at his fellow sailors back on the Callaghan to give him some slack.

Either the winch was not keeping up with Jacobson or there was not enough line on it during this first attempt. In any case, Jacobson soon found himself exhausted by the attempt to swim through the waves to the sailors. Finally, he pulled the harness off and swam to the nearest floating lifejacket. He found himself in the same difficulty as the overboard sailors.

Part of the problem was that, in completing a loop, the Callaghan had come up to the water-logged sailors from down-wind. While the destroyer was stopped, rolling back and forth, the wind was slowly pushing it away from the sailors in the water.

After Jacobson successfully got a life jacket on and started floating along with the overboard sailors, another sailor stepped forward to volunteer for the rescue effort. Leo Jarboe seemed an unlikely candidate. Only age 19, he was a likeable fellow but short in height and light in weight. Yet he had been a lifeguard for several years while in school and had instructed classes in life saving. He had received national recognition for his success in youth water safety programs.

The line was tied on Jarboe this time and he dove in. With powerful measured strokes, he set out for the two sailors who were floating together. He reached the two men and got a grip on them both. The winch was then used to pull the three back to the ship. After the three were pulled aboard, the ship was maneuvered to pick up Jacobson.

It took forty long minutes with those difficulties to rescue the men overboard. It was remarkable that the two men were found and rescued. Once again the Callaghan's professional and well-trained crew came through.

B. Witkowski had suffered a badly broken arm and leg when he was slammed against the side of the ship. As a result, later that afternoon, the Callaghan went alongside the Battleship North Carolina to transfer Witkowski for medical treatment. The refueling was postponed.

Task Group 38 changed course to the southwest. It had been decided that Luzon could be left alone for a couple of days. The next target would be Formosa again.

But first it was necessary to continue the refueling. Admiral Halsey was being careful to keep his escorts refueled since the debacle of the December Typhoon. The heavy weather had prevented several ships, not just the Callaghan, from refueling on the 7th.

Not long after sunrise and breakfast, the Callaghan proceeded to get into position where it could join with a tanker for refueling. At 8:40am it was astern of the tanker Manatee. Another ship was alongside the tanker so the Callaghan spent over an hour steaming slowly along behind. Finally at 10 minutes before 10:00 it was the Callaghan's turn.

Fueling was accomplished with hoses both fore and aft. The weather was better, so the fueling went flawlessly with 1285 barrels taken aboard. When finished, the Callaghan peeled off to take station number four in the escort screen.

The rest of the day was a bore as the rest of the ships were refueled. In mid-afternoon the Callaghan received mail from fellow destroyer, Pritchett. Flight operations were accomplished just before dusk.

With the sun down, Task Force 38 turned northwest and cranked up the speed. It was another high speed run into the target area. Shortly the black gang was called upon to light off all four boilers and get maximum steam available again.

Long before dawn, flight operations began. It was another typical strike day for the Callaghan. Frequent flight operations meant sudden changes in direction for the formation along with an increase in speed. The destroyers always had to maneuver like crazy at higher speeds than the carriers in order to maintain position in the outer screen. It was actually quite dangerous for the unwary destroyer as a carrier could turn to a course that would cause it to steam right at the destroyer. One of the famous photographs from the Pacific war at this time shows a Fletcher-class destroyer boiling along at flank speed while it crossed in front of one of the big Essex-class carriers.

The strikes on Formosa were mostly disappointing. It appeared that the Japanese were avoiding aerial combat while at the same time going to great trouble to disperse and hide their aircraft on the ground. Dummy aircraft made of wood were now appearing in numbers around the various airfields. But all of this meant that the Japanese were not able to mount any offensive operations of their own. So the purpose of protecting the Army's invasion of Luzon was accomplished.

At this point Admiral Halsey decided that the purpose of protecting the Luzon invasion was fulfilled. He now set in motion a raid that he had requested of Nimitz during Nimitz' visit to Ulithi around Christmas. The Admirals knew that the Japanese fleet was basically defeated. But significant remnants still remained in two places. Halsey couldn't do much about the fleet elements in Japan, but he could go after the battleships which intelligence said were in the South China Sea based in Vietnam.

Once again he was breaking new ground. No American carriers had ever been to Vietnam. This area had been a Japanese enclave since mid 1941. Only American submarines had been able to penetrate the South China Sea after the disastrous early days of 1942. Now, with Halsey in charge, the Americans would come roaring back.

The long run to the southwest took three days. The only break in the high speed cruise was refueling on the 11th. The Callaghan took 1775 barrels of oil from the battleship North Carolina. The Callghan immediately steamed away to patrol as soon as the refueling hoses from the battleship were clear.

On the 12th of January, Task Force 38 stood off Camranh Bay. The Callaghan's Task Unit 38.3 was only 50 miles east of the coast of Vietnam.

The 14 fleet carriers sent off wave after wave of blue planes. Although Halsey was eager to find the Imperial Japanese fleet units that were thought to be in the area, he was to be disappointed again. Those units had prudently withdrawn to the Singapore area. Despite this, the planes found good hunting with all the small warships and maritime ships in the area. Over 40 were attacked during their stay in this area.

The air opposition was very weak. About 15 planes were shot down that day. Dozens were shot up on the ground. At this stage in the war, it was becoming obvious to everyone that the Japanese were beaten. They could no longer conduct offensive action of any kind. The Kamikazes were a terrible threat but only as a defensive weapon.

Since no major fleet units were found, Halsey decided to get back up to the Philippines area to support MacArthur's landings on Luzon. Therefore during the night Task Force 38 withdrew to the northeast.

On the 13th it was time to refuel once again. The Callaghan lined up behind the Aucilla. The weather had turned rough again and the deck force had real trouble with the refueling hoses. First the forward hose parted and then the aft hose parted. After getting a thousand barrels aboard, the forward hose parted again and Captain Bertholf called it quits. The Callaghan had enough fuel to get through a couple of days of normal cruising. Since not all of the warships had been able to fuel, there would be another chance for the Callaghan the next day.

That is exactly what happened. The weather was noticeably better when refueling recommenced. The Callaghan stood guard while all the remaining ships fueled. When the last ship was done, the Callaghan went alongside the tanker, Neches. The Callaghan topped off with another 542 barrels of Navy oil.

Two hours later, the tankers left and it was off to the races again for Task Force 38. They were heading back to familiar territory. The air action planned for the 15th included Formosa again. There was a difference though. This time they were coming in from a new direction. The Task Force would be located to the southwest of Formosa. The planes would fly to the northeast to strike the Formosa airfields once again.

Because of the location of the Task Force roughly between the China coast and Formosa, an opportunity to strike in two directions was present. Admiral Halsey was never one to miss out on an opportunity! In the morning, strikes would go in both directions.

Nothing of great consequence occurred over Formosa that day. The Japanese air forces were laying low. The strike that covered the China coast, however, turned up something interesting. The squadron leader of VF 11, Gene Fairfax, was leading a group of Hellcats about 50 miles east of Hong Kong when he ran into a Japanese transport plane with an escort of 4 Zeros.

Fairfax correctly guessed that the transport with an escort of fighters was carrying a VIP. He ordered his division of Hellcats to take out the escorting Zeros first. He shot one of the Zeros down himself while the other 3 were flamed by his wingmates. Fairfax and his wingman then leisurely riddled the transport with their .50 caliber guns. It was a complete victory. Intelligence later revealed that the Japanese Admiral commanding the South China Sea frontier was aboard.

On the 16th Hong Kong itself was attacked for the first time in the war by American carrier planes. It proved to be a tough target. Many valuable tanker and cargo ships were in the harbor protected by a forest of anti-aircraft guns. Task Force 38 lost 22 planes that day, mostly due to the anti-aircraft fire over Hong Kong. But in return, the Japanese paid dearly in ships that they could not replace and were fast running out of.

Late in the afternoon, one of the planes among the 22 ditched in the water about 18 miles away from T.G. 38.3. The Callaghan got the order to retrieve the crew of the divebomber. Captain Bertholf soon had the Callaghan alongside of the rubber life raft containing the airmen. The whaleboat was lowered and the two flyers were soon aboard. The Callaghan returned to the carrier formation with Lt. (jg) E.S. Binder and airmen R.D. Biddle as guests.

Less than two hours later, the Callaghan received the Porterfield astern to pass a spare radar part. This was an example of the "make do" spirit required with these long operations thousands of miles away from base. The ships shared the resources they had in order to keep combat efficiency as high as possible.

That night, just before midnight, the Callaghan left to join the picket station 12 miles from the carriers.
This was a regular event now whenever the fleet was in enemy waters, especially since the Kamikaze threat had become so strong.. Still it was exciting for the Callaghan crew to be out in front where the action was likely to start. The picket station was designed to pick up any incoming enemy aircraft early. Therefore, being in that position meant that the crew would know first if radar had bogies on the screen.

The Callaghan rejoined the screen before dawn. The 17th was another refueling day for Task Group 38.3 but not for the Callaghan. The Callaghan spent most of the day picking up passengers from various ships and transferring them to various other ships. This made the Callaghan one of the largest taxis in the world! The weather was rough again so these ship-to-ship transfers challenged the deck crew. Despite their best efforts, some of the transferees got wet.

The next three days were more of the same; lots of high speed cruising, flight ops and one of the usual refuelings. It was all becoming a blur.

On the 21st, the Task Force was once again off Formosa, this time 100 miles. Strikes went in but no Japanese planes rose to challenge. Only two were shot down although many were claimed on the ground from over a hundred strafing attacks. But the Japanese weren't idle this time.

Task Force 38 was taking a gamble. Since refueling had been difficult in the last 2 or 3 weeks, it had been impossible to get all of the warships refueled on any one refueling exercise. Due to the lack of response from the Japanese to the last several strikes that TF 38 had launched, it was decided to attempt refueling today after the morning strike was launched.. Accordingly, the ships were in refueling formation since mid-morning.

At noon, the first incoming Japanese air attack to be seen in awhile was picked up. There were plenty of fighters available to fight them off. Maybe too many. The radio channels become saturated with the pilots excited chatter. The fighter directors on the ships had difficulty getting through. The result was disaster.

At 12:10, the Callaghan and all the other ships went to General Quarters. At first T.G. 38.3 tried to reform in a standard 13 ship circular formation. This came apart when the first carrier was hit.

The first air attack saw two Japanese planes survive the gauntlet of the combat air patrol and the outer screen. A dive bomber dropped a bomb on the Langley. It immediately erupted into flame and dropped out of the formation.

The standard circular formation was disrupted due to the Langley's inability to maneuver and the fact that a course change was ordered shortly thereafter. When TG 38.3's staff

248

saw that the formation was falling apart, they ordered separate escort for each of the big carriers. The Callaghan and the Laws were designated to stay with the big Essex-class carrier Ticonderoga. The big carriers were now maneuvering independently and their assigned escorts were tasked with keeping up with them as they went into their tight circles designed to throw off the aim of the attackers.

The second Japanese plane to break through, a suicider, went for the Ticonderoga. The Callaghan opened up on it but it was in a screaming dive. It dove straight into the island of the big carrier. The Tico immediately erupted into flames. Nearly everyone topside on the Callaghan had seen what had happened and were stunned by the result. They had not seen one of the big carriers take such severe damage close up and personal like this. It was both fascinating and horrifying.

During all of this sudden and vicious action, Captain Bertholf was finding his seamanship skills tested to the limit. The Callaghan was maneuvering wildly to conform to the movements of the big carriers. As the Ticonderoga was turning in a tight right-hand turn, from northwest to north, the Callaghan ended up off the port bow of the Tico, headed in the opposite direction.

This put the Callaghan directly in position to defend the Tico from a Japanese plane that now appeared from the northwest heading right for the Tico. The plane was sighted at approximately 7000 yards. The director slewed on to the plane immediately and the 5" guns soon opened up. The plane was in a shallow dive from 4 or 5 thousand feet of altitude. The pilot made no evasive maneuvers. That was a bad mistake.

The Ticonderoga's guns were now hammering out salvos of 5" rounds at the on-coming plane. The Tico's burst were seen as mushrooms due to the side angle view that the Callaghan personnel had. The Callaghan's bursts were seen as round since they were viewed from directly behind. As the range wound down to a little over 3000 yards, one of the Callaghan's 5" shell bursts was dead on. Seconds later, the pilot bailed out.

The now pilot-less plane went into a steep dive straight into the sea.

The victory was short lived. Minutes later another plane dove on the Ticonderoga. This one was faster and the attack was shorter. The guns did not stop it. It crashed into the big carrier and a second ball of smoke and flame shot up from the wounded ship.

With grim determination, the gunners aboard the Callaghan kept their fingers on the trigger. Yet another plane appeared and the guns roared out. Luckily this plane got the message quick and did a U-turn. This was fortunate because the plane was a US Navy plane. The plane directors aboard the carriers started warning off any friendlies in the area. Two carriers were now unable to land planes anyway.

The attack was over and the Task Group staff attempted to sort out the mess. The group divided into two; one group formed of the unhurt ships and the other group formed around the two wounded carriers. The Callaghan was ordered to stay with the fully functional ships. As usual, the screen commander elected to keep the Callaghan with the group and send other destroyers to escort the cripples home.

Because refueling had been interrupted by the Japanese air attacks, it was scheduled to start again the next day. In fact, it started unusually early. T.G. 38.3 was in formation for refueling before dawn. The Callaghan lined up to refuel from its old friend, the Battleship Washington just as dawn was breaking. 1070 barrels was taken aboard and the hoses were disconnected by 9:00am! The Callaghan, as usual, took a position in the screen while other ships fueled.

As soon as the destroyers were fueled, the ships went into formation for flight operations. Strikes were launched by the various task groups against the Ryukyu islands (including Okinawa) and the Sakishimas, which was a small group of islands between Formosa and Okinawa. T.G. 38.3 drew the Sakishima islands for its target. It was recorded by Tom Raabe in his diary as "a small island about 350 miles from Japan". In a couple of months, the Callaghan crew would become far more familiar with all of these island groups then it would have dreamed. There were no great losses on either side in these raids but much valuable information was gathered in preparation for the coming invasions of Iwo Jima and Okinawa.

After nightfall on the 22nd, Task Force 38 finally was free to head home (if you could call it that) to Ulithi. It had been a remarkable record-breaking campaign. Never had such a large US fleet operated for such an extended period (nearly 30 days) so far from base (never less than a thousand miles). For most of the operation, the Task Force was not just in enemy waters but also deep inside enemy territory with Japanese airbases all around. It was a prelude to the final phase of the war which would bring Allied forces to Tokyo itself.

A couple of days before arriving at Ulithi, the Callaghan and the other destroyers of squadron 55 were detached from T.G. 38.3 to join Task Force 34. Halsey had the Battleships pulled out of the carrier groups to form Task Force 34. Since the missed opportunity at the Battle of Leyte Gulf to stop Kurita's Central Force with the modern Battleships of the US Third Fleet, a little attention was being paid to the reality that if Battleships were to fight as a surface force, they would have to know how to operate together. While the fleet was heading for the barn, the battlewagons plus a few cruisers practiced surface warfare maneuvering. The Callaghan got to be a part of it.

The truth was that this practice was a waste of time. The Battleships would never again operate against enemy ships on the open sea. The Callaghan's crew was witness to a majestic formation of mighty dinosaurs practicing a form of warfare that would never be seen by mankind again.

The benefit for the Callaghan and its fellow destroyers was that they got in some badly needed gunnery practice. The morning of the 26th, just before arrival off Ulithi, the Callaghan got to fire off several hundred rounds of 40mm and 20mm. Captain Bertholf and the gunnery officers were justifiably concerned about maintaining the edge of the machine gun crews. Task Force 38 had been lucky through most of this campaign but the action on the 21st had illustrated how vital accurate gunnery was with the new Kamikaze tactics. There was no room for error.

At noon, the Battleships started entering Magai channel to Ulithi atoll. As always, the destroyers were last to enter the lagoon. The Callaghan went to the tanker Naverra first to refuel. Then it steamed off to the berthing area where most of the destroyers were anchored. Unfortunately the first berth where the Callaghan dropped anchor was unsatisfactory for some reason. The sailors had to drag the anchor back up and start all over again. This was one of the annoyances of using a forward base in a Pacific atoll that a few months ago belonged to the enemy.

The next several days were spent in the usual routine of trying to resupply and repair the ship adequately for the next campaign. Resupply was becoming increasingly difficult. The US Pacific fleet was now larger than the British and Japanese fleets put together. Supplying this fleet and the soldiers which it would transport to the next target, was becoming a major problem for the United States. Hundreds of merchant ships and tankers were dedicated to this task. Yet the shear logistical problem of routing all of the supplies to the ships and men who needed them was overwhelming the system.

One supply which being taken care of was the beer supply at Mog Mog Island. Each day, a liberty party left the Callaghan to motor over to Mog Mog. The sailors drank the warm beer and participated in the beach sports. The officers, on the other hand, usually waited until the evening to head over to the crude officers club. No warm beer for the officers. They drank hard liquor while enjoying the rare chance to meet with their fellow officers from various ships that were in.

Captain Bertholf led the way in the O-Club activities on Mog-Mog Island. Like many in his generation, Mariner Bertholf was fond of drinking and smoking. Plus he was a very sociable person all his life. And perhaps he liked the hard drinking tough-guy image that everyone expected from the fighting man of the era as depicted by John Wayne in his movies.

But in this respect, he fit right in with the Callaghan crew. The Callaghan had a hard living, hard fighting crew. Captain Bertholf was the same.

Meanwhile the normal socializing went on as well. Tom Raabe visited his friend Gene Kampsen aboard the destroyer tender, Markab. That became real easy on the 1st of February when the Callaghan tied up alongside the Markab for an "availability". This was Navy speak for a repair session by the Tender's maintenance crew. With three other destroyers present, many of the Navy regulars in the crew found someone they knew to renew acquaintance.

The Callaghan spent two full weeks in Ulithi this time. It was one of the longest stays in port the Callaghan had since they left Pearl 9 months prior. During this stay, as with every time in port, men were transferred both on and off the ship. Two of the transfers off were notable.

One was F.P. Jordan, Boatswain. Every "bosun" was a most valuable member of the crew and usually one of the most senior enlised men. As Bosun, Jordan had been the first enlisted man aboard the Callaghan to serve as OOD: Officer Of the Deck. Although he only served as OOD while the Callaghan was in port, this was an innovation that was definitely Captain Bertholf's doing. He would be missed. The other transfer was Jake Heimark, the Executive officer.

Jake had been aboard since commissioning. First as gunnery officer, then as Executive officer since May of '44, Jake had a great influence on the life and success of the Callaghan. Now he was getting what every Executive officer looks forward to: a command of his own. He was being sent back to the states to the prospective commanders school before getting a new destroyer to put into commission.

Jake was a very lucky man. He had been with the Callaghan through all the high adventure of the Marianas campaign and the Battle of Leyte Gulf. He had experienced the great typhoon in Dec. and all of the Philippines strikes. He would not have to experience the horror of the Kamikazes in the coming Okinawa campaign. Plus he had the great joy of going home to his young bride.

Hugh Owens would take over as the new Executive officer. Hugh was not the most qualified candidate for executive officer of a warship due to his limited experience. But this would be compensated for by the very capable and experienced crew that the Callaghan now had. When the new Executive officer needed help it was readily available.

On the 9th of February, Captain Bertholf received confidential orders for the next campaign. He had charts pulled for the Bonin islands area for the officers to study. As always, the quartermasters knew which charts were pulled and therefore, where the Callaghan was going. The rest of the crew had a good clue as well when cold weather clothing was brought aboard. This was the first time that had ever happened since the Callaghan had left the states. Many of the sailors thought that someone in the Navy had lost their mind. Cold weather gear in the Pacific? What for?

At dawn the next day, the crew prepared the ship to leave. At 8:30 the Callaghan left the destroyer nest to join the other destroyers headed out the channel. For the last time, the Callaghan would stand guard outside Ulithi as Task group 58.3 (same as 38.3) would sally forth to take the battle to the Japanese.

Soon after the Task Group had left Ulithi and maneuvered into formation, a few of the destroyers detached to form a line for gunnery practice. Concern had been raised with the Admiral's staff over the complete lack of any type of gunnery practice during the unusually long 2 week stay at Ulithi. As a result, this was the first thing on the agenda as the group started the journey that would lead to Japan.

254

The Callaghan was allowed brief anti-aircraft practice with the 5" guns. After that, the Callaghan rejoined the Task Group. The destroyers then formed a bent line alongside one side of the formation in order to conduct machine gun practice. This was allowed while in formation since the machine guns were far less dangerous to the other ships if something went wrong. The 40mm guns fired off 210 rounds for this practice session. Captain Bertholf noted in the war diary that although it had been some time since the gun crews had fired their guns, the results of the gunnery were excellent.

During late-afternoon, Doc Parker informed Captain Bertholf that he had a patient who would require a surgeon. Word was sent to the Task Group staff. Orders came back for the Callaghan to rendezvous with the Battleship South Dakota to transfer the patient. That evening, just before sundown, Seaman First Quinn was transferred via high line to the South Dakota.

Task Force 58 spent the next 6 days training while the ships steamed on a long indirect route to Japan. First they steamed northeast to the Marianas. The Callaghan found itself back in the same waters where it had spent nearly all of the previous summer. The carrier task force took the opportunity to practice landing support while the Marines hit the beach on Tinian in a giant dry run for the invasion of Iwo Jima.

Continuing the vast semi-circular route, it headed gradually on a more Northerly course ending up a couple of hundred miles to the east of the Bonin Islands. Finally on the 15th, a high speed run was begun to the northwest towards the goal that the United States fleet had sought for over 3 years: Tokyo!

On the last couple of days of the long march towards Japan, the Callaghan crew experienced a drop in the temperature they had not felt since leaving the West coast over a year before. They began to break out the cold weather gear they had been issued at Ulithi. Now the sailors who had thought the supply guys crazy back at Ulithi began to appreciate the planning that went into these great campaigns.

255

A new threat presented itself on this last day before the fleet would arrive off Japan. The Japanese navy had used picket boats to guard Japan since just after the attack on Pearl Harbor. The picket boats were mostly small converted fishing or auxiliary vessels that were capable of spending three or four weeks a couple of hundred miles out at sea without the need to return to land for supplies or for weather reasons. They usually contained a small crew and were armed with whatever guns the Japanese navy could get aboard the boat. That meant that the smaller ones probably were only armed with machine guns but the larger ones often had 3 inch guns that could do damage to a destroyer.

The threat from the picket boats was not a physical one to task force 58. Even with 3 inch guns, the fleet carriers could cruise by them knowing that their 5 inch guns would prevent any picket boat from becoming a modern day David to the US Goliath. Rather they presented an indirect threat from the radios that they had on board. Once having sighted the American carriers, it was a certainty that Tokyo would know the whereabouts of those carriers in minutes. Therefore it was imperative that the picket boats be prevented from making that all-important radio call to the mainland.

The job of taking out any picket boats that got in the way went to the destroyers. A new task was added to the list for the destroyer pickets that steamed out ahead of the fleet by 10 or 12 miles. Now they were on the lookout for Japanese picket boats. The picket destroyers would sink the picket boats.

At dusk on the 15th, just as the run towards Japan was to be started, the Callaghan had to "pull over" to investigate an unusual noise in the steering engine. Captain Bertholf certainly did not want to have steering problems occur while the Callaghan was off the very coast of the enemy home islands. It turned out to be a problem easily fixed by Frank Dunne and his mechanical wizards. The Callaghan quickly rejoined its carrier group.

All night as Task Force 58 made its run towards the coast of Japan, the screen was vigilant for submarines, enemy planes and picket boats. The American carrier force was extremely lucky this time. A combination of bad weather and poor vigilance on the part of the enemy allowed them to reach the launching point at dawn undetected. Most of the picket boats had been avoided on the way in.

Right after the first fighter strike was launched, the destroyer Haynesworth in the same task group with the Callaghan, reported a small enemy picket boat. It quickly sank the boat with gunfire. It did not matter now if a message had been sent or not. With the first strike already on its way to the Japanese coast, it was assumed that Japanese radar would pick them up immediately. The carrier planes didn't need secrecy anymore.

Due to the poor weather with low cloud ceilings and occasional rain, the escorting warships were tense all day watching for enemy aircraft to suddenly appear. Amazingly, it never happened. The air strikes were partially successful in attacking the Japanese airfields despite the bad weather. Nearly a hundred enemy aircraft were claimed as destroyed. However, the American losses were high with over 30 aircraft lost to various causes. Five were lost to mid-air collision directly attributed to the poor visibility.

Nonetheless, the Navy brass were delighted with the ease with which the American carrier force could attack the heartland of the enemy. This was another clear sign that the war was in its last stages.

At the end of the day, the Callaghan picked a lone survivor of one of the Japanese picket boats out of the water. He was immediately transferred to the Bunker Hill for interrogation by the intelligence officers the big carrier had aboard.

At 10:00pm that night a plane was reported in the water. The Callaghan was sent to investigate. After a half hour of fruitless searching, the Callaghan was called back. The formation was cruising at 20 knots at the time, so the Callghan could not search any longer without being left far behind.

The 17th had even worse flying weather than the day before. Several of the scheduled combat air patrols were canceled. The mornings strikes got off with difficulty. With ceilings of 200 feet, most of the strike planes had to fly down at sea level all the way in to the coast. Attempts to fly over the clouds were failures since the "soup" went all the way up to over 30,000 feet. Despite these difficulties and with the cooperation of the Japanese, another 80 Japanese planes were claimed as shot-down.

One of the returning Hellcat fighters had to ditch in the water. It went in just off the right side of the Callaghan, so naturally Captain Bertholf changed course immediately to effect a rescue. For some reason the pilot had trouble as soon as he got out of the plane. It was apparent that the pilot needed immediate rescue. The boat was probably going to be too late.

Sizing up the situation, Lt. (jg) Hongola decided to take action. Hongola was an athlete in school and an excellent swimmer. He was not afraid of the sea. Although stationed in the main gun director atop the pilot house, he removed his shoes and waited for the Callaghan to roll toward the side where the pilot was in the water. He then dove from that great height into the sea. After coming up from the deep dive, he immediately swam out to the aviator. He helped the pilot stay afloat while the whale boat came out to pick them both up. The pilot, Ensign Carl Gustafson was a lucky man. Hongola had saved his life and everyone knew it. Captain Bertholf made a mental note to put Hongola in for a life-saving medal.

At noon, all further strikes were canceled and the formation turned away from Japan. After the usual staff consultations it was decided to give up on Japan and head for Iwo Jima.

First they had to get out of Japanese home waters. All afternoon and all evening the fleet steamed away from the coast. There were numerous air alerts during the day as the

Japanese attempted to find them. Luckily none of the Japanese planes got through.

A couple of hours before dawn the next morning. reports of Japanese picket boats began to come in. As a result the fleet began to maneuver to attempt to go around these contacts. At first it worked, with the carrier groups avoiding coming in contact.

Just before dawn, Task Group 58.3 ran into one too many picket boats. At 5:40am, the Callaghan sighted a picket boat up ahead. The Callaghan and the Pritchett were designated to sink it. A few minutes later the Callaghan opened fire with the 40mm guns.

At first the firing seemed to have no effect. The Japanese built very sturdy fishing vessels out of heavy timbers. The picket boat absorbed hundreds of 40mm rounds. Finally after nearly 20 minutes of steady fire it began to sink. Shortly the cease fire order was given.

The Japanese crew abandoned ship into a life boat that miraculously survived the hailstorm of 40mm fire. The Callaghan got the nod to pick up the crew and Captain Bertholf began to maneuver the destroyer in closer to the little boat.

What occurred next was one of the strangest experiences that the Callaghan crew would have on their great odyssey across the Pacific. A couple of topside crewmen noticed that something was going on in the lifeboat. It appeared to one sailor that most of the Japanese in the boat were holding down one of their members. After careful observation through optics, he came to a shocking conclusion. It appeared that there was water in the bottom of the boat and that they were drowning their fellow sailor!

The boat was finally brought alongside the aft end of the Callaghan. Using the big propeller guards (curved pipes on the outside of the propeller arcs) sailors from the deckforce helped the Japanese sailors get aboard the Callaghan. Several sailors stood guard with small arms while this was going on.

One Callaghan sailor even went down via the propeller guards to get into the lifeboat after the Japanese crew were all out. He checked the remaining face-down Japanese crewman to make sure he was indeed dead. He made a quick check for papers or anything else that might be of value while his buddies from the Callaghan were yelling at him to hurry it up.

The Callaghan had been stopped too long. To be stopped at sea was not natural but to be stopped this long while only a couple of hundred miles from Japan itself was a nightmare come true. Everyone was anxious to get the hell out of there!

Which is exactly what they did. After letting the lifeboat go, Captain Bertholf ordered 25 knots speed to rejoin the Task Group. The Callaghan had one chore left that morning. About an hour before noon, the Callaghan steamed alongside the Bunker Hill to deliver one of the Japanese sailors. The big carrier had Japanese speaking officers aboard who would try to get information out of their new prisoner.

Luckily the rest of the day went by with relative ease as Admiral Mitchner's carriers cleared Japan on the way to Iwo Jima.

On the 19th, Task Force 58 split up. Task Groups 58.1 and 58.4 spent the day refueling. Task Groups 58.2 and 58.3 (including the Callaghan) provided air support for the invasion of Iwo Jima..

The stars of the air support those first days at Iwo were the Marine Corsairs aboard the Essex, the Bunker Hill and an escort carrier assigned to the landing support group. Marine pilots have always excelled at close air support partly because of their basic training which emphasizes infantry skills. The other reason, of course, is because their brother Marines were on the ground taking fearful punishment. Marines always take care of their fellow Marines.

The Callaghan spent the day zigzagging all over the place. Flight operations were frequent all day long with the resulting sharp changes of direction required by the carriers. Luckily the enemy did not intervene with any counterattacks during the day.

Just before dark the enemy finally showed up. Enemy planes were picked up on the picket ships radar but they did not close with T.G. 58.3. General quarters was called anyway to make sure in case of any sneak attack. Word soon came in that the huge old carrier Saratoga had been hit. Two Kamikazes crashed into it causing heavy damage. An hour later another suicide plane crashed into its flight deck near the bow. Superb damage control saved the ship but it was forced to leave Iwo to return to the States for repair. The "Sara" was out of action for six months. By that time the war was over.

An hour after sundown, unidentified planes were much closer to the ships of T.G. 58.3. Orders went out to the destroyers to make smoke.

The Callaghan seldom had used its smoke making ability in the war so far. The easiest way was to simply make the boiler fires inefficient. Extra fuel was added that caused the mixture feeding the fires to get way too rich. This caused smoke to start rolling out of the stacks. This dark black smoke was very unpopular with anybody standing watch on the aft end of the ship.

The other way provided for destroyers to make smoke was to use special chemical generators installed on the stern. These started with a kind of small explosion which often gave off a shower of sparks. Luckily the chemical generator was not used on this occasion. Within 20 minutes an order to cease the smoke came back. Apparently it was inadequate to hide the big fleet carriers.

The rest of the night passed without incident for the Callaghan. T.G. 58.3 steamed all night toward the designated fueling rendezvous set for the following morning.

Just after dawn, the formation turned due north. The Callaghan lined up behind the tanker Taluga. It took almost a half hour before the Callaghan was finally alongside. The destroyer's deck crew soon had the hoses connected and the black oil was pumped aboard.

During the refueling, orders were received for the Callaghan to get mail from the Bunker Hill. As soon as the Callaghan cleared the side of the tanker, it headed straight for the big carrier. In less time than most people can drive to the post office, the Callaghan was alongside the carrier with the deck crew busy again. In a mere thirteen minutes the mail was aboard the destroyer and the lines were cast off.

The Callaghan left at high speed for Iwo Jima. This time the mail was meant for others; not the sailors aboard any of the ships the Callaghan sailed with. While enroute, Captain Bertholf held a steering casualty drill. The Callaghan tradition of drilling to stay sharp and check skills was being upheld.

Just after noon, the embattled island came into view. The Callaghan sailors crowded topside to see the now infamous island and the great fleet that had come to take it away from the Japanese. Soon some of the hundreds of amphibious ships could be seen arrayed around the Southern end of the island.

Among those amphibious ships were the battleships and cruisers whose job it was to help the Marines by throwing thousands of rounds of large caliber gunfire at the Japanese positions. Some of that gunfire was going on while the Callaghan looked for the cruiser Indianapolis.

The Indianapolis was not firing. It was the flagship of Admiral Spruance, the Commander of the Fifth fleet. Command and control was the job of the Indianapolis for this invasion so it did very little firing. The Callaghan hove to not far from the flagship and waited for a boat to come get the mail.

It was a long wait while the destroyer was stopped, unable to anchor. There were still lots of active enemy artillery guns on Iwo that could easily open up on a ship within easy anchoring distance of the island. Until most of them were put out of action, the ships in the invasion force had to anchor several miles out or stay underway.

During this long wait the Callaghan's topside crew had a good view of a major invasion still in progress. Landing craft were shuttling back and forth in a constant stream between the beach and the big amphibious ships. Cruisers and destroyers were firing at distant targets on the island. Some of the shell bursts on the island were clearly visible. Onshore, marine artillery was firing at Mount Suribachi. It was quite a show tempered by the grim reality of the horrendous casualties being reported among the Marines ashore.

Doc Parker was particulary affected by the news of the casualties. He had spent his entire time aboard the Callaghan treating heat rash, minor illnesses and injuries. Here at Iwo Jima was a terrible need for the skills which he had trained for. But he was stuck on a destroyer with no opportunity to help out. He began a letter that day to forward up the chain of command suggesting that doctors no longer be stationed aboard every destroyer. One doctor for each squadron would be sufficient. Years later the Navy would do just that.

Finally after nearly an hour and a half, the boat arrived from the Indianapolis. The mail was quickly passed and Captain Bertholf immediately got underway. Full speed was rung up and course set to the west. Three hours later the Callaghan was alongside the Bunker Hill once again. Mail was passed and then the Callaghan peeled off to go join the destroyer screen.

One last duty awaited the Callaghan that day. Just after dusk general quarters was set, the Callaghan was ordered to take up plane guard duty behind one of the big carriers. The final flights for the day were coming in to land. As soon as the last plane was landed, the formation started zigzagging and the Callaghan rejoined the screen.

The next day was pretty routine. Flight operations were held throughout the day as T.G. 58.3 continued to support the invasion of Iwo Jima. In mid-morning a couple of cruisers and a destroyer division joined the task group.

One of the cruisers was new to the Callaghan and really had a different look to it It was the cruiser Alaska; what the Navy called a "large" cruiser. Before WWII, it would have been called a Battle Cruiser. It was big at around 21,000 tons. It's main battery were 12 inch guns and it looked a lot like an Iowa class battleship but not as big. The Alaska and its sister ship the Guam would spent what was left of the war escorting the fleet carriers to provide anti-aircraft protection with their extensive secondary armament of 5 inch guns and machine guns. Although they had been designed to fight enemy warships, they would never be used for that purpose. The day of the big gun was over.

As dusk general quarters was occupying the attention of all sailors in the task group, radar picked up bogies. It was not clear if they were friendly or not so no alarm was immediately sounded. When it was realized that all friendly aircraft had been accounted for, an alert was broadcast and the formation picked up speed to 25 knots.

Three minutes later a plane came in not far from the Callaghan's position. Unfortunately visibility was poor so the main battery opened fire under radar control. 27 rounds were belted out before "check fire" was ordered. It was several minutes before it or another plane was in range again. The main battery opened up again but this time only 8 rounds were fired.

Night fighters were now aloft so it was decided to let them try their hand while the ships attempted to hide in the poor visibility. The destroyers were ordered to make funnel smoke. The Callaghan rolled the black stuff out behind it for 12 minutes before the enemy planes had been chased off the radar screens.

But it was not over, an hour later the same scenario was played out again. The Callaghan fired 13 more rounds at an unseen enemy plane this time. The formation was put through violent emergency maneuvers. Luckily no enemy planes got through to cause any damage.

The 23rd was a busy day for T.G. 58.3. Refueling was held in the morning for the destroyers with the big ships topping off in the afternoon. Several of the destroyers, including the Callaghan, ran errands after refueling.

The Callaghan first picked up a pilot from the Essex and then three more from the Cowpens. It then took a short trip over to the nearby escort carrier group to deliver the pilots. It then visited the Bougainville, the Admiralty islands and the Windam Bay. It returned to T.G. 58.3 to deliver material to the Bunker Hill. In total, the Callaghan had visited six carriers is two different task groups in less than 5 hours!

About an hour before midnight, the great task force changed course to the north. The Navy brass had decided to hit Japan again.

But first the ships had to deal with an older enemy than the Japanese. On the trip north the weather deteriorated steadily. Soon the destroyers were dealing with huge waves, pounding water and shrieking wind. Once again the pride of the US fleet had run into a typhoon!

For some reason, the weather let up for a short while in the early morning hours of the 25th. Preparations went forward for the planned airstrikes beginning before dawn.

At 7:00am, the first fighter strike was launched. The weather was lousy again so the flyers were expecting a tough time. The planes soon disappeared leaving the ships behind to nervously watch the low hanging clouds. There was very good reason to be nervous because this time the Japanese had discovered the task force on the way to Japan and knew where it was.

Several strikes were launched that morning but all ran into difficulty both with the weather and finding targets. Some of the fighters ran into small formations of enemy fighters resulting in swirling, deadly air combat. Luckily for our guys, most of the Japanese fighters were inexperienced and fought poorly. Only 37 enemy planes were claimed in air combat.

At noon, Admiral Spruance gave into reality and called off further strikes. The weather was getting even worse. He ordered the big task force southwest in hopes that it would be able to strike Nagoya.

But in the middle of the night it became clear that the weather had taken charge. Instead of steaming away from the typhoon, the task force had run right back into it. Weather forecasting was still a very primitive art and the Navy officers in charge of it aboard the flagship didn't seem to have a clue. Again the ships had to select courses and speeds to try to minimize damage to smaller ships.

Sometime around 2:00am, Task Group 58.3 went through the eye of the typhoon. This calmed things down considerably for a short while. When the ships broke back out into the storm, it was worse than before.

This typhoon was not quite as powerful as the one in December, thank God! However, Captain Bertholf must have thought he was getting a master's degree in heavy weather ship handling.

The next day Admiral Spruance gave up on his desire to perform the strategic function of striking at the Japanese homeland. Task Force 58 steamed off to a rendezvous with Servron 6 to replenish. Plans were drawn up to strike Okinawa instead.

On the 27th, the Callaghan took on 1699 barrels of oil from the Neosho. Later that day the Porterfield came alongside to send over the Commodore and his staff. The Porterfield was being detached so the Callaghan was designated the temporary flagship of DesRon 55. Captain Jarrell was welcomed aboard by Captain Bertholf who turned over his quarters to the Commodore as was customary.

One task group was released to return to Ulithi. The rest, including T.G. 58.3 headed for Okinawa. Although the crew did not yet know it, this was to be the Callaghan's last operation with T.G. 58.3. The Callaghan had spent ten months doing what it did best, escort and protect aircraft carriers.

Early on the morning of the 1st of March, strikes were launched. All day long strikes went out to hit the big island. Surprisingly, there was little opposition in the air. At this point in the war, the Japanese were being very careful how they expended their resources. They were very aware of the superiority of the American fighters in the air.

The results of the strikes were judged to be good with many aircraft destroyed on the ground and installations heavily damaged. Extensive photographs were taken for use in the coming invasion of Okinawa. At the end of the day, the task force began the long journey back to Ulithi.

There was time for one more mission for the destroyers, however. Word had come in that a B-29 crew was in a raft near the island of Parece Vela. The air force had requested that Task Force 58 attempt a rescue. As a result, four destroyers were detached to look for the aviators. Since the island was a radar early warning site for the Japanese, the destroyers were also tasked with bombarding the island's installations after the rescue effort.

Starting about an hour before noon, the four destroyers formed a scouting line 10,000 yards apart. for nearly four and a half hours the destroyers searched. With the help of an air-rescue plane from Saipan, the Preston and the Callaghan found the raft with the aviators aboard. The Preston got the nod to pick up the crew while the Callaghan stood by to provide cover.

That evening the four destroyers made their bombardment run on Parece Vela. The Irwin and Cassin Young took the targets on the left side of the island; the Preston and the Callaghan took the targets on the right side of the island. Closing to less than 8000 yards, the Commodore aboard the Callaghan gave the order for the four destroyers to open fire.

To this point in the war, the Callaghan had almost no experience in shore bombardment. It was a satisfying experience to be able to deliver an offensive punch to the enemy with little danger of return fire. The Callaghan started out by delivering several rounds of starshells to illuminate the target.

With the target well lit up, the Callaghan switched over to high explosive rounds and, with it's sister destroyers, proceeded to pound the target with vigor. Many secondary explosions were observed and several towers and buildings disappeared from view. Once it appeared that the objective had been met, the Commodore ordered the four destroyers to leave the scene at high speed.

A course was set back to the task force. In a matter of hours they were among friends again.

After refueling, DesDiv 109, including the Callaghan, joined Task Group 59.1. Admiral Spruance had been convinced by the battleship Admirals that the big dreadnoughts were never going to be of any use in their own right unless they got some practice operating separate from the carriers. As a result, the battleline was formed into T.G. 59.1.

The rest of the trip back to Ulithi was basically one drill after another. The battleships and the destroyers got a needed workout. The problem with escorting carriers was that it provided no opportunity to exercise surface battle skills. Lots of maneuvers and gunnery drills were performed.

In mid-afternoon on March 5th, the Callaghan reentered Ulithi lagoon for another rest and repair period. The first order of business was to reload the ammunition magazines and then to refuel. The Callaghan spent the night tied up alongside the tanker from which it refueled.

The following days were spent in the usual round of repairs, replenishment and errands. This stay at Ulithi seemed to go fairly quickly. There was much to do and the next operation was already shaping up. The Callaghan did not have to spend the entire stay at Ulithi at anchor this time. There was a turn at the tender for availability and there was a period of duty at sea while on radar picket station 45 miles from the great anchorage.

On the 7th, five men were transferred off the callaghan. One of them was Tom Raabe, Electrician's Mate, carrying with him the only known personal diary of a Callaghan crewman to survive the war. Tom Raabe attended the Callaghan reunions faithfully. His diary provided insight and color to this narrative.

On the 13th, the Callaghan slipped away for its turn at radar picket duty. Although this tended to be fairly tame compared to picket duty in front of a carrier task group, it allowed the ship a quiet time at sea to work out minor problems and to concentrate on training. It was refreshing to be at sea as well, where there was always a breeze.

The Callaghan spent a total of three nights on radar picket duty during this stay at Ulithi. Each time the destroyer came back into the fleet anchorage during the day. The extra early warning provided by the picket destroyers was only needed at night. Ulithi, of course, had its own ground based-radar that was quite adequate during the daytime. Aircraft patrols were also far more comprehensive during the day preventing a successful Japanese attack.

On the 17th, a ceremony was held aboard the Callaghan. The Commodore of the squadron presented Lt. (jg) Hongola and BM2c McCarthy with the Navy and Marine Corps Medal for going over the side of the ship to save a pilot from drowning. He also presented a purple heart to Machinist Sims for wounds he received during a strafing attack.

The same day, Ensign W.D. Merrill reported aboard. He was joining the ship just in time for the final campaign. It would be the longest, bloodiest campaign for the Navy's destroyers since the first year of the war. Though it had come through the war mostly unscathed so far, this campaign would hit Destroyer Squadron 55 particularly hard. The luck of the Irish would not hold for the Callaghan this time.

CHAPTER FIVE: HELL ON EARTH

The Callaghan made an unusual two trips to ammunition ships during its stay at Ulithi in mid-March. The destroyers in DesRon 55 were all taking aboard more ammunition than ever before. New places were found to stow 5" shells and 40mm rounds.

The crew found out that the Callaghan and DesRon 55 were going to serve with the bombardment force for the next campaign. For some this was considered a great prospect to see a lot of action close up. For the wise, it was a chilling prospect. They knew that the bombardment force was basically tied to the beach during the first part of an invasion. That meant that the shore guns could use your ship for target practice. Plus the ever present danger of air attack was increased tremendously, simply because the enemy always knew where you were. The beauty of the carrier task groups was that they specialized in hit and run tactics. The battleships of the bombardment group stayed put and had to fight off whatever came their way.

On the night of the 20th/21st, the Callaghan was standing its last radar picket duty 45 miles out from Ulithi. As it steamed back in the morning, the escort carrier Sangamon called saying that a sailor had just fallen overboard. Since the Callaghan happened to be passing at the time, Captain Bertholf directed the destroyer over to where the sailor was in the water. A rescue was quickly affected and arrangements were made to transfer the sailor over to one of the destroyers that belonged to the Sangamon's task group.

The Callaghan would not return to Ulithi lagoon. It waited outside as Task Force 54 sortied. This would be its new home task force. All the topside sailors watched as the old battleships came out. Most of these battlewagons were survivors of Pearl Harbor, having been salvaged, repaired and upgraded during the early part of the war. They were now the expert

270

bombardment force, having been used in that capacity since the invasion of the Aleutian islands in early '43.

The Callaghan joined the screen of the task force and prepared for gunnery exercises. The ships were going to make one last use of the services of the tow planes at Ulithi for some final gunnery practice. The Callaghan fired both 5 inch guns and 40mm's before the exercise was over.

One thing became apparent fairly quickly about service with the old battlewagons. The pace was nothing like it had been with the big carriers. These WWI vintage battleships only had a top speed of about 21 knots. Besides that, they had no need for the constant maneuvering required for flight operations. Most of the time, cruising meant hour upon hour of steady paced zigzagging. In this sense, life had become easier for the Callaghan, at least for now.

The trip to Okinawa took just under 5 days. Everyone had been warned that once in Okinawa waters, the Navy expected a violent reaction from the enemy. There were reports of suicide boats and small submarines that were waiting at Okinawa to repel any invasion force. Although the Japanese aircraft based on Okinawa had been mostly destroyed during previous raids, it was fully expected that the enemy would fly Kamikaze missions from both Southern Japan and Formosa, which were within easy flying distance.

Long before dawn on the 26th of March, the bombardment force arrived off Okinawa. The force divided up into task groups. The Callaghan was assigned to T.G. 54.2, which included the battleships West Virginia and New Mexico along with the cruiser Biloxi. The various groups fanned out to take their assigned positions. At about half past eight in the morning, the heavies opened fire.

So began the longest and most intense campaign the Callaghan would experience. Although for the US Navy it would not be as long as the Guadalcanal campaign, it would certainly be more strenuous in terms of the daily combat operations that went on and on. Okinawa would see far more ammunition fired and more ships damaged than ever before.

All day long the heavies threw big shells at targets on the island. Finally, around 5:00pm, the order to cease-fire went out. The formation soon left for more open water to spend the night. For the Callaghan, however, there would be no such safe haven. It was detached to spend the night alone off the western beaches of Okinawa delivering harassment fire against the Japanese ashore.

What a way to spend the first night! Okinawa was probably the strongest defended island in the entire Japanese empire excepting the home islands of Japan. Over a hundred thousand soldiers defended Okinawa with God knows how many artillery pieces, hidden aircraft, suicide boats and submarines. The Callaghan stood virtually alone against all this. It was enough to make some sailors think that maybe that foxhole wouldn't have been so bad after all!

All night long the Callaghan fired its 5 inch guns in rotation at the island. It was slow and deliberate fire meant not to damage the enemy but rather to keep him awake. The problem was that it kept most of the sailors of the Callaghan awake too!

The Callaghan was steaming slowly to the south near a point on Okinawa called Zampa Misaki about 20 minutes before dawn. The number one (51) mount had been firing at the island for the last shift. It was getting gray in the sky, as the sun was soon to appear over the island to the east. Suddenly a sound was heard from the direction of the island and three planes were spotted coming out.

Someone said "They're ours." A few seconds later one of the officers yelled "Like Hell! They're Japanese, sound G.Q!"

General Quarters started to sound but there was no time. Luckily, Captain Bertholf was only a few steps away from the bridge so he took over immediately. Since the 51 mount was already manned, it started firing right away. But most of the guns were not ready as the planes first circled and then flew over the Callaghan to the seaward side.

The three planes (Val dive bombers) attacked separately, one by one. Captain Bertholf had the helmsman throw the ship through violent maneuvers to try to throw off the aim of the Japanese dive-bombers. The first plane came down in a steep dive from the west trying to bomb the destroyer. The bomb just missed off the port side of the ship.

The plane zoomed back up and circled around as if in preparation for another try. It didn't get the chance. As it completed a half circle around the ship, a 5" round caught it squarely. The plane exploded and fell flaming into the sea.

The second plane immediately began its run on the Callaghan. It was not trying to bomb the maneuvering destroyer. It came almost straight in to attempt a Kamikaze crash. It nearly succeeded. By now the automatic weapons were firing in earnest and got several hits on the plane. It burst into flame but kept coming. Pieces of the plane started falling off. The pilot could not quite hold the plane on a collision course. It made a spectacular show as it flew just over the aft end of the ship and smashed into the water about a hundred yards off the port quarter.

Now it was the third plane's turn. He began his run as soon as the second plane crashed.

Captain Bertholf was careful observing this last plane. He wanted to be sure to make the right maneuver at the right time to throw the Japanese pilot off his aim. This plane had a very steep dive angle making it harder to avoid. The 40mm and 20mm guns were really pouring out the fire but nothing stopped this plane.

Not long after the plane started his dive, Captain Bertholf yelled to the Helmsman "Hard right rudder!"

The helmsman knew what the stakes were and he gave it everything he had. The ship heeled over as it leaned into its turn. For a long moment in time, the men topside watched as the plane came screaming down, only catching fire at the very last. The noise was deafening as the guns roared and chattered. It was a fascinating and terrifying experience.

The pilot was adjusting his dive to try to prevent overshooting like the last plane had. Would the plane hit or miss? Many who watched thought it would hit.

It almost did.

At the last moment, as if in slow motion, the men saw that the plane was hit, the ship was sliding away in its turn and the plane was directly dead center on the ship. The men became aware of the awful scream of the planes engine and then the whomp sound as it smashed into the water just to the side of the ship. A great cascade of water went up and came back down on the still turning ship.

The men had basically one of two responses. Some froze in silent shock. The others yelled out some obscenity or epitaph in involuntary reaction to the violent event. Only then did they realize that pieces of the plane were coming back down on the deck along with the water.

Some of the men noticed that the ship did not entirely escape being hit. The plane had carried away the main wire antenna, strung between the main mast and the aft stack. That's how close the near miss had been!

A quick check of the radar showed nothing on the screen but general quarters was maintained for a few minutes just in case. In cleaning up the debris from the plane, someone found a grim reminder that a human being had piloted the aircraft. A boot complete with foot was found. An officer quickly ordered it thrown overboard.

The attack was reported to the commander of Task Group 54.3. Congratulations on thwarting the attack were sent back. Captain Bertholf soon canceled the G.Q. and the galley crew set about finishing their preparations for breakfast.

The men were still talking about the air attack when they started lining up for breakfast. There was a long line of men down the mid-section of the ship lined up aft of the door to the main mess. One of the men looked down in the water and was astonished to see a pipe sticking out of the water!

Suddenly men were hollering and yelling up to the bridge. "Periscope on the port beam!!" The commotion was so great that Bertholf heard it himself before word was passed in the usual manner. He rushed over to the port side and looked out. He was scanning the water five or six hundred yards out when someone below yelled up to him to look their way.

He turned and saw that the men were pointing at an object that was only about 75 to 100 yards from the side of the ship. The shock of seeing it so close to the side of the ship galvanized him into action. He bellowed orders for the depth charges to be set shallow and to fire the port projectors as soon as ready.

Moments later the three K-guns on the port side fired their depth charges high in the air. When they came back down to smack the surface of the water, most of the men watching realized how slowly the ship was steaming. The Callaghan was only doing about 8 knots at the time. This meant that the 300 pound depth charges were still very close to the stern of the destroyer.

The depth charges went off with an enormous roar due to the shallow setting and the extremely close proximity .The stern of the ship was literally lifted out of the water. Captain Bertholf thought to himself, "Oh my God, I've sunk my own ship!"

Sinking or not, he spit out orders to speed up the ship and put it into a tight turn. General quarters were sounded again for the second time in a morning that had hardly gotten started!

As the ship came around, sonar reported a brief contact with the enemy submarine. Lookouts reported seeing an oil slick in the water where the depth charge attack had just been delivered.

Bertholf ordered another depth charge attack. This time it was a full pattern with the six K-guns firing as well as rolling four of the big 500 pounders off the stern. When this booming attack was delivered, the Callaghan heeled right into another turn to head back. Meanwhile the nearest fellow destroyer, the Porterfield, was steaming over to join the attack.

But no further contact was reported. The sub had been sunk. To confirm the sinking, the Callaghan nosed around the area for a half hour or so, stopping to pick up some debris that was floating in the oil slick from the dead submarine. Then it received orders to rejoin the task group.

Right after the Captain canceled the general quarters, he got a big surprise. A short sailor with a big name came up to the bridge. He brusquely introduced himself to Bertholf as the man who manned the aft steering station. He then did something that astonished everyone who saw it.

The sailor poked a finger upward into the Captain's chest. "You almost sunk us! Don't EVER do that again!" He then turned on his heel and left the bridge.

After a stunned silence, Bertholf said something to the effect of "Well I'll be damned!" He then burst out laughing, turned the bridge over to the officer-of-the-deck and returned to his sea cabin.

The sailors got a belated breakfast to end an amazing morning. The admiral of the T.G. 54.3 sent his congratulations on 3 planes and a submarine in the space of little more than an hour.

After that, it was simply back to business as usual. The Callaghan had experienced in 24 hours, the basic duties it would perform for the rest of its time at Okinawa. First it would guard the big ships from whatever danger would come. Second, it would support the invasion with gunfire; lots of gunfire. Third, it would fight off the planes that would make it Hell for the Navy at Okinawa.

The next couple of days were devoted to bombardment in preparation for the invasion. On the 28th, the big ships did all the firing. But on the 29th, there was a Underwater Demolition Team (UDT) operation.. Since the frogmen were going in to the beach to check conditions and remove obstacles, the destroyers were tasked with covering them with gunfire.

The destroyers moved in close to the beach. At a little after 9:00 in the morning, they opened up, pouring fire in on the beach a couple of hundred yards above the water line. For nearly 3 hours in the first phase of the UDT operation, they cruised slowly back and forth along the beach. While landing craft delivered the frogmen and all during the difficult work of setting explosives to clear beach obstacles, the destroyers stood by faithfully. 5 inch and 40mm rounds flowed in streams over the heads of the frogmen. When the morning's work was done, the Callaghan had fired 245 5 inch rounds and 917 rounds of 40mm.

That was just the beginning. In the afternoon, the destroyers moved back in again. This time it was to provide cover fire for the landing craft while the frogmen were extricated from the beach. Word came back that most of the enemy fire that the frogmen were taking was small arms and machine gun. As a result, the order went out to hose the beach down with the 40mm's. When the Callaghan was finished this time, 1667 rounds of 40mm had been expended, a new record!

The Callaghan crew was glad to rejoin the task group. It was gratifying to hit the enemy directly for a change but it was unnerving to be so close to enemy held territory for so many hours. Not only was there the threat of enemy shore-based fire, but being tied to the beach like that made a ship an easy target for kamikazes. Furthermore there was a known threat from mines off Okinawa. It was simply not the duty destroyermen were used to, or trained for.

The task group left the area of the western beaches of Okinawa and steamed out to get some sea room. The ships steamed that night in an area to the northwest of Okinawa. There was no reason to be out there except that it was away from the island. The only anchorage available to the Navy at this time was the newly won lagoon inside the islands of Kerama Retto, which is precisely where the Callaghan went the next morning As usual, the destroyers patrolled while the big ships entered first. The Callaghan got its turn to steam into the lagoon soon enough and promptly found a particular LST to moor alongside. This LST was loaded with ammunition, including 5 inch Navy rounds.

A work party was formed immediately to take on the unenviable task of loading 5 inch shells and the 5 inch powder cans aboard the Callaghan. 954 shells of various types and 855 powder cans were loaded and stowed below in the magazines. Captain Bertholf immediately ordered the crew to prepare to get underway.

Next, was a trip to the local gas station. In this case, the gas station was the tanker Brazos. In a remarkable display of efficiency, the Callaghan came alongside the Brazos, moored and took on over 1500 barrels of fuel in less than an hour. Then the ship was on its way again.

No time for rest or relaxation here. The Callaghan left Kerama Retto to join the heavy cruiser Salt Lake City and destroyer Abele for a little reconnaissance mission. The Americans were considering the potential usefulness of the small island of Ie Jima located not far from the northern end of Okinawa. This mission was to get a waterline view of the island.

Right around dusk, the Callaghan broke away from the other two ships to join other destroyers on one of the patrol stations that the Navy had set up around Okinawa. These stations were selected to provide what was hoped to be effective harassment fire against the Japanese troops manning positions on Okinawa.

The Callaghan fired a leisurely 150 rounds at the island that night. This was the second night of harassment fire duty for the Callaghan. The most amazing thing was how it ended.

A few minutes before dawn, it happened again. At medium to high altitude, a "Judy" dive bomber appeared. As soon as the lookouts reported it, the gun director was on the target. There was no hesitation this time. The Callaghan went to G.Q. immediately and soon opened fire with the main battery.

The plane turned toward the ship and started an approach, gradually losing altitude. As the black bursts of antiaircraft fire began to appear in its flight path, the plane began a remarkable display of acrobatics. It twisted, turned and jinked to avoid the destroyers AA fire.

In moments the Callaghan was putting out rapid full salvos of five rounds of 5 inch per salvo. As the plane closed to about half the distance between it and the ship, it suddenly turned away. As the Captain put it in his action report "It appeared he was deterred by the AA fire this ship was throwing his way."

Taking no chances, the Callaghan continued firing until the plane was nearly out of range. This was considered a success by the skipper as no attack had been allowed.

The crew was discovering that getting up for morning reveille was not a problem at Okinawa!

The rest of that day went by without incident. The Callaghan spent it back in the screen of the bombardment task group it now knew so well. The big ships were simply marking time. Tomorrow was L day at Okinawa. L stood for Landing day although it was called Love day by most of the brass. All the preparation was going to bear fruit as thousands of army and Marine troops would be going ashore.

The night passed as quietly as the day. An hour before dawn, the Callaghan went to general quarters. Then she turned out of the screen to head for her assigned patrolling station for bombardment duty.

True to Okinawa form, a half hour or so later, an enemy plane was reported inbound. The plane, a Val, was spotted visually about 6000 yards to the rear of the Callaghan. All of the guns that could bear on the target, the aft two 5", rear 40mm and fantail 20mm's, opened up immediately. All of the nearby ships in the task group opened fire as well. There were many heavy ships surrounding the destroyer, so guns were firing all around.

The plane appeared to be diving on one of the heavy cruisers. It crossed far enough to the port that all of the 5" guns plus the port side 40mms were able to fire. Abruptly, the plane was hit and crashed into the sea just 200 yards short of the heavy cruiser. The Callaghan put in a partial credit claim for shooting down the plane.

A mere 10 minutes later, it happened again! A Val was spotted by lookouts as it came out from a cloud strip about 9500 yards away off the starboard bow. The plane was still flying straight and level when it was taken under fire at a range of 8500 yards. About 30 seconds later, other ships on the starboard side joined in. With that volume of fire coming at him, the pilot started taking evasive maneuvers by doing slow rolls to each side. When it was about 6000 yards away from the Callaghan, it started a dive on one of the heavy ships.

After the dive started, the starboard 40mms aboard the Callaghan opened up. The tracers from the 40's were observed to hit the plane's fuselage behind the engine cowling. Seconds later the plane burst into flame and it fell into the water well short of its target.

At 8:00 in the morning, the Callaghan joined the other gun ships in bombarding the shore. The firing was slow and deliberate. A half hour later, the first wave of landing craft began heading in to the beach. The last great invasion of the war had begun!

The Callaghan ceased fire and stood by. The destroyers off the beaches were now expected to be available for "call fire." Each destroyer had a shore fire party assigned to it. The shore party would advise the destroyer of targets it needed bombarded. The Callaghan would get particularly good at this task, earning a vote from their shore party as the "best call fire destroyer at Okinawa."

There was little call for shore fire that first day. Everyone from soldiers hitting the beach right on up to Admiral Kelly Turner himself were surprised at the lack of opposition. They did not know that Japanese General Ushijima had ordered that beaches should not be defended.

Based on the experience of Saipan and Iwo Jima, many Japanese military leaders had decided that the beaches could not be defended against the overwhelming firepower of the American Navy. Further, one of the army divisions had been withdrawn from Okinawa, drawing down the available forces. Therefore, Ushijima had decided that he could make a better defense by fortifying the Southern half of Okinawa into a bastion designed to bloody the American troops when they would turn to attack sometime after the landing.

The Callaghan did get a few short fire missions that first day. Then it was over. Concern turned once again to the sky. Would planes appear at dusk when all ships are more vulnerable in the fading light?

Naturally one plane did show up. But it was flying far enough out that it could not be hit by antiaircraft fire. The Callaghan was ordered to lay smoke. If you can't hit em, hide!

After the smoke screening mission was called off, the Callaghan prepared for the role of night fire support. This differed from day fire support mainly in that the majority of fire delivered was illumination rounds. The soldiers and Marines did not yet have many targets to be destroyed. But they did have a high need to be able to see if the wily Japanese might be planning one of their infamous Banzai attacks.

It was another night of little sleep. It was hard to sleep when on an irregular schedule, the main battery would suddenly open up to deliver a round or two. Worse, the Japanese were sending planes to harass the fleet off Okinawa that night.

The Callaghan was at the readiness level of 1-easy. That meant that the crew was at their battlestations but were allowed to get permission from officers to move around to make the long hours less fatiguing. About 20 minutes after midnight, word was received of a "snooper" coming toward the beach area Apparently, the plane had seen the Callaghan firing starshells.

The plane came out of the darkness suddenly. The guys topside saw the flashing of its machine guns as it opened up to strafe the Callaghan. It happened very quickly with machine gun bullets bouncing off of the metal decks of the Callaghan in all directions. The number two 40mm mount was the only gun to fire off a few rounds at him. It was completely ineffective.

The plane apparently flew a quick circle and then tried again. Only this time he fired at the next ship over, an LCI which was just a few hundred yards away. This was his last attack and he abruptly flew off into the darkness.

But the Japanese pilot had drawn blood. It was discovered that one of the 20mm gunners had been hit. Doc. Parker was called while sailors got the gunner out of this harness and laid him on the deck. It was McCann, one of the ships bakers.

Doc. Parker arrived in just a minute or so but he didn't like what he saw. McCann had a shattered leg; there was lots of blood oozing out and he was unconscious, in shock. Doc. made a quick examination and found worse. The bullet had ricocheted up into McCann's body. There was major internal bleeding. Doc. was sure there was no hope. He could not find a pulse.

He had McCann carried into the ward room. He took another look and declared the sailor dead. He sent word to Captain Bertholf and then ordered the pharmacist mates to clean McCann's body up. He would be prepared for burial at sea.

There was one more action about 30 minutes before sunrise. Tracer fire from other ships indicated that they were firing at a plane. Despite the poor visibility, lookouts spotted it a little over 5000 yards out. It appeared to be a Zero fighter plane that was maneuvering radically to dodge the heavy antiaircraft fire. The Callaghan opened fire with the main battery for just a few seconds. At that point the plane was already falling into the sea. It burst into fire when it hit the water.

At 6:34am the Callaghan secured from general quarters. At 7:00am the destroyer took position to provide call fire support for target area 7996. The main battery crews did not even get a half hour off.
Many of the crew members looked like they were awake in name only. They were getting haggard in appearance.

What saved them was the Japanese lack of defense of the center part of Okinawa. The call fire was over in an hour and 15 minutes. The Callaghan stood by all day but was not called for more fire. Late in the afternoon the Preston came by for a rendezvous to receive some material from the Callaghan. Being a thousand miles away from their support base, the ships were already sharing and trading materials and equipment to keep operational.

That evening the Callaghan rejoined the heavies in the bombardment task group. All night was spent steaming in the clear zone to the west of Okinawa. The next morning the Callaghan went in to the beach area again but with a different purpose this time. After 14 days at sea, with constant operations and the threat of Japanese suiciders ever present, the Callaghan was getting to drop anchor for a few hours.

The sailors were told to get as much rest as they could outside of any duties they had to perform. The Captain was not sure how long they would be able to stay at anchor. Not all of the sailors were free though. Two thirds of the guns were manned as the Kamikazes could show up at any moment.

At 10:00am in the morning, a burial service was held for Thomas James McCann, Baker 2nd class. This was a solemn ceremony that few of the civilians turned sailor had seen. The body had been wrapped in a canvas shroud and covered with a flag. After a few words were spoken by the skipper and a Bible passage was read, a volley of rifle shots were fired in salute. The platform that held the body was then tipped up so that the body could slide free over the side of the ship. The flag was held back so it would not go with the body. In time honored Naval tradition, McCann was committed to the sea.

At noon, sailors catching up on their sleep were rousted out to form a work party. The LST 721 had come alongside to serve as ammunition ship for the Callaghan. It took the rest of the day to load the ammunition. 625 5 inch shells were brought aboard along with nearly as many 5 inch powder cases. In addition, 14 of the heavy depth charges were manhandled aboard.

Before they were through loading the ammunition, some ammunition went the other way. At dusk the destroyers were asked to provide illumination rounds again. Even though anchored, the Callaghan joined in. It was canceled after an hour or so.

The Callaghan finished loading the ammunition and stood by all night to provide illumination support which was required on an intermittent basis. General quarters was called way before dawn at 5:00am. This morning there were no enemy planes to fight off. It was relatively quiet as the Callaghan remained at anchor.

In mid-morning, a request came in for call fire support. The Callaghan fired white phosphorus rounds, a few at a time. The fire control shore party was carefully coaching the rounds in on some target. 43 rounds later the shore party called cease fire.

Another 750 rounds of 5" shells were loaded from the LST plus a huge number of 40mm rounds: over 4000! Finally, at 2:30 in the afternoon, the Callaghan weighed anchor and steamed slowly out of the anchorage.

Three hours later the destroyer joined the bombardment group for another retirement to the west to spend the night at sea.

The Callaghan was shuttled around between three different task groups on the 5th of April. the last mission involved escorting a couple of old APDs which were high speed transports converted from old World War I era destroyers. The

Scribner and Kinzer along with some ampbious vessels, were on a mission to land a Marine battalion to clear Tsugin Jima of any Japanese units or facilities. The Callaghan and Irwin would stand guard off the island all night and part of the next day.

Just after noon on the 6th, the Callaghan was detached along with the Irwin to join the battleship West Virginia . Minutes after joining up, a twin engine plane was spotted flying in the general direction of the ships. It was recognized as Japanese and General Quarters was sounded. Before the guns could open up though, a friendly fighter plane shot the bomber down.

The little group of ships was on the way to join a larger group of fire support ships. Word came in that there was an unusual amount of enemy air activity. Large groups of planes had already attacked other formations of ships all around Okinawa.

At 4:15 the threat became real for the fire support ships. Antiaircraft bursts were observed about 10 miltes off the starboard bow. Lookouts picked up two Vals both low on the water.

One was extremely low and appeared to be closer and faster. The Callaghan fire control team turned its attention on it by slewing the big gun director onto that plane. This plane was flying an erratic, evasive course and varying its altitude as well. The main battery opened fire at 11,500 yards.

The target continued toward the Callaghan until the range was about 7500 yards. At that point the plane turned right and began to open the range from the Callaghan. It finally circled over the destroyer escort Witter at about 9600 yards distance. The Callaghan ceased fire for fear of hitting the DE. The Irwin, was still able to fire on the plane and was getting hits. Shortly thereafter, the plane went into a rapid turning climb. At the peak of its climb the plane nosed over and dove on the Witter. It hit the little ship's bow causing flames to erupt and a big smoke cloud to roll over the ship. This was the second time the

Callaghan crew had witnessed a successful Kamikaze attack on one of its fellow warships. It was a sobering sight.

The Witter lost six crewmen killed and six wounded from the Kamikaze. It limped away to Kerama Retto. The damage was extensive enough that the ship was later scrapped. Many ships were knocked out of the war in this manner at Okinawa.

The primary reason that the last several combats with enemy planes had begun with a visual sighting was that the Callaghan's all important SC radar was inoperative. Within a day or so of L day, the radar's worn out gears quit operating. This was not something the crew could fix themselves. It would require a session at a tender that could replace the worn out gears. Due to the critical need for every warship available at Okinawa, the Callaghan could not be spared to leave for this repair at this time.

The loss of the SC radar meant that the ship could not search for planes at long range. In most cases, planes would have to be spotted by lookouts using binoculars. In rare cases, given an accurate vector on a bogie by the warning network, the FD radar could be coached on to the target.

The FD radar was the surface search radar. It was designed to find ships or land on the surface of the earth. But it would also pick up planes at long range if it was aimed at the correct vector and the plane was at a relatively low altitude. It was not easy and required a sharp eyed operator to pull it off.

On the morning of the 7th of April, the bombardment task group went to general quarters over an hour before dawn. Since there had been such heavy air attacks the day before and planes were reported in the area already, the Admirals were taking no chances. The task group was on a course of 180 degrees which is due south.

The early G.Q. was a wise precaution. The warning net advised the ships of a bogie headed their way at 0525. The plane was reported to be directly ahead flying a course of 0 degrees which was an exact reciprocal of the ships' course.

With this precise information, the Callaghan's fire control team was able to get the big FD radar on the target. There it was, at 20 miles, closing at about 150 knots.

Soon antiaircraft fire was observed from leading ships of the formation. The plane swung out to the right to go around the ships. When it came within 6000 yards, the Callaghan joined the fight with its main battery. 54 rounds were belted out until the plane opened the range to approximately 9000 yards. The cease fire was given.

Although the plane was not hit, this was a significant fight in that the Callaghan fired its main battery while under the control of the Surface Radar! It was a very dark morning so the plane was never seen visually. Using the FD radar to direct the main battery at this plane was equivalent to firing at a PT boat 6000 yards away that was traveling at 150 knots!

Shortly after this incident with the plane was over, the Callaghan was detached to escort the battleship Tennessee to Kerama Retto. Both ships were soon anchored inside the protected area of the anchorage.

While at Kerama Retto that day, the Callaghan transferred one of the stewards mates to a tender for medical treatment. It also steamed over to the Brazos again to fill the bunkers with fuel oil. Late in the afternoon, the destroyer left Kerama Retto to rejoin the bombardment task group which was nearby.

General quarters was sounded well before dusk due to enemy aircraft activity in the general vicinity. 45 minutes later a plane did come in.

Once again the Callaghan was able to pick up the plane on its FD radar. This plane was about 18 miles away, at 5000 ft altitude and traveling about 140 knots. When the plane was about 7200 yards away, the main battery opened up. The plane began to fly toward the far side of the formation of ships which took it away from the Callaghan. As the range went beyond 10,000 yards the Callaghan ceased fire.

287

Right after the main battery went silent, the plane was seen to dive on one of the battleships and hit it. It turned out that the plane had dove on the battleship Maryland and smashed into the number 3, 16 inch gun turret. The plane was evidently carrying a heavy bomb because the explosion penetrated the armor plating on top of the turret. Over 20 sailors were killed and many more were wounded. The topside sailors aboard the Callaghan had witnessed yet another suicide dive that seriously damaged a major unit of the US Navy.

Even though the war in Europe was almost over and despite the complete destruction of the Japanese surface Navy, the United States Navy was facing its most difficult challenge since the dark early days of the war. Before the Okinawa campaign was over, more ships would be damaged than in any other campaign of the war. This happened to the Navy when it was at the very height of its power. Nothing could demonstrate more clearly the central role that aircraft now took in warfare at sea. The kamikazes would be the most serious combat threat the US Navy would face for decades to come. Nothing else came even close.

Oddly enough, that night the Callaghan left the formation to take special radar picket duty between stations Number 1 and 14. Apparently the Navy brass decided there was a potential hole between the first and last radar picket stations off Okinawa. It is strange that they sent the Callaghan to plug this gap when its air search radar was not functioning properly.

The next day the Callaghan returned to the active area off western Okinawa to resume fire support duties. The Callaghan joined the destroyer Laffey to provide fire support in sector No. 7. The next two days were spent alternating fire support duty with other destroyers.

On the morning of the 10th, the Callaghan was sent to relieve the Porterfield on the fire support station off Nago Wan. Orders came to support nearby minesweeping operations so the ship left to do so.

Just after dawn, they secured from general quarters. By 7:30 the Callaghan was on station off Unten Ko. An hour later a disturbing event occured.

Several sailors observed one of the stewards mates, Alexander, at the rail not far from the depth charge throwers. Alexander was the largest and most muscular of the stewards mates. He was considered a little slow mentally because of the way he talked. He had been at odds with another steward named Penn for several months. Penn was a sharp witted, fast talker from the city who liked to needle Alexander. Their disputes had gotten them both in trouble with the officers on several occasions. This was one of the major problems that Doc. Parker had to deal with since he was in charge of the stewards.

The sailors who witnessed what happened would remember later that Alexander was acting strange. He stared into the water intently. His body language showed hesitation and uncertainty. Despite this he climbed up on the rail and immediately jumped off.

The sailors were stunned. Several voices yelled "Man overboard." The word got up to the bridge and the officer-of-the deck immediately ordered a sharp turn on the side Alexander had jumped from. Captain Bertholf was on the bridge in seconds and concurred with the action. He directed a search for the missing man.

But there was no sign of the stewards mate. Doc. Parker told the Captain that he was pretty sure that Alexander could not swim. He apparently went down before the ship could turn around. The man's action had all the earmarks of a suicide. Every spare sailor was topside looking for the man in the water but to no avail. After 20 minutes, Captain Bertholf called it off because the destroyer was needed to cover the minesweepers.

There was a great deal of speculation as to why Alexander committed suicide. Many thought it was his fights with Penn. Some of his fellow stewards noted that he had been despondent. Some thought it was the stress of the Kamikaze threat that everyone aboard felt. The truth will never be known. But this incident illustrates the pressures the crew were dealing with during the Okinawa campaign.

For the next three weeks the pattern had already been set. The Callaghan spent day after day and night after night on fire support duty. when not on fire support duty, the destroyer was either screening the heavy ships of the bombardment task force or getting refueled and rearmed at Kerma Retto.

Luckily there was very little air action close enough to the Callaghan to require a gunnery response during this time. The Callaghan got a break from the Kamikazes even though many other warships were attacked during this period. For whatever reason, the Callaghan missed most of the action for awhile.

On April 21st, the Callaghan received aboard the Commodore of DesRon 55 and his staff. Once again the Callaghan was the flag ship of the squadron.

On May 1st, 6 enlisted men were transferred off the Callaghan for new assignments back in the States. On of these was Ed Kellner. The gunnery officer in charge of the torpedo gang had told them that one man would get to rotate back to the states. Instead of going by seniority, he had the guys cut cards to determine who the lucky guy would be. Kellner won the draw. He would go on to a long career in the Navy, eventually becoming a Lt. Commander.

Two men reported aboard the Callaghan that evening. One was a new Stewards Mate to replace Alexander.

The next three days were a blur of fire support and harassment missions interspersed with the occasional air raid alert. Nothing serious developed for the Callaghan. However on the 3rd, on Radar Picket Station Five off West Okinawa, destroyers Little and Aaron Ward were hit by a mass attack of Kamikazes. The Little was sunk losing 30 killed and 79 wounded. The Aaron Ward was crashed by the unbelievable number of seven Kamikazes and still managed to stay afloat! Although 45 sailors were killed, the heroic crew of the Aaron

Ward put out the fires and got the damage under control. It was towed by the Shannon back to Kerama Retto.

On the morning of May 4th, the Callaghan was patrolling off Haguchi anchorage providing an antiaircraft screen for the transport ships in the anchorage. At 8:45, a plane was spotted diving toward the anchorage from out of the sun. Initially the plane was off the starboard beam but the ship was swinging left so that was changing. The main battery opened fire immediately at a range of 8000 yards. The target, an Oscar, was hard to hit because it was in a fast spiraling dive. When the range to the plane was reduced, 3 of the 40mm mounts opened fire. Fire was maintained until the plane was directly over a light cruiser. The plane then went into a 90 degree dive and crashed into the forward part of the cruiser.

These vicious attacks of May 3rd and 4th were a part of the fifth Kikusui. The Kikusui were organized mass air attacks that were employed during the Okinawa campaign with the express purpose of defeating the US Naval forces involved in the invasion. The Japanese had anticipated that the Allied forces would invade either Okinawa or Formosa during the early part of 1945. They had purposely held back their aircraft to be ready to respond to such an eventuality. This explained the apparent lack of response to the invasion of Iwo Jima and the air strikes that Task Force 58 had mounted against the home islands.

A few minutes before the Callaghan tried to down the diving Oscar, radar picket Station One was hard hit again. Station One was one of the two stations closest to Japan. A fellow destroyer from the Callaghan's squadron, the Morrison, was out there. The Morrison had been damaged along with the Irwin when the Princeton was sunk during the Battle of Leyte Gulf. With the Morrison on Station One was the destroyer Ingraham.

25 Japanese planes headed toward Station One. The combat air patrol intercepted them and shot down several. But many of the planes broke through and began to attack the Morrison and the Ingraham. Three different planes tried to drop bombs on

the Morrison and missed. Then at 8:25, a zero crashed into the Morrison's number one stack and bridge causing severe damage. The electrical systems all went out which crippled the Morrison's war fighting ability. A second zero clipped the number three gun and then smashed into the main deck opening a big hole into the after engine room.

The Morrison might have survived all this. But the crippled ship was now attacked by two old twin-float biplanes. The first crashed into the Number 3 5" gun causing the gun powder to explode in the upper handling room. The second crashed into the Number 4 gun causing more powder to explode. This caused such extensive flooding aft that the skipper ordered the crew to abandon ship. It sank soon afterwards.

The Ingraham did not escape damage. She received two near misses before a zero crashed near the Number 2 five inch gun. The forward fire room was flooded, 14 men were killed and 37 wounded. The Ingraham was damaged so severely that she had to return to the States for repairs. She never got back to the war. In addition, a rocket landing ship, LSM(R) 194 was hit by a suicider and sunk. This little vessel lost 13 men dead and 23 wounded.

The destroyer Luce was also lost out on radar Station Twelve. Several other ships were damaged by Kamikazes that day. All in all, the 4th of May was bloody for the US Navy at Okinawa.

The Callaghan had to spend all the next night on shore bombardment duty. But then it got a break. In the company of the Battleship Colorado and a cruiser, they steamed down to Kerama Retto. The Callaghan spent the next three days in the anchorage; resting, repairing and replacing ammunition. It was during this time that the all important air search radar was finally repaired.

Since the ship was out of the action for awhile, a Captain's Mast was held. One of the sailors, a Seaman First class, came before the Captain with a charge of urinating over the side of the ship. The Captain came up with a very appropriate punishment for this man. He was put on the head detail for the next three months. The "head" is navy lingo for the bathroom and "detail" means a work crew or duty.

Some of the sailors got to go ashore while the Callaghan was immobilized. Kerama Retto was still very primitive with very limited facilities. Still, the men were glad to get ashore for a few hours. There was ever-present danger aboard all of the ships even while at anchor in the lagoon. The Kamikazes had struck at Kerama Retto several times since the Okinawa Campaign had begun.

The other thing about Kerama Retto that was attractive was the islands that it was made of. These were not coral atolls like so many of the islands that the Callaghan had visited since the Marianas campaign. These were real islands complete with rolling hills and honest-to-goodness trees! There was actually something worth exploring here.

There was not much on the "beach" area. Howard Grey decided to go for a walk. He walked away from the beach area and soon found himself drawn to explore the inviting hills. These little tropical hills kind of reminded him of California. After climbing up and down several of them, he headed toward the beach on a different side of the island. Quite a bit of time had passed by now. He was concerned about returning in time to catch the boat ride back to the ship.

When he got back to the official "beach" area, he mentioned to one of the sailors on duty there that he had been up in the hills. The man looked at him strangely for a moment. He then told Howard that there were still Japanese soldiers holed up in caves out there. The Americans were unable to find them during the day. At night the Japanese came out to either steal food or to try to attack any Americans they might find alone. Howard was chilled by the thought of the Japanese eyes that may have followed his every move as he so carelessly wandered the island landscape!

On the 8th, the Callaghan moved back up to the Nakagusuku Wan (bay). Shortly after arriving they were back to providing harassment fire in support of the troops ashore. The ship spent two days on this duty.

The 10th brought an early trip back down to Kerama Retto. The first stop was alongside an LST to perform a duty which we would now call recycling. The Callaghan unloaded its spent shell casings into the LST. These shell casings would be sent back to the United States for reloading. Then it was over to a tanker for refueling. After that, the ship steamed over to the Las Vegas Victory ship to load ammunition.

That illustrates the primary cycle at Okinawa. It began with fire support duty and night illumination. Hundreds and hundreds of rounds would be fired off. Then steam back down to Kerama Retto. After that, unload the empties, refuel and load new ammunition. The cycle would then repeat itself.

There was, of course, the occasional sudden break in the routine to try to fend off Japanese planes.

Just before sundown on the 12th, the Callaghan had just arrived at Haguchi Anchorage where most of the transport ships were anchored. The crew was just getting ready to put the anchor down. Lookouts spotted two strange planes closing from the west. They swung into a wide orbit about 5 miles away. It was impossible, at first, to identify the planes due to the haze and setting sun. One of the old battleships commenced firing on the planes so the Callaghan joined in along with most of the ships in the anchorage. Both planes then went into a steep dive on the old battleship. The lead plane was hit and burst into flame. It crashed just off the starboard side of the battleship. The second plane, close behind, crashed into the starboard side of the big ship's after smokestack.

After a rare quiet night, the Callaghan left the next day for Southern Okinawa to rejoin the bombardment line. A new type of target not seen before by the Callaghan appeared on the scene. A small boat came along the shore while the Callaghan was steaming between positions. After studying the target through binoculars, Captain Bertholf approved a suggestion to use the 40mm guns to fire at the boat. A few dozen rounds of 40mm later, the boat turned in to the shore and the destroyer ceased fire.

At the second bombardment position of the day off Naha, the same thing happened again. Another small boat was observed moving along the shoreline. Again the 40s were turned loose. This time a couple of hundred rounds were fired at the target. After the barrage of cannon rounds ceased and the dust settled, it was evident that these native small boats were very difficult to sink. However, the boat was certainly damaged and probably wouldn't be going anywhere soon.

The evening and all night were devoted to fire support and illumination. In the morning the Callaghan returned to Kerama Retto for another round of unloading empties, refueling and loading ammunition.

During the afternoon of May 17th, the Callaghan was providing cover in support of hydrographic operations. The Callaghan was anchored offshore providing call fire against Japanese guns or installations that might threaten the little boats doing the hazardous job of charting the depths off Okinawa. It is ironic that this job was proceeding in light of what would happen the very next day in virtually the same spot.

At 1445, the operation was completed for the day. The Callaghan had destroyed five machine guns and one medium artillery piece in one target area. In another, it had collapsed two caves and demolished an underpass that the Japanese were using to hide men and equipment. At 1621, the Callaghan got underway and headed back to Hagushi anchorage.

The next day the Callaghan rejoined T.G. 54.3 which was on its way to Kerama Retto. It was time for another cycle of load fuel, ammo, provisions and offload empty shell casings. About mid-morning, word was received that the Callaghan's old friend and sister destroyer, the Longshaw was in serious trouble.

Back in the area the Callaghan had been in the day before, destroyers had been taking turns providing gun support. This was off the west coast of Okinawa near a reef called the Ose Reef. Unfortunately for the Longshaw, someone was careless in plotting their position that morning. With a reef nearby, that could be a fatal mistake.

At about 7:19 in the morning, a sound was heard that no seaman ever wants to hear. A loud growl was heard coming from under the ship as it ground to a halt. The Longshaw was hard aground on Ose Reef.

Immediately her skipper, Lieutenant Commander C. W. Becker, had the engines thrown into reverse. The 60,000 horsepower engines spun the big propellers until the whole ship shook. The hull would not budge and the destroyer remained hung up on the reef.

For over three hours, the crew of the Longshaw tried increasingly drastic measures to get the ship to move. After it became clear that the engines alone were not enough, they tried shifting anything that was not bolted down from the forward part of the ship to the aft part of the ship. That included ammunition.

Moving ammunition was always dangerous. The big magazines were built with special doors and hatches meant to provide the maximum protection possible against anything which might cause an explosion. Getting several hundred 5" rounds and powder cases up out of the magazines required opening up these hatches/ doors and leaving them open for hours. The special protection was gone during this risky operation. Further, there was now a trail of explosive shells and cases stretching the length of the ship.

An urgent call went out to the fleet for help. A big fleet tug like the ones that the Callaghan had met in the middle of the ocean last October was sent to try tow the Longshaw off the reef. The Arikara soon arrived.

The Arikara took up station behind the Longshaw. Towing cables were sent over to the Longshaw and rigged through the stern chocks. Amazingly, even with the mighty Arikara straining with maximum power, the destroyer would not budge. Clearly, the destroyers hull plates were somehow fastened to the coral or rock of the reef.

Of course, all this occurred within sight of the Okinawa shore. The Japanese had noticed the destroyer stopped out in the bay. They recognized an opportunity to retaliate against the hated gunships which had been tormenting them. They immediately began moving big 150mm guns up to a position where they could fire on the hapless destroyer.

At 11:00am, the Japanese battery opened up. Salvo after salvo came out and the Japanese were quick to correct their fire. In a matter of a couple of minutes they were slamming big shells into the helpless destroyer.

The Longshaw tried to fire back but it was not a typical fighting situation for a destroyer. Since they could not move, they could not bring the entire main battery to bear on the target. Worse, the ammunition and the crew who normally handled it were dispersed all over the ship. The return fire was weak and ineffective.

The big enemy shells had a horrible effect. Sailors were torn to pieces and blown off the ship. The fire control equipment for the main battery was soon wrecked. Fires began and ammunition started exploding. The ship was doomed.

Captain Becker ordered "Abandon Ship" even as he was seriously wounded himself. The officers suffered the worst casualty rate with only 9 survivors out of 22. The enlisted men lost 68 of their number. Captain Becker remained with his ship. His body was consumed by the raging fires around the bridge area and never found.

After the survivors were evacuated, the Navy sent in gunships to make sure the Longshaw would not boarded by the enemy and yield vital secrets. The Longshaw was blown apart by thousands of shells poured on it by "friendly" ships. It was an ignominious end for one of the fine warships of DesRon 55.

In the middle of the seemingly endless duty with the shore bombardment group, on the morning of May 25th, the Callaghan was suddenly confronted with danger from the skies.

The Callaghan had been on assignment all night long supporting the troops with call gunfire and illumination from starshells. It was a tired crew that anchored the destroyer in Nakagusuku Wan bay.

The morning was rainy and overcast with a low cloud deck. Despite this, there were air alerts all morning as enemy air activity picked up. After an attack by Japanese planes in a nearby area, it was decided to get the warships in the bay under way. The Callaghan pulled up its anchor and slowly moved out.

At 10:15am, the nearby Battleship West Virginia opened fire with its anti-aircraft guns. The men on the Callaghan who were topside looked in that direction. Suddenly two twin-engine planes burst out of the cloud cover headed right for the Callaghan. The fire control system had to move fast to get into action. There was barely time for the gunnery officer to give the order to open fire.

The gunners reacted automatically with practiced movements hurried by adrenaline. The 5 inch guns immediately began booming out rounds at the most difficult target possible: one coming straight at you. The 40mm guns opened fire at the same time as the main battery. The range was rapidly decreasing and it was clear that the 5 inch guns would have to get lucky to knock down even one of these planes. It was going to be up to the machine gunners and they would have to get on the targets fast.

The ace 40mm gunners, long trained to absolute boredom by Captain Johnson and honed by Captain Bertholf, came through. The 40's hit both planes just before they flew over the Callaghan. A couple of mounts went vertical as they followed the lead plane as it screamed directly over the Callaghan at less than 100 feet of altitude. It was mortally hit. The other plane turned away at the last second and flew off trailing smoke.

The lead plane was now on fire, out of control and immediately crashed into the sea less than 800 yards away. It was a spectacular crash of a large aircraft that had apparently just tried to attack the Callaghan. The guys topside were elated, mesmerized and horrified; all at the same time. Many of them were cheering.

Despite the possible danger, Captain Bertholf immediately stopped the ship. The crew watched two airmen get out of the plane and crawl out on the wing. The Chief Bosun formed an armed rescue party. The whale boat was lowered and the rescue party motored over to the Japanese plane. The two Japanese were returned to the Callaghan.

After the whale boat was hauled back aboard, one Japanese crewman was taken to Doc. Parker and the other to the aft aid station. Doc. tried to save the more seriously injured of the two but failed because of his extensive injuries. The Pharmacist Mates in the aft station treated the wounds of the Japanese Navigator. Eventually he regained consciousness.

The Navigator's name was Hasegawa. He was surprised to find that he was being well treated by the American sailors. But his stay aboard the Callaghan was short. He was transferred that evening to the Battleship New Mexico and disappeared from the life of the Callaghan crew for 50 years.

The Callaghan returned to the gun line off Okinawa and continued its support of the soldiers and marines ashore. Toward the end of this period, one shore party declared the

Callaghan to be the best destroyer at Okinawa for fire support. That was very tall praise indeed! There was other superb gunnery efforts by other destroyers including sister ships Irwin and Cassin Young.

In the end the Callaghan fired over 19 thousand 5" rounds at or over targets on Okinawa. The guns were worn and the fire control equipment was suspect. Problems with the radar have already been mentioned although in the end it changed. The SC radar was back in commission but the calibration was off and needed attending.

The condition of the guns was worrisome enough that the Gunnery Officer talked the Captain into arranging a test of the main battery's accuracy. The test actually revealed that the guns were mostly within tolerances. Only one gun fired at the very edge of the tolerance limit. The overall result was considered acceptable for now. But it was a sign that the Callaghan was in real need of an overhaul.

Problems had come up with the 40mm guns as well. Thousands upon thousands of 40mm rounds had been fired at Okinawa. The guns themselves had fared fairly well but replaceable parts such as the leather seals were worn out. Unfortunately the fleet at Okinawa was at the very end of the longest logistics pipeline the US Navy had ever had to maintain. The little leather seals had not come through the pipeline so that the destroyers could get new ones. Chief Maiwald did what he could but there was always a possibility of failure under prolonged firing conditions.

Equally as important was the fact that the well oiled machine that the Callaghan crew had been was, possibly, not quite so well oiled anymore. A lot of experienced officers and men had transferred to new assignments. There were replacements but they were never as experienced as the men they had replaced. This was particularly acute in the case of one or two officers. The new Engineering Officer was not a Hoskins. That did not matter particularly because Frank Dunne ran the engineering department. He just carried on in his usual "I'll take care of it" mode.

A new gunnery officer came to the Callaghan very late in the Okinawa campaign. He was no Jake Heimark. This was a more serious matter.

The final fire support by US Navy ships on land targets was carried out on June 20th, 1945. Within a couple of days the army and Marines took the last point of land at the Southern end of Okinawa. It was finally over at a terrible cost. Nearly all of the one hundred thousand Japanese troops had been killed. Allied losses were close to 50,000 casualties. For the United States, it was the bloodiest campaign of the Pacific war. Nothing else came close.

The month of July was mostly spent on patrol. The scariest duty was Radar Picket Duty. All destroyers had to take turns at it. There were simply not enough to have any exceptions; including a war-weary Callaghan with questionable equipment.

Ironically, two months after saving a Kamikaze from the drink, another Kamikaze ended the Callaghan's career. During the last week of July the ship had been swept with rumors that the war-weary destroyer would finally get to return to the States for an overhaul. On the morning of the 28th of July the orders finally came in. The Callaghan would serve its last stint on the radar picket line that night. At 2:00am it would be relieved by the Laws and subsequently make the journey back across the Pacific ocean.

The men were ecstatic. Most of them dug into their lockers or sea bags to check on their dress clothes. The laundry suddenly got an overload of uniforms to clean and press. Men were dashing off letters to loved ones to give them the news. It was the first really happy time in the life of the Callaghan since it had come to Okinawa.

It was not to be.

The Callaghan was stationed at Radar Picket station #9 along with destroyers Prichett and Cassin Young. At 12:20am on the 29th a group of enemy planes was picked up on radar. The destroyers all went to General Quarters.

At 12:30 a lone enemy plane made a run at the ships. The main batteries of the destroyers opened up under radar control. The plane veered off. The gunnery men believed it had been driven off by their fire. Whether or not that was the case will never be known. Then it came around again. A rare gunnery mishap suddenly occurred on the Callaghan. Number 3 5" mount began firing smokeless powder instead of the flashless powder required for night fighting. The smokeless rounds going off looked like giant flashbulbs. They illuminated the destroyer for anyone to see.

It was discovered later by the Commodore that there had been another destroyer that reported mismarked smokeless rounds. Apparently a small number of rounds had the wrong label painted on them when they were manufactured. It was such a small number that the Navy had not put out a warning communication about it yet.

The experienced Assistant Gunnery Officer ordered the Number 3 mount to check fire until they got the powder situation straightened out. On the Communications network he heard the new Gunnery Officer countermand his orders. The new guy wanted all of the big guns to fire, flashing or not.

The kamikaze did see the flashes and he turned directly toward the aft end of the ship where Number 3 mount was. It was coming in on the starboard side of the destroyer. As it drew close, personnel topside were astonished to see that it was a biplane with floats. It was flying an extremely slow 85 miles an hour.

This was a major problem because the fire control system was set to track targets at 85 knots and higher! The speed factor in the fire control computer was designed to put the shells out in front of the plane so that it would fly right into the bursting shells. This plane was flying so slow that the shells were probably bursting too far in front of it to have any effect. The gunnery officer could correct for this in a crude fashion by aiming slightly behind the plane. But this was not something they had ever practiced while under radar control. The great concern had always been speeding planes not slow ones.

Further, since the topside sailors could clearly see this plane, the possibility existed that the 40mm guns could be brought into action. It was standard policy at Okinawa to keep the machine guns silent at night for fear that the tracers would provide a lighted path for the kamikazes to follow. Since the sailors could see the plane and the plane was obviously following the ships, adding tracer fire to the equation would not have helped the enemy pilot. An opportunity was missed to shoot the plane down.

With the shells bursting in front of it and the number three gun taking strobe-like pictures of the biplane, the horrified topside crew realized that this plane was going to hit. Howard Grey in his perch high up on the aft stack platform was frozen in amazement. He reported years later that he could clearly see not only the ancient biplane but the pilot in his leather helmet as well!

Like Howard, many crewmen froze. The rest either braced themselves or continued to work their equipment in oblivion. The Kamikaze slammed with a tremendous bang into the starboard side of the superstructure immediately behind mount 3. At the same time the main battery ceased fire.

The roar of the guns was replaced by the roar of flames. The gasoline fed fire leapt hundreds of feet in the air. Many of the crewmen in number three handling room were wounded. The crew of the 40mm mount on top of the aft superstructure were all killed. The plane, or parts of it, apparently punched through into the engine room below. This killed or wounded several of the engine room gang down below. The starboard engine had to be shut down.

For a short time there was frantic activity as the destroyer slowed down but continued to move on its port engine as flames and smoke poured off the ship.

At this time there was a problem to take care of in the number 2 5" gun mount. It seems when the ship ceased fire so abruptly, a shell was left unfired in the number 2 gun. Chief Maiwald was called to ask what to do about it. He saw that the gun was aimed off to the side of the ship and that, at the moment, there was no other ship in the area. He advised firing the gun manually by kicking the spade closed. Leo Jarboe got the nod and did just that. When the spade slammed home on the unfired powder case, it fired. Problem solved.

Within 5 minutes, a large explosion occurred from the aft deck house area. The ammunition in handling room number 3 had exploded. The ship took on a sudden 15 degree list.

Captain Bertholf told the Commodore (Captain Jarrell) that it was probably time to abandon ship. However, he was going to stay aboard with volunteers to try to salvage the ship. The Commodore agreed with the plan and directed his staff to leave the ship. Bertholf ordered the two motorboats to take wounded personnel, the pay records and the logbook to the nearest destroyer.

The Captain then gave the order to abandon ship. Unfortunately, the normal sound and electronic communications were not working to the aft end of the ship. The effort to get the word to everyone was difficult and not always successful. There was a great deal of noise, fires blocking the way, and exploding ammunition which made it hazardous to anyone trying to get back and forth.

At the same time as he ordered the ship abandoned, Bertholf asked for volunteers for his salvage party to stay with him in the attempt to save the ship. The ship was immobilized with no power, very little communications and no electricity. It was down by the stern and had a slight list to the starboard side. But it did not appear to be sinking. Bertholf was not going to give up without a fight to try to get the Callaghan back to Okinawa.

Communications were so poor that many of the men who stayed aboard were not actually volunteers. They simply did not get the word that there was an abandon ship order. In a few cases, sailors who were non-swimmers chose to stay aboard as long as possible out of fear of the water.

The landing craft that were part of the little task group at radar picket station 9 moved in to help. The reason for their presence at radar picket stations was this very situation. The Kamikazes seemed to always go after the destroyers while leaving the small craft alone. When the bigger ships were hit and in trouble, the little guys would come alongside to render assistance in whatever ways they could.

There were plenty of ways to help tonight. At 1:02, LCS 125 came along the port side and immediately got fire hoses going from it's stern to try to hold down the raging fire aft. At the same time it took aboard wounded over the side of it's bow area.

At about the same time both motorboats were launched after having been loaded with wounded. The port motorboat sank immediately. It had been damaged by flying shrapnel more severely than had been visible in the light of the fires aboard ship. Luckily most of the wounded were immediately rescued by men aboard ship or by the nearest LCI.

Aboard the Callaghan there were massive problems. The very stubborn fires that did not want to go out. Along with the fact that virtually no equipment was operating, it was difficult to fight the fire and effect repairs. What they really needed was power. The emergency generator was working but the electrical power was just not getting to most of the ship.

There were many heroes that night. One of them was the Electricians Chief. Along with one of the other Electricians, he headed down into the severely damaged area of the ship where the main circuit breaker board was located. If that could be

305

fixed or bypassed somehow, they might get power to the rest of the ship.

It was a valiant and fatal trip. For in the wreckage below the number 3 handling room was a bomb that the plane had brought aboard. It was a 250 pound bomb such as had devastated many of the ships that the Callaghan crew had seen hit during the war so far. It was probably similar to the one that had sunk the Princeton. It was certainly as deadly.

Suddenly at about 1:30pm, there was a tremendous explosion aft. Many of the sailors all the way forward were knocked off their feet. Anyone near the blast was injured or killed.

This explosion broke the keel of the ship. The keel is the backbone of any ship. Rarely has a warship in the blue water ocean been saved with a broken keel. The keel provides strength to the structure of the ship. Without it, the ship cannot move without progressive damage occurring to the rest of the hull.

The problem for Captain Bertholf was that he did not know this yet. The huge explosion killed or injured several members of his salvage party and gave new fury to the flames. Bertholf sent more than one person aft to try to determine if the keel was broken.

While directing the damage control effort, the Executive Officer, Buzz Buzzetti, descended the ladder at the rear of the bridge. Just as he reached the bottom, he felt a hand grip one of his trouser legs. He looked down and saw Chief Simonton laying on the deck. The Chief had been greviously wounded in the gut. Buzzetti immediately called for some men to come take care of Simonton. The Chief was loaded in the ship's boat along with other wounded sailors. Doc Parker left the Callaghan with this boat.

Finally Bertholf bowed to the inevitable. At 1:43am the skipper ordered the salvage crew and all remaining personnel to leave the ship. The irony was that 2:00am was the original time scheduled for the Callaghan's departure for the States.

Despite the danger from exploding ammunition, the skipper of LCS 130 bravely nosed his craft up until it was touching the side of the Callaghan. His crew fought the fire through the heat and explosions. Bertholf was so impressed by this display of courage and gallantry that he worked hard to get the skipper of the little craft awarded a silver star.

Bertholf, the Commodore and several other sailors from the salvage party were able to jump across to LCS 130. Many of the remaining crewmen who had ignored or didn't hear the abandon ship order now began to jump over the side. The Callaghan was sinking by the stern causing the bow to rise. Several men on the bow were forced to make a much higher leap than normal as the bow rose to 30 feet or more above the water. Leo Jarboe and Chief Maiwald were two of them. They jumped at the same time.

Now, finally, the stern had disappeared, deep in the black water. Only the bow showed now. In moments, it too began its slide to the abyss. A great fighting warship slipped beneath the waves.

Shortly thereafter a deep explosion was heard and felt. Since all the depth charges were put on "safe", the skipper and commodore reported afterward that the boilers must have exploded. It was the last presence of the Callaghan the crew would ever experience.

Meanwhile a frantic rescue effort was under way as the Landing craft and the destroyer Pritchett desperately tried to get the men out of the water. This effort was made difficult by the darkness, the fuel oil coating the water and the continuing danger from Japanese planes. Several crewmen reported hearing the sounds of machine gun fire up above as the night fighters from Okinawa tried to bring down the elusive Japanese planes.

There were a lot of men in the water. Many of them did not have lifejackets on. The strict discipline that required a man to wear his lifejacket to his battlestation had been slowly eroded over time. There had never been enough lifejackets for everybody anyway. It was greatly compounded by the fact that so many of them had been left below decks on the ship.

Now men were struggling to stay afloat using just their lifebelts. A lifebelt was worn around the waist. During an abandon ship crisis, the belt would be inflated either with a CO_2 cartridge or by blowing it up manually just like an air mattress is done today. It was simple to use and easy to wear. The disadvantage was that it was only the size of a bicycle tire. That meant that it would just barely keep a man afloat if nothing went wrong.

Things were going wrong with many of the men. Covering the water was thick fuel oil from the oil bunkers of the Callaghan that had been ruptured by the plane crash and subsequent explosion. It got all over the men and made it that much more difficult to swim and to breathe. Many of the men were wounded. Numerous examples of heroism occured while sailors struggled to save their wounded buddies.

One of those wounded was George Pitts. He was one of the "p" gang that came aboard in Hawaii. He served in the engineering spaces down below. He was hurt badly during the explosion. Someone got him into the water and someone else towed him to a landing craft. Since he was nearly unconscious, he remembered very little of what happened. Decades later at a ship's reunion he met the man who had saved him.

Howard Gray had left his lifejacket below. Although he could swim, he realized right away that he would not make it through the fuel oil and the waves to get to safety. He had to hang on to a sailor who did have a lifejacket. The two of them floated together until a boat came by.

At the same time that the Pritchett was picking up Callaghan sailors, the Cassin Young was patrolling back and forth on the outside of the little group of rescue ships. Everytime an unidentified plane came within range, the Cassin Young opened up with its main battery. There was no thought to hide or to wait for an attack. The Cassin Young was deliberately trying to draw the attention of any potential attackers.

It was a gallant move by the sister ship of the Callaghan. It was extremely dangerous. The Cassin Young was attacked more than once that night. On one occasion, an enemy plane crashed less than a hundred yards from the Cassin Young. The gallant sister ship of the Callaghan fired 400 rounds of 5" shells that night!

Just before dawn, the rescue ships headed in to Buckner Bay. Most of the men were transferred to troopships. The wounded were transferred to a hospital ship. The only advantage to this horrible battle at Okinawa was the presence of the hospital ships. No finer surgical facilities were available in the western Pacific. The men would receive the best possible care in a clean and, by this time, safe environment.

46 sailors and one officer perished.

Admiral Callaghan, for whom the ship was named, was killed on the night of Nov. 13th, 1942. The Callaghan had shot down twelve planes before July 29th, 1945. The thirteenth plane destroyed the Callaghan. The Callaghan was the thirteenth destroyer lost off Okinawa. It was the last United States destroyer lost because of enemy action to this day.

EPILOGUE

The Captain of the Callaghan was ordered to pick one other officer and fly back to Washington D.C. in order to prepare all the reports and paperwork that followed the sinking of a US Navy warship. Captain Bertholf selected Ensign Sheffield because he was from the Washington D.C. area. He also believed the crew would be taken better care of if the Executive officer stayed behind with them.

Captain Bertholf and Ensign Sheffield worked hard to produce reports regarding the sinking of the Callaghan, finish the war diary and other Navy documents. The Captain was even interviewed by a Navy reporter who wrote a short article for a Navy magazine called "Our Navy."

But the most difficult task for the skipper was to write 47 letters to the families of all the crewmen who were killed or missing in action. Captain Bertholf tried hard to personalize each letter that he wrote. These were not cookie-cutter letters. If he knew the crewman personally, he wrote a positive remembrance for the benefit of the family. If he did not know the crewman, he tried to include a report from the officer who was in charge of that man. This was not an easy task for any commanding officer to do. Bertholf did so with grace and humanity.

Meanwhile for the rest of the surviving crew, life was still going on in the far Pacific. It was normal for the surviving crew of a sunken warship to be returned to the States for leave. In this case, the Callaghan crew was already due to return to the States. Despite this, it turned out to be remarkably difficult for the uninjured crewmen to get transport home.

First, they were embarked aboard the USS Hyde for transport back to the US. The Hyde was a nearly brand new attack transport that had been modified to carry a large number of troops. It was ordered to take the crewmen all the way back across the Pacific to the west coast. The Hyde left and everything looked good.

The journey was going to be a long one as they were traveling the formidable distance from Okinawa in the west Pacific all the way to where the Pacific ended at the Golden Gate. The trip would last weeks especially at the slow speed of the transport.

They were making good progress and had made it to Ulithi when great news arrived via radio. The war was over! This meant that they did not have to worry about going back to the combat zone when their survivor's leave was over.

But then the orders for the Hyde were changed. First it was held over at Ulithi far longer than it was originally scheduled. Instead of hours, it remained at Ulithi for 8 days.

Then an incredible thing happened. The Hyde reversed course and started heading back to the West Pacific. The Callaghan crew was stunned! The officers immediately demanded to know why this was happening.

It seemed that once the Callaghan's luck turned sour, it stayed sour for the crew. The most pressing need for the US military immediately after the armistice with Japan was to get transport for troops for the occupation of Japan. Since the Hyde was a converted troop ship, it was ordered to return to the Philippines to pick up US Army personnel needed in Japan.

It did not matter that the Callaghan crew was aboard. It did not matter that they were high on the priority list for transport to the US. They were going back. Morale sunk to very low depths.

The Hyde went to Leyte in the Philippines. There it offloaded the Callaghan crew and picked up army troops. The Callaghan men were transported over to Samar Island, a short distance North of Leyte. There they were stuck in a very primitive camp with crude temporary facilities. They slept in barracks that were little more than huts and took showers from converted 55-gallon drums. They had to get by with donated clothing and gear as they had lost everything when their ship was sunk.

Finally, after the Executive officer vigorously protested through every channel he could, the Callaghan crew was allowed to board another attack transport very similar to the Hyde called the Jean Lafitte. Although the Jean Lafitte was a sister ship to the Hyde, it was older and not as comfortable. For some reason, it seemed to be slower as well.

The Jean Lafitte made its slow, tortuous journey back from the Philippines to the United States. Top of the list of annoyances for the Callaghan crewmen was the quality of the food aboard the Jean Lafitte. The galleys on the attack transports were built to support the ship's crew and a small number of troops. As a troop ship, it was completely inadequate. Hot meals were limited to two a day and were served in several shifts. The destroyer crewmen had depended on three quality square meals a day aboard the Callaghan. Now they experienced something far inferior.

The meal situation was aggravated by the fact that the crewmen were so completely bored on this long slow journey back across the vast expanse of the Pacific. They were no longer standing watches or maintaining their vital equipment. That was all gone and the war over. They did their best to entertain themselves with what little they had. Even the endless card games became a complete bore. The only saving grace was that they were going home.

Home. What an incredible feeling! To be finally going home. Men wrote letter after letter to loved ones even though they knew there was a good chance that they would beat the letters home.

Most of these men were already making plans for civilian life. Almost all of them started out as civilians and most of them wanted to return to that status. Although they were

312

intensely proud of their service in the Navy, they wanted to get on with their dreams of life back in the states. They knew all to well that life in the Navy meant giving up the certainty of life in the states.

They had lived for months on end without experiencing life even close to normal. Months went by without seeing even one female. Years went by without sleeping in a bed on solid land. And all the time, there was the constant threat of the enemy. At sea, a submarine could attack anywhere, anytime. In anchorages, an enemy plane could suddenly cause the panic of rushing to general quarters. In the end, just such a plane had destroyed the one constant they had depended on: the Callaghan.

Finally, one fine September day, the men crowded the rail as the slow transport ship came within view of California. For most of them it had been a full year and a half since they last saw the good earth of the USA. Few people can imagine the feelings of those men. Here was redemption at last; victory at last. Home.

Most of the Callaghan men went back to civilian life. A few stayed in the Navy. Many of them lost touch with their fellow crewmen. But some of them did manage to stay in contact with some of their buddies from the war. This eventually led to some reunions.

In 1972, the first Callaghan reunion was held in Indianapolis. Hugh Slay and Bob Thatch coordinated this reunion. Only a few of the men of the Callaghan showed up. But it was a good start. The next reunion was held three years later to commemorate the 30th anniversary of the sinking of the ship. Reunions followed every other year thereafter for the next 25 years.

In 1985, Leo Jarboe was President of the Callaghan association and directed one of the best reunions ever held in Washington. There were about 50 Callaghan crewmen that attended all or part of the reunion. The crew enjoyed an extensive tour of the Capital building and He remained a very active member of the association thereafter.

In 1995, Leo received an unexpected phone call. A retired Captain from the Navy was trying to get in touch with the remaining crewmembers of the Callaghan on behalf of a Japanese gentleman. It seems that the Kamikaze aviator that the Callaghan had saved after shooting down his plane in May of 1945 wanted to come to the United States to express his thanks.

Kaoru Hasagawa had returned to his family in Japan after World War II. There he worked hard over the years in the box and carton business. He rose steadily within his company until finally he became the President. He was a very successful Japanese executive.

Hasagawa became active in the Japanese naval aviators association. He was asked on a couple of occasions to speak about his experiences in World War II. One question he was asked was the name of the ship that rescued him after his plane was shot down. He couldn't answer that question because he did not know.

Finally, the 50 year anniversary of his suicide mission to Okinawa drew near. He became determined to find out the name of the ship that rescued him and to, in some way, thank the crew that saved his life. He made an inquiry through high ranking friends in the Japanese Self Defense force. They forwarded the request to the Japanese embassy in Washington, D.C. The request was passed along to the US Navy. The US Navy suggested the use of a retired naval intelligence officer, Captain Horn, who had lived in Japan and specialized in research.

Captain Horn used the information he had from Hasagawa to determine what information the US Navy Historical Center had on the battle in which Hasagawa's plane was shot down. His research revealed that the ship which picked up Hasagawa was the USS Callaghan. A request was then made to find a representative of the Callaghan's crew to arrange a possible meeting in May of 1995.

Captain Horn got in touch with Captain Bertholf's widow, Leo Jarboe and Jake Heimark. Arrangements were made for them to meet Mr. Hasagawa when he visited Washington, D. C. in late May, 1995. They all met at the Navy Memorial on Pennsylvania Ave. with both local Television and a CNN crew present. A segment about the reunion of a Kamikaze pilot and the men who rescued him was aired that day on several Washington D.C. stations and on CNN.

The next Callaghan reunion was held that summer in Pidgeon's Forge, Tennessee. It was a memorable reunion because of the attendance of Mr. Hasagawa and his wife. The Callaghan crewmen in attendance shook hands and many had their picture taken with Mr. Hasagawa. He made a speech through a translator in which he thanked Captain Bertholf and the crew of the Callaghan for saving his life.

During a story telling session, Buzz Buzzetti told Mr. Hasagawa the story of how on May 25, 1945, he was put in charge of the boat that went out to the Japanese plane that was floating on the water. He related how they pulled the two flyers out of the water and took them back to the ship. He also told Mr. Hasagawa that he ended up with Mr. Hasagawa's watch that day. More incredibly, he told Mr. Hasagawa that he still had the watch somewhere in his attic. Buzzetti told Hasagawa that he would try to find it and return it.

In 1999, the Callaghan reunion was held in Minneapolis, Minnesota. Mr. Hasagawa was again an honored guest. At a dinner which he held for the Callaghan crew, he sat at the head table along with Captain Horn and Callaghan friends. Buzzetti got up to make a very special presentation. He returned to Mr. Hasagawa the Japanese Naval Aviation watch which Hasagawa had worn that fateful day over 54 years ago. For a few moments, Hasagawa was stunned speechless while the audience applauded. It was a fitting end to a saga of war and humanity that took twists and turns that no-one would have predicted.

As the final Callaghan reunions are being held as are all the final reunions of all the World War II veterans, the stories are being recorded and archived for future generations to study. The one common desire of all is that never in human history shall such a war be fought again. Maybe the future generations will learn from the story of once fierce and deadly combatants that have now become friends. It is clear that this is a lesson we must learn.

47197136R00179

Made in the USA
Lexington, KY
01 December 2015